FOUNDATIONS OF CONTEXTUAL THERAPY

Collected Papers of
IVAN BOSZORMENYI-NAGY, M.D.

FOUNDATIONS OF CONTEXTUAL THERAPY

Collected Papers of
IVAN BOSZORMENYI-NAGY, M.D.

BRUNNER/MAZEL *Publishers* • *New York*

Library of Congress Cataloging-in-Publication Data
Boszormenyi-Nagy, Ivan, 1920–
  Foundations of contextual therapy.

  Includes bibliographies and index.
  1. Contextual therapy. I. Title. [DNLM: 1. Family
Therapy—collected works. WM 430.5.F2 B747f]
RC488.55.B67 1987   616.89'156   86-26846
ISBN 0-87630-449-8

Copyright © 1987 by Ivan Boszormenyi-Nagy

Published by
BRUNNER/MAZEL, INC.
19 Union Square
New York, New York 10003

MANUFACTURED IN THE UNITED STATES OF AMERICA

This book is dedicated to my father Istvan Boszormenyi-Nagy, whose firm commitment to fairness in relating has been a lifelong guideline in my search for the essence of therapy, and to my wife Maria and my son Stephen (Istvan), whose patient understanding enabled me to devote countless hours to writing.

Foreword

These *Collected Papers*, covering a period of almost 30 years, will allow the reader to trace the developing thought of one of the world's seminal family therapists and theoreticians. I gladly accept the opportunity to write a few words that might add a perspective to Ivan Boszormenyi-Nagy's writings.

To me, in addition to their being based on a wealth of clinical experience, these writings reveal a characteristic familial, cultural, as well as national heritage. Let me begin with the latter. Ivan Boszormenyi-Nagy grew up in Hungary. Here he witnessed how his native country was conquered and subdued by two totalitarian powers: Hitler's Germany and Stalin's Russia, these being the two latest foreign invasions in Hungary's long history. Hungary, we may remind ourselves, is a small country, yet one that has produced many outstanding artists, scholars, and—last but not least—psychotherapists. (Her language seems also unique: it appears distantly related to the Finnish and Estonian languages, but to no other European language.) Within the European community of nations, Hungary represents a prototypical small nation culture. It could only survive by, on the one hand, opening up to diverse cultural influences, while, on the other, asserting and preserving its own unique features. This seemed possible only on the basis of a strong group loyalty and cultural vitality.

Here I see one of the sources of Ivan Boszormenyi-Nagy's lifelong concern with the underdog, that is, the disadvantaged minority, be this the minority of a disadvantaged child in a family, a disadvantaged family in a community, a disadvantaged subculture, or a disadvantaged nation in the world community of nations. Who, we find him constantly asking, will defend the interests of those religious, cultural, or na-

vii

tional loyalty groups that have no voice and that have no forum (such as the United Nations) to which they can turn in order to obtain justice? But further: We find in his genealogy several generations of judges, some of them holding positions comparable to those of justices of the United States Supreme Court. Such family "legacy"—a term he has imbued with special meaning—seems also to account for his unusual concern with, and sensitivity to, issues of accountability, loyalty, justice, and fairness in human relationships.

There are other qualities of his thought and writings which may be better appreciated when we view him within a European tradition of scholarship and philosophical inquiry. I have in mind a special reflexivity and erudition coupled with an integrating power that allow him to bring to a creative juncture such seemingly disparate scientific domains as psychoanalysis, family dynamics, social science, medicine, and intergroup justice. Here I find him not unlike Gregory Bateson, a scientist, another European thinker with a philosophical bent who, like Ivan Boszormenyi-Nagy, a therapist, found his eventual home in the United States and who also, like Ivan Boszormenyi-Nagy, exerted his originality at the interfaces of different scientific domains. (These were, in the case of Bateson, mainly cybernetics, biology, anthropology, and formal logic.) But there are, of course, also major differences between the two thinkers. As a thinker, Bateson often gives the appearance of meandering, as when he, following his own advice, seems to alternate between a "strict" and "loose" thinking, whereas Ivan Boszormenyi-Nagy seems to develop and expand his concepts with seeming single-mindedness and dogged perseverance. Evidently, there are different ways in which original contributions can be made.

Today it becomes ever more evident that Ivan Boszormenyi-Nagy for a long time has been broaching issues and concerns to which many other family therapists are now belatedly turning—or more correctly, returning. These are, of course, first of all issues of a relational ethic. Thus, many family therapists are now discovering—decades after Boszormenyi-Nagy made this discovery—that notions of justice, accountability, and entitlement represent perhaps the most important—individual as well as family—"maps" (or epistemologies) which guide behaviors, determine the fate of relationships, and provide therapists with leverage for (reframing) interventions. And there are, intertwined with the above, all those issues that are illuminated through the kind of multigenerational perspective which Ivan Boszormenyi-Nagy has opened up. We might say, by opening up this coherent therapeutic perspective he has made systems thinking three-dimensional, as it were. For example, I view it as a particularly bold and original application of systems thinking when he came to view a child's illness or a spouse's self-destructive behavior leading to the breakup of the marriage as an expression and consequence of a deep loyalty to one's own parents. Clearly, it is foremost in the ethical dimension of relationship where Ivan Boszormenyi-Nagy broke new ground, where he became the fore-runner or, perhaps better, forethinker for many others who often no longer know, admit, or acknowledge that they are following him.

To be sure, the very fact that Ivan Boszormenyi-Nagy so often shows himself to be ahead of his times or is setting himself apart from the mainstream cannot but make him a controversial figure. Also, what some will see as the bedrock of his creativity, namely his earlier mentioned single-mindedness and conceptual perseverance, others will no doubt interpret as a manifestation of rigidity, if not a questionable dogmatic moralism. Be this as it may, these papers — along with his by now classic work, *Invisible Loyalties* (co-authored with Geraldine Spark) — make it evident that he is one of the original thinkers in our field, a pioneer of the first generation of family therapists whom nobody who tries to get a solid grounding in family theory and practice can afford to neglect.

Helm Stierlin, M.D., Ph.D.

Contents

Introduction

This book represents a broad spectrum selection of my writings aimed at a search for the nature and treatability of behavioral-emotional disorders. For many years it appeared to me that the more severe forms, especially schizophrenic psychosis, hold the key to understanding. Since even Freud's genius could not offer sufficient psychological clues about psychosis, first I turned to biochemical avenues of investigation. After three years of consistent efforts had failed to yield significant results, only then did I return to clinical investigation.

My biochemical studies started in 1945, in the second year of my psychiatric residency at the University Hospital in Budapest, and continued at the Illinois Neuropsychiatric Institute in Chicago. This work preceded the arrival of the psychotropic drugs. It was eminently logical to assume that because certain schizophrenics were described as having abnormal glucose tolerance curves and were treatable by insulin-shocks, the effect of insulin upon their basic cellular chemistry should be studied. The reference system I chose was the glycolytic metabolism, the common energy source of all types of cells. Since blood cells were the only human cells obtainable for experimental purposes, I aimed at the effect of insulin upon the glycolytic enzymatic rates of the blood cells of psychotic inpatients and "normal" control persons. After years of studies I found that the one statistically consistent enzymatic deviation finding was probably due to the dietary composition of meals in one hospital.

Having been inspired by Kalman Gyarfas, formerly of the Department of Psychiatry, University of Budapest, later Director of Chicago State Hospital, I had a long-standing curiosity about the significance of relationships in regard to psychotherapy. This interest has informed my career ever since 1957, with my appointment at Eastern Pennsylvania Psychiatric Institute as program director of a relationally based research psychotherapy unit for the treatment of schizophrenia.

Most of the papers included in this volume represent my search through object-relations theory of the British School, hospital management, therapeutic community, intensive individual therapy, family therapy, multiple family therapy—all in the interest of finding the specific helping moment. First the interest was focused on schizophrenic inpatients, but since the mid-1960s it has shifted to the whole spectrum of psychiatric conditions.

Gradually, it became clear to me that an integration of the insights of both individual and family therapies has to be achieved in order to reach to the core of both systemic levels: motivation and relationship. The relational core of personality has been the traditional focus of psychoanalytic, especially object-relations, theory. Conversely, the patterns of here-and-now relationships have been family therapy's arena of interventions. Obviously, the internal and interpersonal realms of relatedness are overlapping but also discrete and often critically discordant.

In the end, after long struggle with the methods of both individual insight and transactional patterning of behavior, the bridge between the two realms emerged by the late 1960s. The therapeutic bridge that allows for the optional resolution of the polarities of internal versus real relating lies in the ethics of close relating. The papers in this volume show the range and evolution of the concepts of family transference, counterautonomous superego, collusive postponement of mourning, mutual confirmation, loyalty, being the object of the other, intersubjective fusion, relational stagnation, loyalty implications of transference, overloyalty, ledger of merit, entitlement versus indebtedness, legacy, rejunction, the four dimensions of relating, multidirected partiality, multilaterality, accountability for consequences, the priority of posterity's welfare, intrinsic relational tribunal and transgenerational solidarity.

They constitute the chain of concepts that define the ethical dimension, the core of both relating and healing. The term "contextual" refers to a therapy that focuses on the ethical dimension as its core guideline.

I first used the term in the title of Chapter 13 of *Invisible Loyalties* (1973) and "contextual therapy" has become the standard name of my and my associates' approach both in the United States and in Europe. A current summary of the therapeutic methods of this therapy constitutes the subject of *Between Give and Take: A Clinical Guide to Contextual Therapy* by Ivan Boszormenyi-Nagy and Barbara R. Krasner (1986).

INTRODUCTION TO THE CLINICAL PAPERS

As in the case of most early family therapy ventures, the origins of contextual therapy can be traced to a long-term concern with helping schizophrenics. Earlier I pursued this concern through existentially and dynamically based individual therapy (1944–1959) and research (1950–1954). In the 1950s many therapists were trying to expand Freud's method into the realm of the therapy of psychotics. Inspired by the writings of Ronald Fairbairn (1952), my initial involvement with family therapy originated from object-relations thinking as applied to the therapy of psychotics. A relational redefinition of Freud's work was the therapeutic rationale of the 24-bed research therapeutic department I founded and directed at Eastern Pennsylvania Psychiatric Institute in 1957. It operated as the Department of Family Psychiatry until 1980 when, out of budget policy considerations, the entire structure of Eastern Pennsylvania Psychiatric Institute was dissolved by state authorities.

The initial research therapeutic unit at EPPI was a model program. It was generously staffed with psychiatrists, psychologists, social workers, nurses and attendants, all of whom were exceptionally devoted to their work. It was possible to offer the patients a giving nurturance and empathy, a chance for cathartic expressiveness, intensive individual therapy with interpretation of transference manifestations, strategic understanding of oscillations between paranoid and dependently depressed phases of the psychosis, ready communication and contact in the face of obvious deep withdrawal, and personal engagement of the entire staff in daily community meetings and hour-by-hour interaction.

Yet the real hope for progress came from the involvement of close relatives in weekly therapeutic community meetings.

From the beginning, relational dialectic was approached from the ontological vantage point of *being* rather than from the epistemological viewpoint of *knowing*. The "thesis" of one relating person is met with the "antithesis" of the partner. Their respective needs were not perceived primarily from a psychological angle of development, form and content of thought and affect but from the point of view of an irreplaceable, mutually constitutive interdependence of being. It was at this existential or (philosophical) anthropological juncture that the reading of Martin Buber's writings represented such a significant input. The point of view of the "dialogue," the core of Buber's thinking, matched the clinical observations of a persisting "ontic dependence" between closely relating people. In this interdependence lies the ultimate contextual resource of close relationships, regardless of the degree of actual contact or of the content of feelings and thoughts in either partner's psyche.

Expanding the treatment focus to the relatives led to improved effectiveness. Even the (bizarre), withdrawn patient became a meaningful, even vital, member of the family. The therapist's extended perspective became the source of a broadened and deeper understanding. Instead of losing depth, the therapeutic focus deepened at the true locus of individuation—the relational context. This led to the dialectical view of individual autonomy and helped to retain concern with the person as an entity in an increasingly systemic-relational view of therapy.

The discovery of the enduring significance of close relationships regardless of psychotic or otherwise "pathological" behavior did more than inform the therapist. It expanded the therapeutic concern to more than one person. Besides more effectively helping the individual, the multiple therapeutic contract facilitated the shift of emphasis from symptom to underlying process. Not only did the symptom yield to a depth focusing on personality, as is the case in psychoanalysis, but in family therapy even the identity of the "patient" becomes relativized. The treatment of psychotics became much safer as the support and emotional resources of the patient's relatives were included in the therapeutic context and as helping the relatives also was added to the therapist's agenda. Despite the recalcitrant claims of conservative individual therapists, it became clear that the dynamic target area of therapy has deepened as a result of the multipersonal contract of relational therapies.

Gradually, a fuller understanding of the enduring significance of close relationships led to theoretical and practical insights into the nature of relating itself. As a corollary to the therapeutic goal of helping through a multidirectional partiality (Boszormenyi-Nagy, 1966), the ethics of fairness and its underlying substance of relational accountability came to be viewed as the fundamental programming, regulatory and sustaining principle of close relationships. As a result, a capacity for responsible concern about relational consequences had to be regarded as the most challenging but also the most reliable criterion of autonomous individual maturity. The chief source of failure of individuation was therefore seen to be in ethical stagnation or disengagement in families. As a corollary, continuity of self implies responsibility for the consequences of one's total spectrum of relational involvements.

A traditional linear, nondialectical view of individuation alleges that through actualizing himself, the individual can create and control his whole relational spectrum, rather than just his personal side of reality. In turn, a nondialectical, circularly systemic family therapist may presume that through his interventions he can "create" his client's reality. The contextual therapist, however, assumes that between people there exists a relational reality, an interlocking of their respective spontaneous motivations. The growing recognition of the clinical significance of intergenerational relationships has led to a reordering of priorities. Human life, like animal life in general, cannot survive without some regard for transgenerational solidarity. On the one hand, callously expedient big business or absolutist authoritarian government can threaten the survival of a liveable environment on earth. On the other hand, disregard for the reality of family relational consequences can interfere with the emotional welfare of posterity.

Without regard for the consequences of our actions for others, both individuals and groups are liable to contribute to an "age of narcissism." A disregard for consequences to children in adult living arrangements is just as detrimental to posterity's relational reality as colonial or dogmatic conquest of one society by another has been on a larger scale.

The claim to adult freedom frequently covers a subtle disregard for or exploitation of posterity's rights and entitlements.

In the contextual sense we cannot really gain freedom at the expense of our children's rights. Freedom to serial or simultaneous multiple partnership, chosen single parenthood, carrier pregnancy or destructive parental battling should not be understood as a license to ignore the young child's welfare. To settle the adult issues and simply to expect the small child "to understand" is intrinsically unfair. And unfairness to one's child cannot, in the long run, stand in the parent's interest. Genuine freedom results from a balance between individual spontaneity and accountable caring about the reality of consequences to others, especially to a defenseless posterity.

Considerations of fairness as the basis of trustworthiness, itself the foundation of relational viability, requires a therapeutic method built on relational accountability. This underlying relational ethic is not an ethic of sacrifice and self-renunciation. Instead, it is an ethic that requires benefits both for the actor and for his partner. Only such a multilaterally fair principle can do justice to the principle of fair accountability, the basis of genuine dialogue. The combination of due self-assertion with fair consideration of the partner represents the contextual formula for mature individuation. This formula yields both freedom for active commitment in life and freedom from self-destruction.

Currently, the contextual orientation stands between the various individual therapy approaches on the one hand and all family therapy approaches on the other. Ever since the formulation of the four dimensions of relational reality—facts, psychological needs, transactional systems, and relational accountability (Boszormenyi-Nagy, 1979)—the approach has become an explicitly integrative framework. But the central integrative principle of all therapies rests at the core of the helping relationship—the ethics of relating, that is, the accountability for consequences to others. This "dimension four" is the umbrella under which the contextual therapist subsumes the various, mutually untranslatable dimensions of relational ontology and epistemology. Finally, the ethical dimension will provide also the clue for the synthesis of therapy and prevention. The criteria for serving posterity's interests provide crucial guidelines for today's health.

Furthermore, the formula of fair multilaterality will serve as a bridge between the generations. The very ethical priority of fair availability is the foundation of transgenerational solidarity, the fiber of all higher animals' species survival. In humans this also includes accountability for a safe environment and for trustworthy parent-child relating. Transgenerational solidarity is a natural guideline for the rejuvenation of community fellowship and also for a rebuilding of a more trustworthy and democratic intergroup and even international community. Contextual therapy is thus inseparable from its prospective broader societal applications.

REFERENCES

Boszormenyi-Nagy, I. (1966). From family therapy to a psychology of relationships: Fictions of the individual and fictions of the family. *Comprehensive Psychiatry 7*, 408–423.

Boszormenyi-Nagy, I. (1979). Contextual Therapy: Therapeutic leverages in mobilizing trust. Report 2 Unit IV. *The American Family*, Philadelphia: The Continuing Education Service of Smith Kline and French Laboratories. Reprinted in Green, R. J. & Framo, J. L. (Eds.) *Family therapy: Major contributions*, pp. 393–416. New York: International Universities Press (1981).

Boszormenyi-Nagy, I., & Krasner, B. (1986). *Between give and take*. New York: Brunner/Mazel.

Boszormenyi-Nagy, I., & Spark, G. M. (1973). *Invisible loyalties*. New York: Brunner/Mazel.

Fairbairn, W. R. D. (1952). *Psychoanalytic studies of the personality*. London: Tavistock.

Acknowledgments

The author wishes to express his gratitude to Dr. Catherine Ducommun, of Lausanne, Switzerland, for her assistance in the selection of papers to be included in this volume and for her critical review of the commentaries that connect the individual chapters of the book.

The author also gratefully acknowledges permission received to reprint each paper:

Chapter 1. **Correlations Between Mental Illness and Intracellular Metabolism.** Reprinted from *Confinia Neurologica*, 1958, Vol. 18, pp. 88–91. By permission of S. Karger AG, Basel.

Chapter 2. **Hospital Organization and Family-Oriented Psychotherapy of Schizophrenia.** Reprinted from *Proceedings of the Third World Congress of Psychiatry*, 1961, pp. 476–480. By permission of the University of Toronto Press.

Chapter 3. **The Concept of Schizophrenia from the Perspective of Family Treatment.** Reprinted from *Family Process*, 1962, Vol. 1, No. 1, pp. 103–113. By permission.

Chapter 4. **The Concept of Change in Conjoint Family Therapy.** Reprinted from *Psychotherapy for the Whole Family*, edited by A. S. Friedman et al., 1965, pp. 305–317. Springer Publishing Company, NY. By permission of Alfred S. Friedman.

Chapter 5. **From Family Therapy to a Psychology of Relationships: Fictions of the Individual and Fictions of the Family.** Reprinted from *Comprehensive Psychiatry*, 1966, Vol. 7, No. 5, pp. 408–423. By permission of Grune & Stratton, Inc.

Chapter 6. **Relational Modes and Meaning.** Reprinted from *Family Therapy and Disturbed Families*, 1967, edited by G. Zuk and I. Boszormenyi-Nagy. Science and Behavior Books, Palo Alto, CA. By permission of Gerald Zuk, Ph.D.

Chapter 7. **Loyalty Implications of the Transference Model in Psychotherapy.** Reprinted from *AMA Archives of General Psychiatry*, 1972, Vol. 27, pp. 374–380. By permission. Copyright 1972, American Medical Association.

Chapter 8. **How I Became a Family Therapist**. Reprinted from *The Book of Family Therapy*, edited by A. Ferber, M. Mendelsohn, and A. Napier, 1972, pp. 84–85. Science House, N.Y.

Chapter 9. **Ethical and Practical Implications of Intergenerational Family Therapy**. Reprinted from *Psychotherapy and Psychosomatics*, 1974, Vol. 24, pp. 261–268. By permission of S. Karger AG, Basel.

Chapter 10. **Behavioral Change Through Family Change**. Reprinted from *What Makes Behavior Change Possible?*, edited by A. Burton, 1976, pp. 227–258. By permission of Brunner/Mazel.

Chapter 11. **Comments on Helm Stierlin's "Hitler as the Bound Delegate of His Mother" in History of Childhood Quarterly**. Reprinted from *The Journal of Psychohistory*, 1976, Vol. 3, No. 4, pp. 500–505. By permission of the Association for Psychohistory, Inc.

Chapter 12. **Clinical and Legal Issues in the Family Therapy Record**. Reprinted from *Hospital and Community Psychiatry*, 1977, Vol. 28, pp. 911–913. By permission of the American Psychiatric Association and Neal Gansheroff, M.D.

Chapter 13. **Contextual Therapy: Therapeutic Leverages in Mobilizing Trust**. Reprinted from *The American Family*, 1979, Report 2, Unit IV, pp. 1–10. By permission of Smith Kline and French Laboratories. This paper also appeared in *Family Therapy: Major Contributions*, edited by R. J. Green and J. L. Framo, 1981, pp. 393–415. International Universities Press, NY.

Chapter 14. **Trust-Based Therapy: A Contextual Approach**. Reprinted from *American Journal of Psychiatry*, 1980, Vol. 137, No. 7, pp. 767–775. By permission of the American Psychiatric Association.

Chapter 15. **Contextual Therapy: The Realm of the Individual (Interview with Margaret Markham)**. Reprinted from *Psychiatric News*, 1981, Vol. XVI, No. 20, October 16, p. 17; Part II in Vol. XVI, No. 21, November 6, p. 26. By permission of the American Psychiatric Association.

Chapter 16. **The Contextual Approach to Psychotherapy: Premises and Implications**. Reprinted from *Annual Review of Family Therapy*, edited by G. Berenson and H. White, 1981, Vol. 1, pp. 92–128. By permission of Human Sciences Press.

Chapter 17. **Commentary: Transgenerational Solidarity—Therapy's Mandate and Ethics**. Reprinted from *Family Process*, 1985, Vol. 24, pp. 454–456. By permission.

Chapter 18. **Transgenerational Solidarity: The Expanding Context of Therapy and Prevention**. Reprinted from *The American Journal of Family Therapy*, 1986, Vol. 14, No. 3, pp. 195–212. By permission of Brunner/Mazel.

Chapter 19. **Contextual Therapy and the Unity of Therapies**. Reprinted from *The Interface of Individual and Family Therapy*, edited by S. Sugarman, 1986, pp. 65–72. By permission of Aspen Publishers, Inc.

FOUNDATIONS OF CONTEXTUAL THERAPY

Collected Papers of
IVAN BOSZORMENYI-NAGY, M.D.

1

Correlations Between Mental Illness and Intracellular Metabolism

This paper summarizes the rationale of my years of research on red cell metabolism in schizophrenia. The crucial personality parameter pertaining to psychosis is seen in one's capacity to utilize earlier identifications in approaching new people. The hypothesis then assumed that whether or not it is genetically determined, the biological substrate of such a relational capacity should be correlatable with the intracellular metabolism of the brain or perhaps of all body cells. This hypothesis was underlying the study of phosphorus metabolism in red blood cells (Boszormenyi-Nagy, 1955; with Gerty, 1955; with Gerty & Kueber, 1956).

REFERENCES

Boszormenyi-Nagy, I. Formation of phosphopyruvate from phosglycerate in hemolyzed human ethrocytes. *Journal of Biological Chemistry, 212*(1), 495–499, 1955.

Boszormenyi-Nagy, I., & Gerty, F. J. Diagnostic aspects of a study of intracellular phosphorylations in schizophrenia. *American Journal of Psychiatry, 112*(1), 11–17, 1955.

Boszormenyi-Nagy, I., Gerty, F. J., & Kueber, J. Correlation between an anomoly of the intracellular metabolism of adenosine nucleotides and schizophrenia. *Journal of Nervous and Mental Disease, 124*(4), 413–416, 1956.

It appears that there is an increasing realization of a need for a thorough reconsideration of our psychiatric nosological framework. The psychiatric thinking of the last few decades has shifted the focus of attention away from the medical frame of reference. This has been especially apparent in the United States, where some of the important contributions to the cultural and social applications of psychiatry have been made. This paper is intended to examine the implications of biological studies in general, and of intracellular metabolism in particular, for psychiatric nosology, especially in view of the mentioned shift of emphasis in our thinking.

What is the cause of this change in psychiatric thinking? Does the shift of emphasis toward cultural and social factors mean a new and better understanding of etiology, or does it represent only a swing of the pendulum toward a preference for theories on spiritual factors of causation?

It is impossible to answer this question without the clarification of our fundamental attitude toward the causation of what are called psychiatric conditions or illnesses. Most of us will probably agree that, in the majority of psychotic pictures, the question about bodily and environmental causal factors is not an either-or proposition. Instead, the correct question should sound: How much of the determination comes from either of these two areas? After consideration of the available amount of information regarding psychosis, we have to conclude that it has not been proven that in a phenomenon as complex as mental disturbance either inherited constitution or human environment could be completely excluded as a possible etiological factor. It is clear that human behavior is, to a great extent, determined by the hereditary traits of both species and individual.

Although it is impossible to describe the hereditary determinants of our behavior in detail, the whole of these traits may be viewed as an inborn strength or capacity for survival. It can be assumed that each of us presents a certain amount of this potential "strength" toward our social environment at the beginning of our interpersonal functioning.

It is also obvious that such an inborn "strength" has to be based on a certain kind of efficiency of the organism in general, and of its structures responsible for the organization of its behavior in particular. Theoretically, it should be possible to assign to each newborn child a single value expressing its strength for the complex task of successful human adjustment. Such a measurable property would be expected to give a Gauss-curve shaped distribution in populations. Yet, even the knowledge of this hypothetical value would not be sufficient for us to predict the actual extent of future adjustment in a given individual. Very few among us would doubt that there are significant differences as to the extent to which human environment can support or inhibit the process of personality development. Only a combined knowledge of the extents of both inherited flexibility of the organism, and of the total influence of its environment, would enable us to predict the actual level of healthy mental functioning in a given individual.

Consequently, other, more concrete questions can be asked. What is the physical mechanism of this constitutional disposition or of the bodily determinants of behavior? Since the subject of the question is in the biological frame or reference only, the answer is relatively easy. The inherent properties of the germinative cells determine the range of potentialities of the inherited characteristics of the individual. Such potentialities pertain to size, shape, color, the relative inferiority of organs, intelligence, etc. The mechanism by which these determinations are implemented must be part of the complex chemical operations of resting and dividing cells. In this sense, in each individual, the various kinds of tissue cells "inherit" certain patterns of metabolism, which eventually will determine the efficiency of the function expected from the corresponding tissue.

Some individual, for instance, may inherit a circulatory system of less than average resistance, another an immunity to certain infections, etc. In certain instances, a generalized constitutional metabolic deficiency of all cells of the organism might be manifested as a disturbance in the function of one of the organs or tissues. An example of this could be the phenylpyruvic disease in which, apparently, a generalized enzymatic failure manifests itself as a "behavioral" condition: oligophrenia. It is logical to assume that, although the enzymatic abnormality is generalized, it is the cells of the brain that have the lowest resistance to this interference.

The next question will pertain to the relationship between two sets of occurrences: the one of publicly observable data, and the other, the field of inner experience. Namely, if the implementation of hereditary traits of behavior rests ultimately on the cellular-biochemical level, we have to assume that there are certain fundamental determinants of behavior in the "psychological" frame of reference which correspond to these biological traits. In other words, what are those inborn fundamental behavioral patterns, characteristic of an individual, which would be discernible in spite of modifying effects of any possible environment? Or, in what manner would a given individual handle life experience differently from others in the theoretical case of all having an exactly identical environmental history? We know of the existence of such fundamental genetically determined behavioral variables in the case of the above-mentioned phenylpyruvic disease. There, intelligence is affected as a result of a generalized enzymatic deficiency concerning the metabolism of aromatic amino acids. We know, on the other hand, that in schizophrenia it is not the intelligence function which is responsible for the behavioral disturbance. The crucial problem of these patients appears to be a less efficient or less flexible interaction with people, especially in emotionally meaningful relationships.

The next question is, can we conceive of a specific personality parameter, pertaining to psychosis, which is as fundamental a characteristic as for instance, intracellular enzymatic properties are fundamental to the organism? Although the answer to the last question, at the present time, most likely is negative, certain hypotheses can be formed. We know that the environment contributes to the formation of the ego or of the representation of the self in a human individual by two main ways. One is by providing the very facts of existence which the individual has to learn, whereas the other way is by providing models in the process of maturation, with which to identify. The classical example of above is the role of the mother who is the first catalyst of human interaction potentials, as well as the first model object for identification. Later on, the other significant adults play similar roles for the child. At a certain phase of development, the internal representations of outside people will not only provide us with "ready-made" learned patterns of behavior, but they give content to our own self. Only after this has taken place can we deal satisfactorily with complex human situations, helped thus by our capacity to identify with the very roles played by ourselves, as well as the ones played by others. In this sense the extent of our capacity to utilize earlier identifications in approaching new people, determines the efficiency of our dealings with human situations or, of our interpersonal flexibility.

It is suggested here that impairment of the latter capacity of the human mind is the pertinent factor in "emotional illness" or psychosis. This potential or capacity has to have its mechanism in the brain just as operative intelligence has its own. Such mechanism ought to be dependent on the integrity of the structure and function of the brain. The functioning of the brain, on the other hand, as that of any organ, is dependent on various energy-producing intracellular metabolic patterns. Some of these patterns might be hereditarily vulnerable in the brain or in every cell of certain organisms. Such a deviation might conceivably be identical with a postulated "constitutional factor" in emotional illness in general, or schizophrenia in particular.

Our project at the Eastern Pennsylvania Psychiatric Institute endeavors to establish the descriptive criteria of fundamental interpersonal patterns by long-term observation of acute schizophrenic patients who are in intensive psychotherapy. Consecutively, the possibility will be tested whether some of the fundamental interpersonal patterns will correlate with patterns observed in the intracellular metabolism of the red cells of certain schizophrenic patients. At the same time, we realize a great need for a systematic comparison of various biological findings of different centers around the world for the study of the intercorrelations of these parameters, either on the same clinical material or with the help of more careful clinical description of the pertinent patient material, of the various studies.

2

Hospital Organization and Family-Oriented Psychotherapy of Schizophrenia

[This paper was written with James L Framo, Ph.D.]

This paper, first presented at the Third World Congress in Montreal in 1961, encompasses the early phases of conceptualizations as they grew out of family-based work with inpatients at the Department of Family Psychiatry of Eastern Pennsylvania Psychiatric Institute. The search for hypotheses concerning the effectiveness of the family-based approach extends into object-relations theory.

Regarding the phenomenon of transference, family therapy is described as a new perspective for the direct observation of some of the relationship patterns that in individual therapy or analysis are able to be inferred only from reenactments of early family relational attitudes between patient and therapist. This observation is expanded to the exploration of the dynamics of hospitalization. It is, therefore, hypothesized that behavior toward the hospital staff and other patients may replicate familial patterns of relationships.

Since the various family members share their regressive tendencies toward continuing to relate to their internal objects through alleged relating to real others, their, often painful yet strong, need-complementarity leads to a form of stagnation that prohibits separation and mature individuation. Their resistance to change may be so violent that other family members may take on paranoid or otherwise psychotic-like attitudes.

Another combination of "family transference" with internal object relations was described in this paper. In her delusional world a psychotic was observed to remain in the company of the endopsychic representations of regressively gratifying early relationships. Consequently, the patient may displace (transfer) onto the persons in the hospital environment not only these early familial images but the interactions among internal objects as well. Therefore, whole family climates can be transferred upon unsuspecting others, often instantaneously. Naturally, the shifts of family transference onto strangers did create significant conflicting "loyalties," a term first used in this paper.

All of the complex relational phenomena of hospitalizations were elicited and made further observable through the introduction of family day activities, partial care of the patient by her mother, multiple family therapy groups with their combined familial group dynamic processes and many others.

This paper has evolved from our work on a research treatment unit, where attention has been given to the interaction of three major therapeutic factors: intensive individual psychotherapy, family therapy, and ward milieu therapy. The organizational design of this project is based on an assumption that the most pertinent focus of schizophrenic psychopathology is the dimension of relatedness. Most of the workers who have conducted intensive psychotherapy of the schizophrenic conditions agree on the supporting and egoconstructive influence that good relationships can have upon the "weak" ego of the schizophrenic (Federn, Sullivan, Fromm-Reichman, Eissler, Sechehaye, Rosen). The same principle is implicit even more specifically in the work of the pioneers of the family-based treatment of schizophrenia (Lidz, Bowen, Wynne, Jackson). Moreover, the entire therapeutic effect of the psychodynamically oriented psychiatric hospitalization is also translatable into a relationship psychology. In this way we strongly contrast psychiatric hospitalization with the service-based therapeutic concept of the general hospital. In other words, in general medicine or surgery, the patient is helped by specific acts being done to him, whereas in the psychiatric hospital help largely consists of furthering the capacity of the patient to utilize human relationships. Thus, the emphasis in psychiatric hospital treatment shifts strongly from *what* is being done towards *by whom* it is done and in what manner.

Thus far we have stated those theoretical foundations of our paper that do not appear new or controversial to the expert student of psychotherapy with schizophrenic patients. The specific main point of view of this presentation, however, may not be readily acceptable to those workers who have not shared our several years' experience with the family treatment of schizophrenia and have not familiarized themselves with publications of workers in this field. We feel, specifically, that the study of the psychopathology of schizophrenic family interaction can develop into one of the basic sciences for hospital psychiatry. For one thing, the bizarre symptomatic behaviour of the schizophrenic patient in the hospital can often be decoded as a repetitious meaningful message within the context of family living. When the patient enters the psychiatric hospital the uniform and routine aspects of her first contacts leave her with a feeling of isolation and loss of meaningful human relationships; she then has to recreate a living space of relationships and can only fall back on past experiences and fantasies. Just as in the psychoanalytic situation the patient is forced to respond with early infantile patterns because of the frustrating, one-sided nature of the relationship, similarly, certain facets of psychiatric hospitalization (such as its perceived impersonalness) foster "transference" of the patient's attitudes from the family to hospital personnel. The study and utilization of these unconscious, reconstructive patterns has been the purpose of the organization of our research hospital unit and of this present report on its activities. We do not intend to give here a detailed report on the psychology of families of schizophrenic patients; rather, we will use the dynamics of these family situations in order to introduce a framework for the philosophy of a therapeutic approach.

Before getting into the specifics of our findings it would be apropos at this point to describe the nature of the situation from whence our observations have been derived. Our observations originate from a special psychotherapy unit of the Eastern Pennsylvania Psychiatric Institute. The unit was organized four years ago, for the purpose of obtaining a better understanding of schizophrenic psychopathology and learning more effective methods of treatment. The project has had as its bias psychological methods of treatment, particularly intensive psychotherapy. From its inception, furthermore, relatives have been involved in the treatment as well as ward personnel. The therapeutic staff consists of two full-time and three half-time psychiatrists, two psychologists, and a social worker. Inasmuch as the unit consists of 20 beds, there is intensive individual and family therapy coverage, and sufficient time for the staff to have frequent conferences for the exchange of observations. It should be added that a large proportion of our patients would be described as "hard core," chronic schizophrenic cases.

Each patient receives individual psychotherapy at least three times a week. Daily group meetings are held with all the patients, nurses, and ward administrator in order to foster communications on the group level, where the most important transference reactions so often take place unnoticed. We have established a variety of ways of stimulating emotionally meaningful relationships. For instance, once a week the community meetings include the therapists as well—and a family-conference-like quality is further emphasized by the reading of a report by one of the nurses on one or two patients' recent behaviour. These reports consist of confronting statements about the patient; they state, in effect, "this is what you have been doing; this is how others see you." The patients then have an opportunity to respond to these reports (which are sometimes critical) in the presence of the other patients and staff. Opinions frequently are divergent as the patient may dispute the report, and this situation frequently stimulates family transference and countertransference reactions. Powerful reality-testing tools are brought to bear when the therapist can point out that something the patient resists "seeing" is seen so clearly by others. It is rare that other patients will side with the staff, but occasionally this happens, and then sibling-like resentments come to the fore as the "accused" patient feels she has discovered a traitor in her midst. We have often noticed that the semisocial context of these meetings tends to dilute the tension of the patient-therapist or patient-nurse relationship to the point where it is safe to express highly personal, positive feelings. We have found, for example, that these sessions have helped in those cases where the fear of homosexuality has interfered with expressions of need for affection and warmth.

Another therapeutic activity has been conducted on a once-a-week basis, where all the patients and some of the staff meet together with the relatives of the patients—usually at least one parent of each patient. This complex meeting has come to be a source of considerable support for many of the parents, some of whom continue to attend even after their daughters have left the hospital. We have confirmed in our studies the striking social isolation of these families as described by other authors (R. Gibson); indeed, for some, it is the only place during the week that they have to go. Occasionally, conflicts between subgroups of parents and patients have developed here on the basis of newly discovered loyalties: for example, patients have sometimes banded together against parents as though they were the common enemy. Patients and relatives tend on occasion to manipulate each other and hospital staff according to patterns remarkably similar to the intra-family battles that had occurred at home.

The most intensive form of treatment for the family occurs in the regular family therapy sessions, where a single family, including the primary patient and two parents (although occasionally including "normal" siblings and grandparents), is seen together by two therapists. We have had ten families in treatment, lasting from several months to three years.

In addition to these regular activities, certain relation-oriented therapeutic activities are organized as the occasion demands it. For example, we have found *ad hoc* organized psychodrama sessions useful in situations where the powerful delusional transference relationship between patient and therapist blocks the treatment. On such occasions the patient may playfully assign a role to a third staff member that fills out the plot of a family drama that the patient is attempting to master. The patient frequently projects unwanted aspects of herself onto this third person and then reacts to this person with a more observing ego attitude, thereby by-passing her habitual paranoid defensiveness.

On other occasions it has proved useful to have the mother of a regressed and self-destructive patient come to the hospital several hours a day to minister to her daughter. The reports of this mother during family sessions along with the nurses' observations comparing their own to the mother's struggle with the regressive, ambivalent communications of the patient proved to be invaluable aids in understanding her.

All the observations from the various approaches are eventually fed back in the form of appropriate interpretations into the two main therapeutic activities of the unit: individual and family therapy. With all of this information the family therapists are able to work with the most important dimensions of unrecognized, elusive, and unconsciously defended family psychopathology.

We have increasingly recognized the need for two therapists in the family situation. Not only do the two therapists support each other's role but they may divide roles between them, one attacking the paranoid projections that the patient automatically transfers to the critical person, and one escaping the "bad mother" role and accepted as more helpful. When the pathological, bizarre types of behaviour can be interpreted in their relevant interpersonal meaning—i.e., in the family context—their rigid dominance in the patient's defences and the attraction of the unconscious revengeful, omnipotent, self-destructive goals become less irresistible.

The family-oriented approach to schizophrenia has been based in the past on such hypotheses as those of the "schizophrenogenic mother," "parental seductiveness," "rejection," etc. Those who have actually observed these families in treatment have advanced thinking far beyond what were found to be oversimplified, naïve concepts. New theoretical frameworks have developed in centres where intensive, sustained family treatment is being conducted by those well grounded in individual therapy of schizophrenics. In family treatment it is often seen that patterns that in individual psychotherapy could only be inferred from transference reactions become directly observable as manifest interactional patterns in the family. The patient's need for symbiotic attachments, for instance, may turn out to be one component part only of an amorphous sticking together of the family as a whole. Various terms have emerged for the description of these states: Wynne mentions pseudomutuality (1), Bowen talks about an undifferentiated family ego mass (2), and one of us has described this family symbiosis as pathological need complementarity (3). Whether the illness of the primary patient is a direct consequence of the several mutually reinforced pathological patterns in these families is still open to question, but all workers in this field tend to agree that the family members respond to the exploration of these types of behaviour with similar defensive resistances as individuals do when in treatment.

Patterns of relationships are mediated in these families through distinctive styles of communication, affective responses, and action sequences. The early infantile fantasies as translated into inappropriate behaviour are not only tolerated or condoned by the family, but they can trigger these types of behaviour actively in the overtly regressed primary patient. We have frequently observed family members co-operating jointly in unconsciously defending their right for their "pathological," complementary adjustment patterns. Resistance to a change can become so violent that another member, i.e., a parent, may temporarily appear overtly paranoid, self-destructive, or physically ill. This unconscious resistance to change is understandable because the parents' repressed infantile needs appear to be gratified by those features of the psychosis that seem to dovetail with these needs in complementary fashion. At the same time the psychotic behaviour may enforce in the parents behavioural mechanisms that are complementary to the patient's unconscious needs. At other times the psychosis seems to be a mere compliance with the parents' unconscious wishes for immobilization of the patient's growth toward autonomy. These considerations suggest that some of the parents' unconscious needs can only be fulfilled if the patient remains psychotic. Even if the coalition of therapeutic influence along with the autonomous tendency of the patient is strong enough to produce a symptomatic improvement, the unconscious motivational forces of both patient and parents still must be dealt with. If these unconscious forces are not recognized and handled they will defeat the well-meaning, conscious efforts of parents, therapists, and patient. This important consideration often remains neglected in symptom-oriented treatment programmes of psychotic patients.

A young schizophrenic girl, after five years of hospitalization, finally attempted to obtain a typist's job by taking a typing performance test. Yet, in a family session, her father, an intelligent and successful man, derogated her effort by pointing out that her moderate rate of typing speed in no way compared with the performance of an expert typist. This first tentative gesture of the patient toward a realistic life goal was thus completely missed. The father's implied disparaging attitude was so inappropriate to this moment of long-awaited optimism and so much in contrast to his consciously supportive and liberal attitudes that it startled everybody in the room.

In the case of another chronically regressed patient the father was enthusiastic about family treatment so long as the patient remained incoherent. When she, however, started to make more sense in the sessions he became visibly uncomfortable, suggested that her illness was organically based, and wondered whether a pill or injection might be found that could cure her.

These examples indicate how resistant parents can be toward growth in the patient; and how a genuine movement toward independence (improvement) would threaten the unconsciously desired family symbiosis, through loss of the needed object. Despite conscious distress on the part of the parents, however, the separation from the patient by dint of hospitalization is not nearly as threatening to the symbiotic togetherness as is maturation and the prospect of marriage, implying permanent separation. In its extreme form the parent's unconscious wish aims at an immobilization of the patient, preferring even hospitalization to separation. This is because the patient represents for the parent an internalized parental love object that must be possessed; so that the original feelings of attachment to the parent can be restored. Conversely, the psychotic, in her delusional dream world, remains in the company of the intrapsychic representations of a more gratifying family circle than her actual family could be. In the company of these internalized representatives of her early family she can act out in fantasy the weirdest instinctual strivings, whereas the recognition of the parents in their contemporary real form would often foil her imaginary gratifications. Consequently, the patient often prefers to project these early parental or other family images upon members of the hospital personnel or upon other patients. We would also like to emphasize that *interactions* among several of these internalized representations can also be projected upon interactions between real persons of the environment. Transferred feelings and attitudes can thus be directed toward interpersonal situations or whole "family" climates rather than being directed at a particular individual.

Without going into detail on this extension of the transference concept at this time, an illustrative example is offered. A young female patient, who had been living out her delusional Oedipal fantasies, reacted to a nurse with sudden, murderous hostility when the nurse approached her in the company of the patient's father, even though she had been generally friendly toward this nurse previously. However, in the described triadic situation, she reacted to the nurse with a vehemence reminiscent of the rivalrous Oedipal "battle" with her mother. Similarly, in many situations when her father met the nurses in her presence, she demanded that he side with her in her grossly inappropriate claims for protection against the maliciousness of the nurses. As evidence that she reacted to this situation as a replica of her family threesome we offer her repeated statements from individual therapy that her father had never taken her side against her malevolent mother.

Another dependent, affection-hungry patient often attempted to manipulate a giving and mothering nurse into more devotion by cleverly provoking competition between her and another nurse. She then maintained a childishly possessive "control" over the two captive love objects in a manner similar to her earlier hoped-for control over her mother and governess.

Physical touching of the patient by ward personnel is often provoked by the regressive behaviour of the patient; these experiences tend to stimulate a transfer of early childhood feelings to the nurturing atmosphere of the hospital. We have described in an earlier paper (4) how the very authoritarian structure of the psychiatric hospital itself, as well as the rescue motivations of its personnel, merge in a complementary fashion with the regressive needs of the patient.

It may seem superfluous to add how often the countertransference reactions of the staff are a function of these manoeuvres of the patient. Whereas everyone would agree that staff members develop countertransference, we are emphasizing here that these countertransferences are remarkably similar to attitudes seen within the families of the patient. Just as for example children play one parent against the other through the parents' mutually felt jealousy, patients can utilize the latent jealousies among staff members for intricate manipulations of hostile and dependent attitudes. The staff member's feeling reactions to her real relationships with other staff members colours her countertransference responses to the patient. These phenomena are analogous to but more complicated than one-to-one countertransference responses to the patient. The structure of these complex interactions is hard to conceptualize because they involve both communications and fantasy distortions of more than two persons. Sometimes we can get clues about the intrapsychic representations in the patient by noticing what the patient provokes various members of the staff into feeling.

CONCLUSIONS

A great deal of attention is being given nowadays to individual psychotherapy on the one hand and to "social psychiatry" on the other. The workers in these two areas adhere to different philosophies and they search for theoretical frameworks in different directions. Whereas the former group is mostly concerned with intrapsychic symbolism and transference in a one-to-one interpersonal relationship, the second group looks mostly for explanations from that form of social psychiatry that is based on the objective social-psychological studies of small-group behaviour. We know a great deal about how unconscious motivations operate in deep psychotherapy and psychoanalysis, but except for the Oedipal triadic situation there is no consistent theory to explain the deeper, subjective psychology of group interactions.

It must be emphasized that the essence of this paper's point of view is not that the hospital should be transformed into a family-like organization, but to recognize that its therapeutic structure is responded to by patients and relatives as family-like in their feeling attitudes. Their transference to the hospital as a home is even extended to the hospital's physical, inanimate characteristics, in accordance with Searles' recent emphasis on the importance of the relationship to the non-human environment (5).

As can be anticipated, the inclusion of family members in the hospital treatment programme does create certain difficulties in the staff, particularly in conflicts over role relationships. The gain through increased insight, however, tends to outweigh the disadvantages, and the therapeutic goals become much better defined for the entire ward staff when the meaning of the psychosis is exposed in its family context. Concepts like "narcissistic withdrawal" and "inappropriateness" as applied to schizophrenic behaviour may eventually become replaced by a knowledge of the coded interactional messages as specific indicators for suitable kinds of therapeutic management.

What are the implications of the principles presented here for the therapeutic organization of the psychiatric hospital? The methods of therapy that were applied at our research hospital unit were set up for the purpose of studying the most personal, the family aspects of the human situation involved in hospitalization. Thus, these methods served observational as well as therapeutic purposes and can be considered as examples or pilot projects only for the preparation of their systematic incorporation into the policies of hospital organization. We do not claim that we can propose a definitive model for the ideal hospital organization to meet modern society's mental health needs. We *do* feel, however, that the family orientation can serve as a sound and meaningful guiding principle for the understanding of the deepest human needs in psychiatric illness and that this dimension deserves more attention in hospital administration.

REFERENCES

1. Wynne, L., Ryckoff, I. M., Day, J., and Hirsch, S. I. Psychiatry. *21*: 205–20, 1957.
2. Bowen, M. Family treatment in office practice (unpublished), Conference on Family Treatment, Temple University, Philadelphia, March 30–31, 1961.
3. Boszormenyi-Nagy, I. The concept of schizophrenia from the perspective of family treatment, *In* Symposium on the Family Treatment of Schizophrenia at the Annual Meeting of the American Psychological Association, Chicago, September, 1960 (in press, Family Process).
4. Boszormenyi-Nagy, I., Framo, J. L., Robinson, L. R., and Holden, E. Family concept of schizophrenia and treatment organization of the psychiatric hospital, Read at the 117th Annual Meeting of the American Psychiatric Association, Chicago, May, 1961.
5. Searles, H. F. *The Non-human Environment in Normal Development and in Schizophrenia*. New York: International Universities Press, 1960.

3

The Concept of Schizophrenia from the Perspective of Family Treatment

This article is based on a paper read at the annual convention of the American Psychological Association in Chicago, September 1960. One of the hypotheses of this writing is need-complementarity, a dovetailing between the deep motives of closely relating members. This is both a resource for each individual and a cohesive force for relating. The prototype is heterosexuality. The male's needs are complemented by the female's needs. At its primitive manifestations need-complementarity can lead to fusion and undifferentiation. The sick child's guilt-laden needs for self-destruction may collude with the possessive needs of the parents. On a more differentiated level, one party's evolving identity demarcation promotes the emergence of the other member's autonomous individuation.

A persistent early contextual theme was the "dialectical" construction of the person-interrelationship. The self is viewed then as the "figure" that ontically depends on its "ground," the other. This dialectical view of the person-relationship juncture is in obvious contrast with a simple adoption of the general systems model. The self's ontic dependence on the other is an indispensable component of relating, even if the mode of relating is "regressive" or psychotic. The private experience and meaning of a close relationship is seldom captured through "communicated objectively observable meaning." It was at this point where familiarity with Ronald Fairbairn's object-relations theory promised a bridge from Freudian to relational understanding. An internal model of ego-object relating replaced the classical notion of ego-id-superego structure. The

20

motivational base of the individual is thus extended from his own singular psychic realm to that of the dialogue. The ego-constitutive function of relationship is to be contrasted with ego-dissolution resulting from a lack of self-delineation between persons. Thus, the configuration of the individual's deep needs depends not only on his "fantasized relatedness" but also on the thesis-antithesis function of the real self and other relationship.

It is in psychosis that a great part of the self-other dialectic may retreat to the realm of internal relating. At the point where the "pathology" of overtly symptomatic relating fails, the psychotic person may show excessive preoccupation with "regressively gratifying introjects". Hallucinations (Hollender & Boszormenyi-Nagy, 1958) and delusions can represent regressive but reassuring internal relationships.

The specific hypothesis of this paper was founded on several assumptions. One is that schizophrenics struggle with difficult compromises between interpersonal relational ties and those early internalized parental imagos which led to the demarcation of the self. It is further assumed that parents tend to regard the preschizophrenic child as a parent-like figure. (In later contextual literature this process is termed "parentification," Boszormenyi-Nagy, 1965). Furthermore, it is assumed that the preschizophrenic child surrenders his autonomy in submitting to the parental demand. The concept of this giving availability is a predecessor of the later explorations of the role of loyalty in psychotherapy (Boszormenyi-Nagy, 1966, 1972; Boszormenyi-Nagy & Spark, 1973).

Another important contextual concept first formulated here is that of interpersonal consequences. There is a difference between one's stated intentions and the outcome of one's actions. Such an important consequence is the inculcation of an unshakable moral imperative, a "counterautonomous superego," into the child. Thus, a lasting, personality-forming influence is transmitted to the child. Counterautonomous superego reactions are then directed against any assertion of the child's autonomous tendencies rather than against transgressions of instinctual taboos. The child becomes a captive object of the parent's conscious and unconscious longings, and the parent's attitude is transformed into the child's intrapsychic relationship. In sum, the two individual realms and the relational realm are two different systemic levels, but they are intrinsically connected.

REFERENCES

Boszormenyi-Nagy, I. A theory of relationships: Experience and transaction. In I. Bos-zormenyi-Nagy & J. L. Framo (Eds.) *Intensive family therapy*. New York: Brunner/Mazel, 1965.

Boszormenyi-Nagy, I. From family therapy to a psychology of relationships: Fictions of the individual and fictions of the family. *Comprehensive Psychiatry, 7*, 408–423, 1966.

Boszormenyi-Nagy, I. Loyalty implications of the transference model in psychotherapy. *AMA Archives of General Psychiatry, 27*, 374–380, 1972.

Boszormenyi-Nagy, I., & Spark, G. M. *Invisible loyalties*. New York: Brunner/Mazel, 1973.

Hollender, M., & Boszormenyi-Nagy, I. Hallucinations as an ego experience. *AMA Archives of Neurology and Psychiatry, 80*, 93–97, 1958.

The concept of a disease in the customary nosological sense is based on distinctive diagnostic and etiologic criteria. Since the criteria of the etiology of a physical illness are usually connected with organic, heredito-constitutional or acquired causal factors, physical medicine expects to find the causal mechanisms within the biological boundaries of the diseased individual. Psychiatry, on the other hand, is generally concerned with concepts of causation that are quite different from those typically used in medicine. Schizophrenia, in particular, is not exhaustively described by the traditional nosology, as the results of various studies including the present one undertaken at the Eastern Pennsylvania Psychiatric Institute suggest.

It is perhaps justifiable to say that schizophrenia is a diagnostic entity. But only if it is looked upon as a state of acute confusion or psychotic disturbance of thought and volition can it be regarded an analogous to certain etiologically well-defined syndromes of disordered brain functioning. A shift in the focus of observation to the interlocking between the patient's psychotic symptomatology and the patterns of his family life clearly raises the possibility of a need for a new nosology. Such a nosology requires terms based on a psychology which transcends concentration on determinants within the individual patient to include an operational consideration of the unconscious, hidden motivations in the other, presumably healthy, members of the patient's family, motivations which act as external determinants of the patient's behavior.

This paper, then, will address itself to the problem and mechanisms of close, family relationships, the total interactional field of the family with special emphasis on the determining influence exerted on the patient by the unconscious motivations of other family members. Since family life can be considered as simultaneously determined by genetic-historic as well as present interactions among members, the dynamics to be discussed will pertain to both aspects. Furthermore, a hypothesis will be examined, according to which schizophrenic personality development may in part be perpetuated by reciprocal interpersonal need complementarities between parent and offspring.

Interactional dynamics can either be understood in terms of observable patterns of communication or analyzed as to the underlying intentions of the participants. For instance, it may be essential to know whether an interaction is aimed at cooperation or competition. Yet the accompanying patterns of communication may tend to disguise rather than express the main intent of the interaction. In this sense certain aspects of family living can be compared to performing on a stage. The same role can be enacted in a number of ways according to the individual actor's interpretation. Just as in a good play, in real life it would usually be difficult to predict the course of a character's actions without first intuitively grasping the main configuration of his deepest intentions. In this sense, a person's intentions are called "deep" if they correspond to long range goals and attitudes of his life. Depth in this sense does not connote the degree of hiddenness, but it refers to the extent to which any motivation reflects holistic aspirations within the personality.

Similarly, in the study of parent-child interactions it is possible to focus either on the ongoing communicational feedback patterns between the two participants or on the lasting, personality-forming, or genetic aspects of the parent's past influence upon the growing child. Although the parents' contribution to the child's superego is naturally very complex it is possible to concentrate on any one of the various aspects of these parental influences, such as control of impulses, discipline, resultant unconscious identifications, etc. The aspect to be explored in this paper is the way in which the parents' own unconscious possessive needs for the child contribute to the shaping of his moral reactions. In a way, these influences render the child's dependence on the parent not only a source of needed control and support but an unshakable moral imperative. We also intend to explore the personified qualities that internalized objects (imagos) or the superego itself take in the child's mind. What, for instance, was originally a controversy between the parent's controlling influence and the child's wishes, becomes transformed into an intrapsychic dialogue between the child's superego and his autonomous ego aspirations (1). This intrapsychic situation—even if one is cautious about personifying theoretical concepts—resembles, or is an equivalent of a dynamically meaningful relationship and becomes an explicit interlocution in some hallucinatory and delusional stages of psychosis. Perhaps even the primitively destructive and excessively harsh superego of the psychotic is a valued companion when compared to the horror of inner loneliness and desertion.

What, then, are the means by which the parent's attitudes and actions get transformed into the above characterized intrapsychic relationship situation? Although one cannot disregard the importance of the study of the communicational aspects of the process of superego inculcation, once the superego is formed, the child's communication processes become much more complicated due to intermeshing intrapsychic feedback nechanisms. External input becomes fused with internal input from an early stage of internalized object relationships. In the following we shall be concerned with conceptual problems of this incompletely understood area of anaclitically distorted intrafamily interactions as they are apparent from family treatment situations.

In order to understand the intricate private aspects of family relationships, an appropriate conceptual framework is needed which can account for both intrapsychic and interpersonal psychological aspects. Such a relationship framework would have to deal with the overlapping aspects of what is "real" and what is mere fantasy or projection in person A's attitude toward person B. As has often been described, the psychotic patient alternately relates to the real attributes of a person and to an image displaced to that person via projective identifications. Terms such as "inappropriate" or "bizarre," as applied to the patient's behavior, can be interpreted as a merging of the patient's capacity for truly mutual relating and his needs for fantasied relatedness. For example, the psychotic patient who orders the attendant to bow to him, the emperor of France, at the same time will accept the lowest work assignment from the attendant. If the patient is capable of maintaining this partial contact with reality, why can't he modify his delusions? Probably because even the most intelligent patient feels that his delusional beliefs are so vital for him that he is blindly dependent on them; it seems to him as if the integrity and existence of his personality depend on them. These internal relationships (exemplified in the quasi-dialogues of delusion and hallucination experiences) are so highly invested emotionally because they persist on the basis of the early internalized parental imagos which led to the demarcation of the self and to the abandonment of primary narcissism. The family relationship conduct of the schizophrenic suggests a compromise between internal and external relational ties.

Instead of attempting further to characterize the nature of a generalized psychological theory which would compound man's total spectrum of relationship needs, this paper will explore its implications for family interaction in schizophrenia. Consequently, the theoretical considerations of this paper are not intended to embrace the full range of a family-based psychopathology of schizophrenic psychosis. They offer, rather, a particular emphasis on a certain dimension of family interaction which is considered most fundamental yet is perhaps least understood. This dimension is characterized by that aspect of togetherness which is based on fitting reciprocity rather than on identical sharing. The reciprocal relationship is gradually established by the mutual feedback characteristics of need expression and need gratification between members. The underlying subjective needs of the participants are conceived of as originating from both instinctual sources and requirements of the identity of each individual. Viewed from the standpoint of the individual then, this dimension of mental activity entails psychic homeostatic processes which form a best compromise among a person's various relationship needs.

The observations underlying these theoretical considerations were collected during three and a half years of intensive psychotherapy of young schizophrenic females and concurrent conjoint psychotherapy of their relatives at our research-treatment unit at the Eastern Pennsylvania Psychiatric Institute. Intensive, sustained family therapy has been conducted in ten cases with the attendance of the patient, her parents and two therapists, in regular weekly meetings. The concurrent individual psychotherapy, milieu therapy observations and frequent conferences enabled the workers to study various interrelated dimensions in connection with observations on family interaction. The purpose of the present paper, however, is to offer certain theoretical notions rather than to report on the therapeutic principles and practice of family treatment.

One of the fundamental considerations to be introduced here pertains to the assignment of the sick role itself to a family member to be designated later as the psychotic patient. Generally speaking, the pathological quality of a person's behavior is established when it fails to conform with the expectations of a) society at large, b) the family, or c) the individual himself. We have found, at least in the case of the young adult female patients we have seen, that the expectations of the family (parents) constitute the most frequent yardstick operative in determining the appropriateness of the patient's behavior. In cases where it is safe to assume that the parents themselves have pathological unconscious expectations toward the patient, the patient's behavior gets labeled as "sick" either as a result of her blind conformance to or because of her failure to meet the parents' deepest expectations. The intrafamilial meaning of the psychosis can thus be conceived of either as a shared effort to maintain a status quo or a rebellion of one member against the expectations of the others.

The main purpose of this presentation is not merely to stress the causal significance of the pathogenic expectations themselves which the members of the family may have toward the schizophrenic. Rather the characteristic interlacing between the unconscious need configurations of the parents and of the primary patient will be focused on. An obvious handicap in exploring this phenomenon is that any individual's deeper motivational trends are ordinarily hidden from observation. Even if the repeated occurrence of certain observable interactional patterns — e.g., sadomasochistic ones — enables us to infer underlying needs, our interpretations concerning the most relevant need levels can only be intuitive and arbitrary. A "sadomasochistic" behavior pattern can certainly be interpreted as a sequence of aggressive and sexual discharges between the two partners. Yet, on a deeper level, this behavior pattern may serve as the principal means of overcoming the participants' helpless feelings of isolation through the only type of meaningful human relationship available between them. Furthermore, it is possible that the main unconscious intent of a sadomasochistic behavior between two family members is for the benefit of a third party, who is a participant observer. A loving attitude may be disguised by vexation, not only for outside observers but for the participants themselves too. To summarize: the private experience and meaning of interactional behavior does not always coincide with its communicated, objectively observable meaning.

One of the fundamental problems concerning the relative strength of a person's various motivational aims is whether his autonomous growth aspirations are stronger than his "symbiotic" strivings. A full discussion of this question is impossible without extensive and penetrating philosophical analysis of the ultimate psychological values in human living, which is not the purpose of this paper. The question however can be rephrased in a more concrete form: does the attainment of his own integrity and fullest personal identity promise such measure of satisfaction that the individual is willing and able to alter his originally symbiotic relationships? We can also ask another question: for full living, just how much dependence on others is indispensable even in the most "independent" person? In fact, independence may have no meaning for a basically unrelated, lonely person, who first has to obtain his ego's definition and inner substrate through hoped for, satisfying close relationships. In this sense the schizophrenic state resembles the presymbiotic, normally autistic stage of childhood (2). All of the foregoing suggests that one of the greatest difficulties in causally interpreting any person's behavior lies in the lack of knowledge of his most relevant motivational formula. In clinical work, whenever we observe a repeated contradiction between a person's stated intentions and the outcome of his actions, we customarily assume that the latter correspond to more fundamental motivational forces. Consequently, the often observed failure of the parents to encourage the patient's moves toward separation suggests that there are lasting unconscious cohesive forces of great power in the family of the schizophrenic. We specifically postulate that these cohesive forces are based on the members' complementary needs which dovetail in the resulting symbiotic togetherness. The force of these unconscious needs makes up perhaps the most powerful single pathogenic circumstance in the development of chronic schizophrenia.

Another assumption to be examined is the following: can the patient's psychosis in itself satisfy an important unconscious need in the parent? Can a prepsychotic, or later on a psychotic child, be more gratifying to the parent than a child with a healthily growing personality? We postulate that the characteristic personality development of the schizophrenic, and later on the psychotic condition, may represent his unconscious compliance with the parent's deep-seated desire to suppress his emancipation. Since arrest of personality development leads to a diminished capacity to relate to members of the opposite sex, the likelihood of losing the child through heterosexual attachments outside the family becomes practically eliminated. Naturally, the physical maturation of the adolescent and the young adult will press for new instinctual gratifications, which create special problems in family living. Yet, if holding the child in a captive relationship is the parent's main unconscious goal, suitable, bizarre family adjustments will have to develop to gratify these needs in the patient. Varied erotic and sadistic stimulations may be applied to the schizophrenic under some disguise, even actual incest or open seductiveness may be condoned.

What configuration of needs leads to this destructively possessive and symbiotic parental attitude pattern? It has been assumed that a parent who is fixated on the loss of or separation from his own parent will unconsciously seek the recovery of the lost relationship first in the marriage mate and later in the child. Avoidance of the pain of the early loss will necessitate the mobilization of powerful, unconsciously determined devices, in order to prevent a repetition of the experience of the loss. Our clinical material tends to substantiate the prevalence of emotionally nonfulfilled marriages among the parents of the schizophrenic. This marriage situation on the other hand, tends to involve the primary patient in a pathologically reinforced bind with one or both parents. A mother, whose catatonic 21 year old daughter has hardly said more than a dozen sentences in the past two years, commented that her daughter's life was a wasted one and "God could take it any day." Yet she hardly missed a single visiting day at the hospital because, as she also stated, her daughter has been the principal source of affection all of her life. Her history revealed that at the age of four she had been sent to an orphanage following her mother's death. It is conceivable that her daughter, either intentionally or inadvertently, by being psychotic is maintained in a state of "captivity" as a substitute object of the mother's symbiotic longing.

Considerable clinical evidence has been gathered from our observations of families in support of the assumption that the parents tend to regard the preschizophrenic or schizophrenic child as a parent-like figure. We have heard parents overtly complaining of their child's "unwillingness" to listen to the parent's life problems or "to give enough time to planning for the family." Often the patient appears to have been loved in her childhood only because of her prematurely serious, responsible, behavior. In slips of the tongue parents frequently call the patient "mother."

Even though the parent's postulated unconscious need for symbiotically retaining their child as a quasi-parental object would account for many of their observed attitudes, an explanation is needed for the willingness of the child to surrender his autonomous life goals—unless a constitutional under-endowment of his autonomous potential is assumed. Also, one has to distinguish between direct responses to external, undermining and manipulative influences, and to intrapsychic dynamic factors in the child himself. The actual dynamic forces which counteract the patient's movement toward growth and independence originate in part from a specifically thwarted superego structure. In order to have the patient's superego develop into a manipulatable force, the parent may unconsciously shape the child's early internalized value orientation according to his own symbiotic needs. We postulate that a "counterautonomous" motivation is gradually inculcated into the child by the parent who intuitively "conditions" the child to fulfill his own unconscious symbiotic needs. The most important moral injunctions are directed not primarily toward destructive or sexual impulses, but toward any attempt at increased autonomy. One of our mothers reported how she used to warn her children that they should avoid the sexual immorality of present day youth; yet she constantly impressed them with her bitter disappointment about marriage. Thus all extrafamilial erotic interests were penalized. In a slip of the tongue this mother implied that unconsciously she did not expect her children to get married. A seventeen year old patient was accused by her parents of neglecting her family because of her rather infrequent and timid attempt to have dates. That a mother can be aware of her superego distorting influence on her daughter is illustrated in the case of a patient who maintained consummated incest with her brother for some time prior to hospitalization. At the end of an interview with the patient's therapist, amidst profuse tears, the mother stated: "Whatever wrong she did, she didn't know she was doing wrong, because I have never told her the facts of life . . . I should have explained it to her more plainly." The mother's tacit condoning of the incest is further hinted at by the greatly delayed timing of her implicitly seductive warning to her incestuous son: "If you don't cut that out . . . you'll have to get out of here . . . If you have no respect for your sister you'll have no respect for your mother."

It appears that once a counterautonomous superego has been built up in the pre-schizophrenic child, a simple, apparently innocuous trigger signal from the parent, or even from others, is sufficient to produce a painful and perplexing feeling of guilt over any semblance of emancipation. The patient's psychotic productions often contain clues about their awareness of this ambivalent, futile internal situation. One of our patients, for instance, reported that each time she felt interested in a boy, she had the feeling that her mother was watching disapprovingly over her shoulder. She also had a matching delusion that her vagina was abnormally small. Several patients reported a general feeling that somebody had taken or was taking their freedom of action away, that they are constantly being disapproved of by someone, or that they are controlled by robots. At other times their delusions take the form of a psychotic rebellion and patients may disown their parents. Parents are also among the most frequent subjects being killed or harmed in the patients' dreams.

What is the role of specific patterns of communication in the establishment of the above described pathological split of aspirations (autonomy vs. symbiosis) observable in the young adult schizophrenic? No doubt the confusing injunctions originally must have been of a "double bind" (3) type. But later on, the structure of the patient's own motivational forces becomes such that the greatest inner resistance is mobilized against anything that could lead to independence, and the parent's communication at this stage may only represent a comment on the patient's impotent *internal* situation. A mother, for instance, has only to validate mildly the patient's exaggerated concern about her moderately large size as an incapacitating barrier toward marriage.

Although it is possible to include in this presentation only a few supporting fragments, the evidence of the study that led to the foregoing considerations is substantial. Yet the hypothesis of intrafamilial need-complementarity as a psychogenic factor in maintaining schizophrenia is not meant to supersede or exclude other known explanations. For example, we do not want to underestimate the undischarged instinctual forces which impel the patient to seek primitive gratifications at all costs. Although we have plentiful evidence that parents can seduce their children into various types of regressive indulgence, it would be injudicious to exclude the possibility that the child's own biological make-up could contribute to such fixations or regressions. We maintain, though, that the contribution of the personal relationship needs of parents has not been paid adequate attention as superego-forming influence. Often it is easy to infer from observable facts that some of the guilt-laden forces in the patient "collaborate"with the symbiotic needs of the parent. The verification of these forces does not have to depend on clues from observable behavior. A permanent attachment to an inner "presence" of the parent, even long after the latter's actual death, has been described in cases of chronic schizophrenia (4). The intrapsychic object or the staff member upon whom the former may be displaced, takes then the place of the original parent.

In conclusion, I should like to distinguish the hypothetical constructs of this paper from those published by other workers who have studied the familial dynamics of schizophrenia. While all the theories must consider the interrelations of individual and group psychologies, our need-complementarity hypothesis views schizophrenic family (and perhaps individual) pathology as an epiphenomenon of characteristic structural needs (identity defects) of the personalities of the members. A distinction is made here between structurally determined and instinct-based origins of deep unconscious needs. The most important structurally determined needs from our point of view, pertain to the experience of *relatedness*. It is largely out of relationship needs with respect to early important object relationships that the ego came to have its identity.

Keeping the ego-constitutive function of relationships in mind, it is conceivable that a "symbiotic" attachment is maintained between family members among other reasons, for the economic one of keeping anxiety connected with threatening identity dissolution at a minimum level. Thus, what appears to be a mutually possessive and captive relational feedback between parent and child may represent a gain which brings satisfaction on a regressive level of ego integration, even if independent growth of both participants is hindered.

Wynne et al.'s concept of pseudomutuality emphasizes that aspect of schizophrenic family living which is permeated with an illusion that rigid relationship ties among members secure them against the recognition of divergent aspirations (5). Whereas the concept of pseudomutuality connotes a "sense of relation" which becomes a "hollow and empty experience" (5), the concept of need-complementarity stresses a regressive, but "meaningful" experience of relatedness between family members. The complementarity of deep needs among the various family members, along with other factors, such as specific communication patterns (3), or internalization of the "overall family role structure" (5) help to make up a "homeostasis" (6). The end result of this type of adaptation is in part accountable for the characteristic social isolation of the families of schizophrenics. The psychotic state of the primary patient, on the other hand, often represents a rebellion against the rigid family ties which are manifestations of the powerfully binding need complementarities.

It is clinically observable that inner feelings of loneliness do not depend on outside circumstances; this has little to do with loneliness in a physical sense. In other words, the total network of relationship possibilities is complicated by the fact that the ego can react to the more or less personified introjects with a subjective experience of relatedness. The psychotic condition produces many instances of an apparent exclusive preoccupation with regressively gratifying introjects, perhaps as the only resort from the bind of symbiotic family ties on the one hand, and threatening personality disintegration on the other.

REFERENCES

1. Freud, S. *The Ego and the Id.* *1927,* London, Hogarth Press Ltd., 1950.
2. Mahler, M. S., Furer, M., & Settlage, C. F., "Severe Emotional Disturbances in Childhood: Psychosis," in Sylvano Arieti (Ed.), *American Handbook of Psychiatry,* New York, Basic Books, 1959, pp. 816–840.
3. Bateson, G., Jackson, D. D., Haley, J., & Weakland, J., "Toward a Theory of Schizophrenia," *Behav. Sci.,* 1, 251–264, 1956.

4. Hill, L. B., *Psychotherapeutic Intervention in Schizophrenia*, Univ. of Chicago Press, 1955.
5. Wynne, L. C., Ryckoff, I. M., Day, J., & Hirsch, S. I., "Pseudomutuality in the Family Relations of Schizophrenics," *Psychiatry*, 21, 205–220, 1958.
6. Jackson, D. D., "The Question of Family Homeostasis," *Psychiat. Quart. Suppl.*, 32, 79–90, 1957.

4

The Concept of Change in Conjoint Family Therapy

This chapter was devoted to a formulation of change in the "multi-personal" texture of psychological health and illness. This familial, systemic level of motivations is addressed as the substrate sought to be altered in family therapy. It is suggested that this systemic level is connected with the "long-term gratification economy" of all participants.

It is hypothesized in this chapter that a collective "family pathology" opposes each participating individual's autonomous growth needs. This raises the question of directionality of change. Whereas all life processes are composed of chains of continual change, some of these changes are desirable, while others are detrimental for the self-preservation of the individual. It is proposed here that certain dynamic facets of the family's life support individuation whereas others are conducive to stagnation. Also, some of these forces foster "identity indoctrinations," unconsciously instigated by the parents' superego or ego requirements.

The chapter's specific hypothesis for obstacles to individuation focuses on a "collusive postponement of mourning" over relational losses. This follows the basic Freudian assumption that the road toward personal growth passes through inevitable relational losses, such as weaning and learning to walk without adult support. The absorption of these losses constitute entry points to new relational involvements, always requiring a degree of relinquishment of the reliance on a secure past relationship. Successful transition depends on the completion of the mourning over loss, without which there is no "distinct ego boundary formation" and therefore no complete "self-object delineation." The facing of loss is a painful process, however. Therefore family members not only resist their own share of acknowledgment but also become accomplices in a shared postponement of maturation. Their need-complementarity turns them into unconscious conspirators of sacrificed growth.

Here lie elements of what in my other writings (Boszormenyi-Nagy, 1965, 1967) was described as being the "object for the other." From one family member's vantage point the other member's merit through availability entitles the same to be spared from pain of relational loss. Later on this discovery of obligated complicity led to the emergence of the concept of loyalty (Boszormenyi-Nagy, 1966, 1972). The parent may have the need to hold on to his or her own deserting but desired parent object, and he can do so through displacing the parental image onto the child. The child may then unconsciously conform to the parent's object restorative efforts by surrendering his own growth and individuation. In this sense psychotic symptoms such as delusions and hallucinations can represent efforts at avoiding pain of mourning and at a collective object conservation and thus lack of change.

REFERENCES

Boszormenyi-Nagy, I. A theory of relationships: Experience and transaction. In I. Boszormenyi-Nagy & J. L. Framo (Eds.), *Intensive family therapy*. New York: Brunner/Mazel, 1965.

Boszormenyi-Nagy, I. From family therapy to a psychology of relationships: Fictions of the individual and fictions of the family. *Comprehensive Psychiatry, 7,* 408–423, 1966.

Boszormenyi-Nagy, I. Relational modes and meaning. In G. H. Zuk & I. Boszormenyi-Nagy (Eds.), *Family therapy and disturbed families*. Palo Alto: Science Behavior Books, 1967.

Boszormenyi-Nagy, I. Loyalty implications of the transference model in psychotherapy. *AMA Archives of General Psychiatry, 27,* 374–380, 1972.

B ecause of its relevance for pathology, the assessment of change is
of fundamental significance for the psychotherapist. Pathology,
whether it is conceived in physical or psychological terms, traditionally
connotes a deviant (altered or changed) state of an organism. As to
psychiatric conditions, that which has been altered can be best defined
either in intrapsychic or in interpersonal terms. It is apparent that of
all recent developments in psychiatry, family therapy has been most
emphatic concerning the multipersonal texture of psychological health
and illness. This chapter is specifically concerned with questions of
individual and interactional changes, accompanying conjoint psychotherapy of families comprising at least one clinically schizophrenic
member.

I shall first discuss general criteria of change; then an hypothesis for
the main dynamic dimension of change; and finally, the implications
of insight for change, along with some general concluding considerations.

CRITERIA OF CHANGE IN FAMILY THERAPY

The literature on evaluation of change effected by psychotherapy
is far too voluminous and multifaceted for a review here. From the
point of view of family therapy, it is especially premature to focus on
detailed questions of evaluative methodology before the main conceptual issues of the criteria of familial change are clarified. Furthermore,
family therapy experience teaches the therapist new dimensions of
evaluation regarding even individual psychotherapy. However, even
from the vantage point of individual psychotherapy, one cannot escape
the conclusion that it is impossible to define change in the total dynamic
functioning of a person without reference to his most intimately interpersonal, familial exchanges.

A truly systematic discussion of change in families undergoing psychotherapy ideally ought to be based on operationally definable process
concepts of psychological health and maturity of both individuals and

families. At the other extreme of the scale, a clinical-empirical evaluation of change may simply rest on the presence or absence of descriptive
psychiatric (symptomatic) evidences of traditionally defined pathology.
Since space does not permit even a tentative utilization of such a highly
useful conceptual analysis as Hill and Hansen (1960) identification of
interactional, structural-functional, situational, institutional, and developmental frameworks that are applicable to family studies, the
observations in this chapter will be based on the author's six years of
experience with conjoint (institutional, home, and office) family
treatment and on team discussions held at the Philadelphia Psychiatric Center and the Eastern Pennsylvania Psychiatric Institute.

The family therapist has to develop a long-range process view of
therapy in order not to get lost in the sequence of kaleidoscopically
changing "microscopical" events. For the moment, an event may strike
him as an impairment, while seen in its overall temporal context the
same event may represent an important element of progress. A large
category of phenomena classified under "regression in the service of
the ego" (Kris, 1952) belongs here. Temporary disorganization of a
formerly always composed member, for instance, may indicate the
beginning of a rearrangement of his contribution to the total family
pathology. Loewald (1960) characterizes the course of psychoanalysis
as consisting of "periods of induced ego-disorganization and reorganiza-
tion." In the same significant paper, he suggests a guideline for the
analyst in his evaluation of the direction of movement and the placement of his interpretations. The guideline issues from a construction,
even if rudimentary, by the therapist of a reference image of the patient's
core personality. In other words, according to Loewald, the analyst
extrapolates into the future that intrinsic construction of long-range
change which he has inferred from the minutiae of his observations
of the patient's here-and-now behavior as well as of his conscious and
unconscious account of his past.

Many an apparent change in families turns out to be a simple manifestation of a never-ending relational seesaw movement. Several of our
treatment families have come to use the term "Yo-Yo" for this pseudo-
progress quite spontaneously. It is only through understanding the long-
term gratification economy of all participants of the symbiotically close

familial relationship that the therapist can learn whether, for instance, a young girl's leaving home means increased autonomy or rather a travesty of individuation through the subsequent intensification of her symbiotic involvement. In other words, any apparent change may actually contribute to reinforcement of the underlying developmental stagnation.

Developmental (directional) concepts underlie any dynamic consideration of psychic health. Change is the essence of life processes and the direction of change points from conception to death. On the other hand, certain changes, e.g., physical growth, are appropriate for the young only. Slowness of the aging process irks the adolescent, whereas it is most welcome to the elderly. Turning now to relational development, personal overinvolvement and underinvolvement appear to be phasically alternating requirements and goals throughout the individual's lifetime, although the general direction of change points to more involvement on a more individuated (mature) basis; early infantile uninvolvement as a start yields to more and more complex and deep involvements throughout adulthood.

Although it is difficult to apply developmental process concepts in evaluating anybody's emotional maturity, at least it can be categorically stated that the individual's life adaptations ought to be aimed at the preservation of his own self. The same criterion of health cannot be applied, however, to the nuclear family. If the nuclear family remains ideally adjusted to self-perpetuation after the offspring have grown to biological maturity, one can assume that certain dynamic facets of the family's life support stagnation. Perhaps the parents cannot let the grown-up children go, despite their best conscious intentions; or the children may have grown up to be frightful of true individuation and of genuine extra-familial involvement. Naturally, the period in which the offspring attains separation age (launching stage) is stressful for any family. We have found, especially, that many families comprising schizophrenic members are close social systems which tend to discourage such intruders as boyfriends, girlfriends, potential marriage mates, etc. Of the many possible criteria of family health or maturity, we can emphasize the one which, by a flexible preparedness for giving up the family's togetherness itself, allows individuation and separation through formation of new relationships on the growing offspring's part. We can epitomize our developmental outlook with the statement that "family maturity" is not determined by the extent of individual accomplishments or of manifest discord, but by the state of the equilibrium between forces supporting individuation and those building roadblocks to personality growth and relational diversification in various members.

Considerations of developmental arrest lead us to the more general and rather central concept of *fixation*, fundamental to post-Freudian psychiatry. It is customary to consider a rigidity or lack of flexibility as the central factor in all psychopathology. Searles (1961), in a paper centering on the significance of change in psychotherapy, describes change itself as a major source of life anxiety. Some therapists claim that *any* change in response to psychotherapy is beneficial. With qualifications, this holds true of family therapy. In this connection it is interesting to note that whereas the student of psychopathology tends to look upon illness as fixation, stagnation, or arrest of change, members of the family often view psychosis as a change for worse from the patient's "good" pre-psychotic, static condition. Family members often wish to change the primary patient back to what he used to be prior to the onset of psychosis and, according to good clinical evidence, unconsciously they wish him to remain there.

Directional considerations of familial change can highlight the intricate connections between intrapsychic and interpersonal dimensions of change. In this regard, it has to be recognized that, thanks to the contributions of Freud, Abraham, Melanie Klein, Fairbairn and others, intrapsychic changes can be formulated in the interactional terms of a quasi-interpersonal conceptional dynamic. To use a common example, any act of actual, interpersonal "giving" alters the giver's emotional balance not only with regard to the receiver, but with regard to his own super-ego as well. Another example highlights the manner in which a seemingly new relationship essentially represents the elaboration of an internalized old one. For instance, the apparently interpersonal, here-and-now relationship of a young woman with her baby may be — dynamically speaking — the heir of her relationship with her own mother (Benedek, 1959). To the extent that she is excessively fixated to an old relational tie in a new relational context, the mother's attitude will become the source of major family pathology (Boszormenyi-Nagy, 1962).

The evaluation of observed interactional changes is, of course, of primary importance for the family therapist. The interlocking of developmental changes ("epigenetic" changes, Erikson, 1959) of individuals no more reveal the overall family process than adding the properties of hydrogen and oxygen reveals the properties of water. Since the family is a multilevel organization, its changes have to be conceptualized on each of its significant levels. The emergence of any simple event, e.g., a heated discussion, can signify change in a) an individual member's habitual behavior, b) the nature of dyadic or other sub-group interactional patterns (coalitions, displacements, etc.), and c) the overall style of the entire family. Changes observed on each of these three levels will have to be integratively evaluated in terms of long-term process considerations. Naturally, the life of an individual is just as much a process as is the life of the brother-sister infatuation or of an entire nuclear family.

While not losing sight of possible evidences of changes in individual members, the family therapist has to maintain an eager interest in noting changes that occur in the dyadic or triadic patterns of the family system of relationships. For instance, newly emerging trends of father-daughter or mother-son involvement may characterize a certain phase of family therapy. One can be drawn into detailed examination of the Oedipal features of these involvements and yet the true significance of such relational changes cannot be evaluated without an understanding of the qualitative changes of each participant's subjective need gratification systems. A father who, returning home late in a drunken state, accused his daughter of promiscuous behavior, turned out be struggling with a projected resentment toward his long deceased mother rather than with heterosexual jealousy in a father-daughter context. The impact of such changes to other dyadic or triadic configurations is even more important to note. Perhaps the most significant dynamic consequence is that a newly emerging need-gratification system between two members will inevitably effect the balance of relational gratifications as far as the other members are concerned. In the above example, there seemed to be no evidence of jealousy on the mother's part, who rather appeared to be a co-beneficiary with her daughter in a wished for, emerging expression of her husband's needs for family. Ultimately, the question of change has to be decided in the context of the total relational system, involving all members.

Many typical examples of dyadic or triadic changes can be cited from clinical experience with families containing a psychotic member. Quite frequently the initial phase of conjoint therapy with such families is characterized by an ostensible parental alliance feuding with an unmanageable "sick" child. The parental alliance is all the more obvious since the parents share the responsibility for the psychiatric hospitalization of the psychotic member. This arrangement, however, tends to yield to one in which the psychotic child gains immense significance as a mediator in the middle of a meaningless, often emotionally "burnt out" parental marriage. This picture may easily change again into one in which the most significant pseudo-alliance in the family appears to be a hostile, ambivalent, primary identification type relating between a forceful, phallic mother and her psychotic daughter. In the case of families with a young psychotic male, a corresponding configuration often is a homosexually tinged, ambivalent attraction between a mothering type father and his son. This inverted Oedipal phase then is apt to yield to a heterosexual arrangement within the family's inter-member involvements. The latter may in turn coincide with extra-familial heterosexual experimentations on the offspring's part, whereupon a defensive closeness between the parents may reoccur as a transitory defensive maneuver and the whole cycle may start again, causing the observer to wonder whether he has seen anything but phases of cyclic oscillation in an essentially unchanging conspiracy of static relationships.

Change is the direct opposite of conformance with fixated family ideologies or "family myths" (Wynne et al., 1961). One has to develop a sensitive ear to parental statements like: "What a pity that Loretta (twenty-one-year-old daughter) has such a poor figure; otherwise she would have been engaged or married a long time ago." With the help of the therapists' warm interest in her femininity, this schizophrenic girl learned that she was not as incapable of attracting men as suggested by her mother, and she started to date afterwards.

Certain family myths can distort the personality development of the offspring by stamping a configuration of negative identity upon them. The most insidious of these identity indoctrinations take place unconsciously, instigated by the parents' superego or ego lacunae (Johnson & Szurek, 1952). By this is meant that the parents' consciously disapproved though not deeply repudiated anti-social impulses may find their outlet through their unintentional encouragement of anti-social behavior in the offspring. These unconscious encouragements usually have typical double binding characteristics, especially when they come in the form of cautions against the child's potentially dangerousness anti-social impulses. An interesting form of power schemes used by mothers can be built on the family myth of the dangerousness of the members' impulses. The mother can then be seen engaged in complicated schemes of protecting each member from the potentially dangerous effect of his impulses upon another member. Such complex, shared mechanisms of impulse discharge and control clearly cut across individual ego boundaries and their change can only be defined in terms of the overall family system. When the family therapist becomes convinced that almost any change in the rigid family myth would be beneficial, he may find it difficult or impossible to revert to his earlier positions where he expected change in terms of character or impulse-defense configurations of individuals.

A HYPOTHESIS OF THE BASIC DYNAMIC OF FAMILIAL CHANGE

It is proposed here that psychological sequelae of object loss are of the most profound significance for the two main criteria of maturity: personal identity and capacity for interpersonal relationships. The incomplete mourning process which in its most general sense diffusely penetrates man's entire individuation, prevents the formation of distinct ego boundaries and leaves one preoccupied with the inner representation of the partially delineated, past relational objects. The incompleteness of the self-object delineation is conducive of an unconscious tendency for projecting the lost person's internal image upon persons of one's here-and-now actual environment. In its extreme, this tendency manifests itself in transference neuroses and delusions; in its milder form it pervades all our closer (familial) ties. This basically object conservative or restorative effort can be very costly as far as the prospects of healthy interpersonal relations are concerned. Various members, especially the growing child, will unconsciously conform to and pose demands for reciprocally shared restorative efforts aimed at retaining deserting though desired early parental images. In certain families the inability for object relinquishment may increase progressively from generation to generation, due partly to physical absence, but even more likely to the inadequate parental model of ego-delineation.

Family pathology then can be conceptualized as a specialized multi-person organization of shared fantasies and complementary need gratification patterns, maintained for the purpose of handling past object-loss experience. The very symbiotic or undifferentiated quality of transactions in certain families amounts to a multipurpose bind, capable of preventing awareness of losses to any individual member. Another aim of the "symbiotic" family organization is the prevention of threatened separations. Separations can occur on interpersonal-interactional and on structural levels. The maturation of a sixteen-year-old daughter, for instance, can cause anxiety in the parents both on account of threatened actual parent-child separation and on account of a reinforcement or return in the parents through identification with their daughter of their own fear of individuation. These fears may compel the parents to revitalize their involvement with the daughter through guilt, scapegoating, infantilization, parentification, or some other means. In one family of this type, the parents developed a concomitant "myth" according to which their only real problem was a marital disagreement over how to discipline their seventeen-year-old daughter. Their discord with each other became so violent that it took close listening and observation on the family therapists' part to detect how the parents' shared role-playing helped them to deny and act out at the same time their anxiety concerning the daughter's maturation.

The above, hypothetical core dynamic of families is assumed to be the determinant of both family need-complementarity (Boszormenyi-Nagy, 1962) and family myth (Wynne et al., 1961). Family pathology amounts to a sensitively regulated system of interdependent displacements regarding the members' affected responses and object choices. The stronger the system as a whole, the less it permits meaningful and mature relating among the members. Deceptive pseudo-involvements, required by the family myth, serve to obscure the incomplete state of individuation of the participants of the system. Vicarious gratifications, projections, and revenge fantasies transferred from early lost love objects prevent the members from definitively working through those steps of maturation which are concerned with the painful process of relinquishing archaic internal objects. The unconscious conspiracy for preventing each other's maturation can therefore be hypothesized as the causative dynamic, underlying the members' symbiotic partnership.

As far as change is concerned, these family systems present well disguised but powerful obstacles. An implicit aim of family pathology is to immobilize real growth in another member because growth leads to the eventual loss of the other member: the source of real or imaginary satisfactions. Inasmuch as imaginary familial satisfactions are partly of a transference nature, they are analogous to certain phases of cling-ing-type therapeutic transference. Whereas the intrapsychic part of the interrupted object relinquishment process is essentially identical in both situations, in family neurosis the individual member is faced with an accomplice in shared postponement of maturation instead of an agent of the secondary process in the person of the therapist. This is an additional, interactional reason why the consequences of the psychotic member's separation from his family so often produce in him overtly familial object-restitutive efforts as symptoms (delusions or halluci-nations).

If the various manifestations of family pathology (projections, in-complete individual boundaries, vicarious gratifications, projective and distorted identifications) are useful only as a means for maintaining the delay of mourning work, the family may itself come to symbolize for its members the denied lost object, perhaps the mother (Josselyn, 1953). Furthermore, it is conceivable that the individual members' primary process needs become largely submerged in the family system and consequently the members become more or less free of typical neurotic (intrapsychic) symptoms. If, on the other hand, one member "changes" with respect to his reliance on the system, one or several of his complementary partners will suffer from "individual symptomatology." The family homeostatic forces will then resume their work as the "betrayed" partners start exerting pressure on the escaping member so that he should resume his compliant family role. Thus, explicit scapegoating often originates from one member's attempts at escape. If scapegoating alone does not compel the escapee to return, he can often be driven into overt psychotic despair with consecutive physical expulsion (hospitalization). The unconscious purpose of the whole game is restoration of the family system, i.e., the imaginary possession of a primal family on the part of most or all members.

Having learned about the underlying mechanisms that prevent genuine interpersonal growth in the family of the schizophrenic does not relieve the frustrations of the therapist who is concerned with change. The therapist will be eager to "attach" any one of the pseudo-involvements manifested between family members, yet he will soon discover that the causal roots of these "sub-system" manifestations involve the total family system. Without affecting the shared motivation of *all* family members for denying and deferring external and internal object losses, the therapist's efforts are largely wasted on mere symptomatic manifestations.

Naturally, the outlook for ultimate change will be determined by the balance between deeper motivational forces of growth or stagnation in the family; and the therapist's role is divided between being a point of crystallization of these forces and an active technician of change. He will, by necessity, have to enter the family system while at the same time protecting himself against being absorbed into it.

The family therapist has to remember that, in any type of psychotherapy, the development of a deep (regressive) relational experience and subsequent exploration are the *sine qua non* of lasting therapeutic effect or change. Criteria of depth are the same in family as in individual psychotherapy. Great intensity of affect may be generated and emotionally charged past attitudes may get forcibly projected (transferred) on other members or on the therapists. Gradually, the barrier against the expression of angry, frustrated or rejecting feelings toward one another will be overcome. Experimentation with trial separations unleashes long repressed frustrations and fosters a more genuine intermember relating. The process of piercing a pseudo-involvement on one member's part stimulates, if motivation permits, a replication on another member's part. With each experience of newly achieved freedom for rejection of transference distorted pseudo-involvements the wheel of arrested mourning processes turns and the family equilibrium advances one step from symbiosis toward potential individuation.

One treatment family came to a meeting with the explicit agreement among father, mother, and married daughter that the psychotic son was to be helped through hospitalization rather than through family therapy. They were unanimous in their opinion that all of their other problems were routine and their only real trouble resided in the intolerable behavior on the boy's part. The therapists' adamant refusal to consider any therapeutic planning other than full conjoint family sessions, gradually led to a violent outbreak of marital disagreement and a decision on the father's part for continuing family explorations instead of hospitalizing his son. In the ensuing, highly emotional exchange, the mother described how she used to scratch her son's back for long intervals while refusing him the right to occupy himself with any hobby of his own. The daughter subsequently admitted to her own marital unhappiness and ascribed her "bad" nature to similar traits in her and in her mother's personality. The session ended in a generalized relief of tension, probably as a result of more genuine, emotionally free relating. That the family system could yield this quickly was probably possible only on a transference-cure basis. The strong stand taken by the therapists established them as targets for transferred parental object needs.

The stage of regression or primary process-type relating brings the family therapist deeply into the family system. A sensitive and suspicious, socially highly accomplished father appeared to be heavily relying on support from one of the therapists for his surprisingly angry rejection of his martyr-like wife. In the subsequent session he displayed a highly ambivalent and guilt-laden behavior toward the therapist. The next day he called to announce that the family wanted to halt therapy for several weeks. As he later associated, the therapist became the heir of a desired yet hated, deserting parental figure who would have to be rejected either symbolically or in reality in order to allow individuation to take place. Often the family terminates at this point or provokes the therapist into terminating treatment. However, as far as long-range change is concerned, even though such termination is premature and the subsequent reunion of the family has a paranoid flavor, it might foreshadow a more mature, more individuated pattern of acting at least on the part of one or possibly all family members.

Premature termination may not be in itself a desirable treatment goal but its prognostic significance merits conceptual exploration. A family's arrested life process may pick up from the point of termination and its homeostatic steady state might get adjusted on a new functional level. More specifically, since we have hypothesized that the main cause of stagnation was a fear of object-relinquishment, an ability to relinquish the therapist as a quasi-familial object may, though it does not have to, signify a newly-won capacity for growth through an emancipation effort in the context of transference.

A family's prognostic evaluation can be made from the balance between the changes they have made and their resistance to change while undergoing conjoint therapy. The first ominous prognostic sign usually is a proof of genuine unwillingness by one or several family members to become deeply involved in an intensely emotional thera-peutic group process.

A twenty-one-year-old psychotic girl who used to write bizarre suicide notes to her family, soon became non-psychotic in her overt behavior shortly after family therapy had been started. Yet even while she was overtly asking for discontinuation of the family therapy ses-sions, she kept sending disturbed letters to the therapists, most likely in order to document her deeper needs for help. Quite in contrast to the daughter, the mother consistently refused to become involved in the therapy process. In the beginning she showed her resistance by not having anything to say or by considering the repetitious discussion of the few "crazy" symptoms of her daughter as the only valid subject area. She consistently refused to talk about her own past memories and fell more and more into the habit of discouraging even the other members of the family from doing so. In the end she began missing sessions and she only occasionally darted through the room where the meetings were held. Finally, she told the therapists not to come any more because her daughter was well now. The therapy had to be discontinued. Several months after termination the mother called to tell the therapists that her daughter had been admitted to the local state hospital and that she hoped she would be cured there by means of physical treatment.

The following example illustrates the thesis that a mere capacity for regressive, deep involvement is not in itself sufficient for an ultimate good prognosis. The mother in this family of a nineteen-year-old schizophrenic boy started out rather cool and aloof in the conjoint treatment sessions and remained so for several months. She would have nothing to say except for well-guarded conventional statements until, approximately at the end of the second year of treatment, she became childishly flirtatious and talkative. Thus, in this sense there has been a definable behavioral change in the mother, yet she was unwilling to connect this behavior with associations from her past. She specifically refused to agree to having her father attend a single session. In one of the last sessions with this family, in which the members seemed to be emotionally freer than ever before, she asked to be excused or else she would have to "do" on the sofa. A few weeks later the family terminated therapy in an abrupt manner, at a point where evidences of change in the family seemed insignificant.

CHANGE IN THE FAMILY SYSTEM
VS. CHANGE IN INDIVIDUAL MEMBERS

Without intending to question the validity of individual-based concepts of psychotherapeutic change (Luborsky, 1962; Siegal and Rosen, 1962; Wallerstein, 1963) for the family therapy situation, we would like to stress the importance of developing a conceptual system for evaluating change on the level of family interaction as a system. Regardless of whether one agrees with the collectively deferred mourning process as the fundamental dynamic mechanism of the pathology of the family system, some kind of a dynamic regulatory principle has to be assumed to operate on a collective group level of the family. It has to be postulated that the emotional gratification economy of each member is, to a high degree, regulated by the nature of the family's group transactional process. It is logical to assume that the system's change cannot be expressed in terms of a mere additive summation of each family member's shift from id to ego mechanism, decreased anxiety, or other criteria of individual structural rearrangement.

The following is an example of a family system of gratification: a family was referred for conjoint therapy because of the psychotic behavior of a sixteen-year-old, extremely muscular son. This boy had quite openly threatened various family members with murder. Curiously, the mother was not nearly as much concerned about her son's threats as were the father and the recently married ("escaped," in her own words) nineteen-year-old sister. As it turned out, the boy's threatening, unreasonable behavior represented a vicariously displayed manifestation of the mother's own, warded-off, murderously hostile attitude toward her husband and her daughter. The latter two gave evidence of their deeply isolated feelings of anger toward the mother through occasional, surprisingly direct and intense outbursts of angry denunciations. Yet, it was also obvious that the son's "craziness" filled the role of a welcome "lightning rod" for all members' explosive tensions and thus his behavior, although consciously censured, was reinforced by the "pleasure economy" of the homeostatic family system.

The question as to the family-therapy counterpart of the Freudian expectation that where there is id, ego shall be, remains unanswered so far. We have claimed that family therapy cannot become productive without a transitory phase of regressive, "free" interaction. This question appeared related to the requirement for a regressive therapeutic transference relationship in psychoanalysis. Naturally, in both cases successful therapy ought to result in a better integration of all functions, leading to more satisfaction in life. Man's satisfaction depends, to a great extent, on his capacity for channeling innate drives into socially and biologically workable patterns of action. The process principle of change demands that the organization of every member's patterns of action be flexible enough to keep pace with the changing requirements of the individual needs for "self-actualization" (Maslow, 1954) and society's expectation for the emergence of new nuclear families from old ones. The very existence of such a purposeful normal adaptation suggests that a surpra-individual family principle has to regulate what ostensibly appear to be the satisfaction goals of individuals. Any lasting change in any member or in the family as a whole has then to fit into the dynamic constellation of the timetable of the family's growth process.

It would be an exaggeration to assert that in family therapy the only significant criterion of change is that which occurs on a group level of the entire family. Changes in the configurations of libidinal or aggressive needs as well as in the degree of the autonomy of ego functions of each and every member have to be watched for significant *indicators* of rearrangements on a multiperson level. One father, for instance, achieved the status of an independent entrepreneur during the treatment period, for the first time in his life. Another father who had been essentially idle for many years decided to undertake a work-training course. In several families parents became able to sleep together again after many years of relational defeat and mutual avoidance. In quite a few cases, the psychotic offspring—under the impact of family therapy—resumed school work, dating, or employment. All of these changes in individuals or in interacting dyads and triads involved complementary changes on all other members' part. The main guideline in evaluating the degree of healthy contribution of any family change issues from the members' joint capacity for replacing gratification systems of stagnant possessiveness with those of fresh, new involvements and with pride in everyone's gain toward individuation.

The family therapist finally has to be cautioned against overlooking, for reasons of his own needs, *lack* of significant change. Although verbalization of previously non-verbalized behavior is ultimately conducive to many new insights, some family therapies are maintained for reasons other than motivation for change. Certain families may continue conjoint family treatment only because they obtain dependent support from and a convenient target for parental type transference in the therapist. Dynamically then, rather than changing the family system, the therapist becomes merged with that aspect of the system that stands for a generalized parent object. Through his own altered emotional position in the family, he may be inclined to distort his perception of the family's interaction. In other words, what may represent a change from the therapist's point of view, may not really be a change for the family's pleasure economy.

In summary, I wonder whether any pathological family system can have a good prognosis as to significant change unless there is evidence that the members can meet the following minimal criteria in a relatively short time: 1) a sufficient emotional spontaneity for the creation of an atmosphere in which they are impelled to make statements which they feel uneasy about after the session; 2) an ability to explore their past emotionally significant relational ties in relation to the interactional structure of the current family and the family therapy situation; 3) a willingness to include any of their relatives or friends, or whomever else the therapists suggest, in their meetings; and 4) evidence of changes in the family's patterns of interaction, e.g., changes in long-established sleeping arrangements, tolerance of the offspring's social experimentation, etc.

REFERENCES

Boszormenyi-Nagy, I. The concept of schizophrenia from the perspective of family treatment. *Family Process, 1,* 103–113, 1962.

Benedek, T. Sexual functions in women and their disturbance. In Arieti, S. (Ed.) *American handbook of psychiatry.* New York: Basic Books, 1959.

Erikson, E. H. Identity and the life cycle, Selected Papers. *Psychological Issues, 1* (1), 1959.

Hill, R., & Hansen, D. A. The identification of conceptual framework utilized in family study. *Marriage and Family Living, 22,* 299–311, 1960.

Johnson, A. M., & Szurek, S. A. Genesis of anti-social acting out in children and adults. *Psychoanal. Quarterly, 21,* 323–343, 1952.

Josselyn, I. M. The family as a psychological unit. *Social Casework, 34,* 336–343, 1953.

Kris, E. *Psychoanalytic explorations in art.* New York: International Universities Press, 1952.

Loewald, H. W. On the therapeutic action of psychoanalysis. *Internat. J. of Psychoanalysis, 41,* 16–23, 1960.

Luborsky, L. The patient's personality and psychotherapeutic change. In H. H. Strupp & L. Luborsky (Eds.), *Research in psychotherapy, Proceedings of the conference APA, Division of clinical psychology* N.C. May 17–20, 1961, American Psychological Association, 1962.

Maslow, A. M. *Motivation and personality.* New York: Harper Bros., 1954.

Searles, H. F. Anxiety concerning change as seen in the psychotherapy of schizophrenic patients — with particular reference to the sense of personal identity. *Internat. J. of Psychoanalysis, 42,* 74–85, 1961.

Siegal, R. S., & Rosen, I. C. Character style and anxiety tolerance: A study in intrapsychic change. In H. H. Strupp & L. Luborsky (Eds.), *Research in psychotherapy, Proceedings of conference APA, Division of clinical psychology* N.C. May 17–20, 1961, American Psychological Association, 1962.

Wallerstein, R. S. The problem of assessment of change in psychotherapy. *Internat. J. of Psychoanalysis*, 44, 31–41, 1963.

Wynne, L. L. The study of intrafamilial alignments and splits in exploratory family therapy. In N. W. Ackerman (Ed.), *Exploring the base for family therapy*. New York: Family Service Association of America, 1961.

5

From Family Therapy to a Psychology of Relationships: Fictions of the Individual and Fictions of the Family

This paper preceded the unifying notion of justice as a relational dynamic (Boszormenyi-Nagy & Spark, 1973). It does, however, lead toward the formulations of justice and ethics as major determinants of close relationships. Thus, family relationships are assumed to be the vestiges of important resources rather than rigid systems that impede individuation. Naturally, the ethical perspective also allows for the possibility of exploitation of one family member by the other.

The dialectical view of relating (see also Boszormenyi-Nagy, 1965) is aimed at an integration of the newly evolving systemic model with the traditional individual-based view. The context envisaged by the dialectical view is the dialogue, a perspective distinctly different from systems (patterns) of observable behavior. The dialectical framework assumes that the person is in part a product of self/other antithesis and that only whole persons can enter into a meaningful dialogue. The invisible linkages connecting relating partners are different from the dynamic unconscious of each person, taken as a separate psychic universe. These issues have complex but important implications for such phenomena as undifferentiation, fusion, symbiosis, pseudo-mutuality, and enmeshment. Conversely, the "mechanisms" of autonomous individuation closely connect with issues of the dialogue. As a corollary, inducement of traits by antithesis has to be added to that of inducement by imitation.

Even though the ethical nature of relational dynamics is not yet formulated here, the goal of family health is defined as rich interaction among "well differentiated and responsibly acting members." Poorly differentiated families are seen as avoiding personal responsibility and commitment. An important criterion for the dialogue is mutual confirmation, which, from today's perspective, includes mutual self-delineation and self-validation (Boszormenyi-Nagy & Krasner, 1986).

Conversely, the possibility of corrupt exploitation lies in the lack of responsibility for the outcome of, for example, confusing communications, rather than in the diagnosable pattern of the dysfunctional transaction itself. Especially, the child can become entrapped in this type of victim role, that is, become exploitatively parentified. The (multigenerational) consequence of behavior is more crucial than any pattern of behavior by itself.

Different from individual unconscious, both in a dynamic and in a configurational sense, are "unconsciously collusive patterns of interactions." Why do all members comply with them? The notion of "loyal support" introduces the term "loyalty" into the literature of psychotherapy, to be further elaborated later in this volume (Boszormenyi-Nagy, 1972) and in Invisible Loyalties *(1973).*

Finally, it is in this paper that the key contextual therapeutic methodological principle, multidirected partiality, is described. This method is a corollary to the therapist's empathic support for a genuine dialogue between partners in close relationships.

REFERENCES

Boszormenyi-Nagy, I. A theory of relationships: Experience and transaction. In I. Boszormenyi-Nagy and J. L. Framo (Eds.), *Intensive family therapy*. New York: Brunner/Mazel, 1965.

Boszormenyi-Nagy, I. Loyalty implications of the transference model in psychotherapy. *AMA Archives of General Psychiatry, 27*, 374–380, 1972.

Boszormenyi-Nagy, I., & Krasner, B. *Between give and take*. New York: Brunner/Mazel, 1986.

Boszormenyi-Nagy, I., & Spark, G. M. *Invisible loyalties*. New York: Brunner/Mazel, 1973.

Family psychotherapy, an approach hardly a decade old, is growing in recognition by both professionals and lay public. In recent years the number of invitations to speak on the subject has been increasing and the attendance at lectures on family therapy has mushroomed. It is becoming more and more common that families coming from the so-called "intelligent lay public" know about and ask for treatment as a whole family. Although it is difficult to evaluate the efficacy of any psychotherapy, especially if new, it seems that family therapy has its results in its favor. Nevertheless, the real contribution of a new field may depend on the soundness of its theoretical assumptions, explicit or implicit. This paper is aimed at the examination of some of the theoretical questions posed by family therapy.

For the purposes of this paper family therapy has to be defined broadly. First, it is a psychotherapeutic approach, and as such it is distinguishable from material or purely educational aid needed by many families. Second, even though there are many ways of treating families, all family therapies share the ideal goal of affecting a superordinate family gestalt of relationships which is more than the sum of the "dynamics" of individual family members. Most family therapists insist on working with the actual interaction among family members on a conjoint basis. Others may treat alternately various individual members and subgroups of families, but they do it from a point of view which focuses on relationships, rather than on analysis or support of individuals.

The circumstances that led to the emergence of family therapy are too complex to be fully enumerated. Contemporary psychiatry appears to be in a state of undeclared war among factions whose differences are either real or grossly exaggerated. Ostensibly, the limitations of the individual-based framework of the otherwise conceptually impressive and technically thorough psychoanalytic tradition contributed to treating entire families. Indeed, most of the early family therapists developed their concepts through either expansion of or partial rebellion against traditional Freudian viewpoints. Yet, it would appear to this writer that all thoroughly explorative and personality-change-oriented therapies belong basically in one big camp, jointly opposed by impatient or antipsychological critics.

The latter often propagate efficiency based methods of social engineering as psychotherapy, and disregard or discredit schools of therapy which are guided by concepts of *personality change* and *growth*.

The reasons for querying the value of psychoanalytic or dynamic psychotherapy are manifold and certainly broader than the critics' resistance to change. There is a need for critical self-examination on the part of the practitioners of dynamic psychotherapy. Actually, cautious and conservative psychoanalysts have never claimed efficacy of analysis beyond the realms of the neuroses. Patients with conditions based on fundamentally weak ego organization, extreme disintegrative anxiety, or globally dependent life orientations are not recommended to undertake psychoanalysis. Other recent critics question the broad applicability of analysis on the basis of social transition. They maintain that contemporary man lives under different types of stress than the "Victorian" ones typical of Freud's Vienna. Patients with typical neurotic symptomatology have become rare and they are being replaced by increasing numbers who manage to "function" while threatened by both lack of personal meaning and feelings of generalized inner emptiness.

Sociologists note the retreat in significance of the time-honored institution of the extended family. Others claim that religion has lost its importance as a regulating value in modern life. The coldly rational world of materialistic science and its technological applications threaten life with the prospect of nuclear death. Even many of the behavioral sciences threaten to lead ultimately to perfecting methods of manipulation and exploitation of the individual human being. The family then is believed to be the last bastion of uncontaminated privacy and human rights in modern life, and it is natural to turn to it with hope as to a renovator of existing lives and guarantor of prospective "healthy" ones.

Although the vigor of the newly developing "unit" or "conjoint" family psychotherapy approaches is impressive to watch, critical observers rightly wonder: What is the real contribution of these approaches to psychiatry? Will the actual observation of man from the vantage point of his close relationships contribute to new psychological theories or to a new application of old ones? The present paper assumes an affirmative answer: The observation of and work with actual family relationships will require a new *psychology of relationship*. The author is in accord with a position taken in a lucid and thorough manner by Handel,[11] who commends interpersonal relationships rather than interaction as the basis of studying families. We cannot afford to neglect the familial mechanisms of pathogenicity and of therapeutic change. The emerging psychology of relationships will have to integrate elements of various existing and future theoretical frameworks—for example, depth psychology of individuals, transactional and communicational theories, and existential-phenomenological theories.

Though the family therapy "movement" obviously needs a conceptual framework of its own, the development and dissemination of the concepts is likely to face formidable resistances. Family relationships in their truly personal aspects have been the most respected and least intruded upon areas of human life, barely touched even by modern civilization. Their study would lead to exposure of some of the hidden roots of the most cherished and vital group forces of humanity: national feelings, religiocultural group struggles, prejudices, hypocritical scapegoating practices, etc.

A more specialized, strong resistance to the development of the new psychology of relationships will originate from professionals rigidly committed to a particular point of view. Many deny the need for any new outlook and maintain that approaches which focus on the family (e.g., social work, child-guidance work, etc.) have existed for years. They will continue to discuss and teach family therapy which they have never fully experienced themselves except in microscopic and well-insulated dosages, such as family diagnostic interviews, occasional conferences with parents, etc. Others advise us dogmatically to put aside all theoretical knowledge about individual dynamics while conceptualizing about the family therapy setting. Conversely, other colleagues suggest that we need no new theories other than the ones we have been using while treating individuals.

A significant theoretical orientation focuses on "system" levels of group behavior in families—for example, transactional, communicational, and contextual. Enthusiastic investigators in this important area may claim that this emphasis should replace rather than complement the subjective, intrapsychic, or experiential dynamic in formulating pathology or therapeutic change in families. Paradoxically, but perhaps not unexpectedly, this extreme position may turn out to be less objectionable to "conservative" individual or psychoanalytic therapists than a synthetic effort that would require an appropriate reexamination and amplification of some of the fundamental Freudian principles in the light of our actual experience with relationships and families. It is likely that the debate between family therapists and other psychotherapists and even among schools of family therapists, will temporarily mask the real issues of the import of this form of psychotherapy. It is possible furthermore that on the verge of accomplishing a mature synthesis of the best of humanistic traditions and modern scientific ideas, psychotherapy faces the danger of becoming the butt of pseudo-intellectual "objectivism" or the victim of the clearly anti-intellectual, antihumanistic "caveman" in modern man.

Conjoint family therapy is probably the most insightful way of studying and affecting family relationships. Various social agencies as well as systematically inquiring social scientists have long been interested in the description of the family's social functions and in social norms and values governing family roles. Social workers and child-guidance agencies have focused on the interactional ramifications of the various psychopathologies of individual family members. Family therapy deals directly with the jigsaw puzzle of interlocking dynamic identity and need configurations of family members, as manifested through interactions and other observable resultants of motivations.

Naturally, not all family problems are of a psychodynamic nature. Much has yet to be learned about the lasting psychological effect of detrimental early life experiences. The effects of physical handicaps of a member, poverty, and lack of educational opportunities cannot be discounted in favor of elegantly reasoned psychodynamic formulations. On the other hand, it is equally true that the implications and ramifications of theories emerging from close studies of family relationships will produce new dimensions of understanding the dynamics of society at large. An example of this is the thus far incompletely understood way in which, through its symbolically grandparent-like role, the school can act as a welcome scapegoat, often caught in the middle between parent and child. School and teacher are often thought of as representing society and as such being above the power level of parents, and accused as the only cause of the lacking social and intellectual accomplishment in the child.

In developing the outlook necessary for a competent family therapist, a transition is necessary from the closed-system viewpoint of the individual to that of the family system. The former is typical of traditional psychiatry and the latter of social psychology. A piece of interaction between a "sadistic" and a "masochistic" family member, for instance, can turn out to be a meaningful component of a scapegoating transactional system. However, in the present author's view, as a next step in professional development, it is equally important that the family therapist should learn how to integrate the individual and system-determined components of motivational determination into a whole. It takes a certain family system and a certain individual personality makeup to both stay in or move out of any transactional family system.

THE FICTIONS OF THE INDIVIDUAL
AND THE FICTIONS OF THE FAMILY

It is a basic fact of human psychology that the baseline for all strivings in most, if not all, individuals is the experiential process which culminates in the sense of a distinct identity of the self. The sense of self implies a unitary integrative function centering around a single point of reference: the experiences of one human organism throughout developmental phases and across the entire range of social roles and situations. That this *sense* of self and its implementation in consistent and responsible motivation and actions is a task of dynamic "becoming" rather than an automatic given of biological life, tends to be overlooked in most current theories of family interactions. ˜

The integrated relationship theory demands a somewhat remodeled outlook on the individual. Consequently, a person is thinkable only in a *dialectical* framework as a synthesis of self-other antitheses.[4] The identity of the self is inseparable from its counterpoint: the other as a differentiating ground. Regardless of any interaction or transaction, therefore, personal existence in a psychological sense is by principle inseparable from relationship. Such dialectical view of persons and relationships is distinctly different from relationship concepts based on particular behaviors or interactions among persons as finite units — for example, power triangles, love-hatred transactions, games of control, and scapegoating. Instead, on deeper levels, relationships reflect action organizations based on reciprocal need templates, patterned according to the interlocking identities of members.

The implications of the dialectical theory of self-differentiation requires a thorough methodological reorientation concerning the psychological *boundaries* of the individual. Much of what is ordinarily described as interactional or relational behavior between two or more discrete individuals actually can in our sense be considered as part of a multiperson action organization. For instance, the type of fateful shared dependency, often referred to as "symbiotic" inseparability, is more appropriately described in terms of multipersonal structural fusion than interaction between persumably distinct individuals. Although this conceptual dichotomy may be difficult to illustrate, it is hardly questionable that alliance between two differentiated persons is not the same as the Siamese twin-like inseparability of undifferentiated partners. Their mutual dependence can be called "ontic" as differentiated from mere functional dependence.[4] Ontic dependence is absolute; it is not based on any concrete functional need. Such basic undifferentiatedness can be revealed, for instance, by unconscious slips of the tongue. A mother may say: "My daughter wouldn't *confined* in me," or "She got so angry, she almost jumped out of *my* skin."*

The concept of ego boundary stands in the focus of interpreting the information obtained in the course of family psychotherapy. By ego boundary I do not mean mere cognitive differentiation; rather, I refer to a motivational delineation of persons as entities or systems of action. When, for instance, the family therapist assumes that the symptoms of one member maintain the balance of the family system, he uses a motivational or determinative concept which transcends the boundaries of the individual. The situation assumes an even higher order of com-

---

*I am indebted for this latter example to Dr. Murray Bowen.

plication if questions of etiology or developmental causation are raised in connection with family systems of motivation; which one came first—individual pathology or pathogenic family system?

In family therapy it is natural to think of an interaction sequence as started by one member, yet the boundaries of functional autonomy and responsibility of individual human beings are difficult to ascertain while engaged in close relationships. For example, an amorphous fusion of the motivations of parent and child can be assumed if the former is seen to participate in an unconsciously vicarious way in the latter's delinquent act, even though the parent's conscious disapproval indicates cognitive differentiation of the two identities. It is probable that in a family of four, comprising a hospitalized schizophrenic, therapists couldn't readily agree on who is the *really* sick member. One therapist would regard the docile, overly "well" sibling as sicker than the designated patient; the other would see the children engulfed by a symbiotically manipulative mother; another might view the passive aggressiveness of the father as most crucial. Actually, many family therapists would say that the illness resides in the family as a system and that there is no sense in calling any one member sick. Such confusion of opinions reflects the magnification by the family perspective of what is a built-in contradiction between overt and covert levels of behavioral criteria, applied to diagnosis and dynamic interpretation.

The question of the authentic delineation of individual versus family or group motivations is therefore the *key issue* of family therapy and probably of human psychology. There are many ways of subtle, unconscious fusion and vicarious motivational sharing among members of most families. As a rule, most overtly disapproved or deplored behavior displayed by one member is covertly condoned and rewarded by one or several other members. Yet when it comes to serious legal consequences of delinquent acting on the part of juveniles, for instance, society has to respond through its court in accordance with the "myth" of the individual, based on the fact of the parents' overt disapproval of the adolescent's behavior. Unfortunately, on a deeper level, an ambivalent disapproval by others of a child's actions may be the only—even if negative—confirmation of his person. For example, what could be more meaningful confirmation than *being the object of* mother's constant passionate scorn, especially when at the same time it is also obvious that the rest of her emotional investments leaves her with a feeling of empty purposelessness? Since some of the most powerful unconscious motivations originate from another person's overt disapproval and covert rewarding, one can rightly wonder why does in one child overt approval, and in another overt disapproval, lead to a compliant motivational development. I believe the answer will come from a better understanding of multipersonal laws of unconscious configurations of interactions and transactions in families.

There are family therapists who speak of "curing" the "sick" family. In my opinion they expose themselves to conceptual confusion through extending the age-old, individual-based notion of pathology to a group, and they contribute to the fiction that there is a psychological being called family. The reification of the family as a living creature and its mythical adoration is one of the neurotic defensive games of mankind. The myth of the family has long served as a cover under which a multitude of personal needs, exploitations, and gains remain hidden and obscured. The disorder of a family is a *pathogenic* condition which can lead to various pathologies in individual members.

Traditionally, health and maturation are conceived of in individual terms. It is common, for instance, to picture maturation as an increasing integration of reality with inner strivings, as a more ego-based functioning, etc.; yet differentiation from one's formative or close relationships can also be conceptualized as a dimension of maturation. In turn, if one assumes that family interaction should be conceived as "occurring at the personality level,"[11] one can consider family health and individual maturation along the same continuum. Ideally, the goal of family (and individual) health is a relational situation which is characterized by rich interaction among well-differentiated and responsibly acting members.

At the opposite pole there are poorly differentiated families with extreme symbiotic-type togetherness, shot through with vicariousness and fusion as their style. They develop various ways of avoiding personal responsibility and commitment. They may live according to particular family myths that require, for example, scapegoating of a member, assignment of sick roles, reversal of generation or sex differences, etc. The observer may often get the impression that when one member would want to break away from such family system, he would be punished for trying. However, a more accurate description of this situation may be that all members are committed to and gratified by the maintenance of the system. In other words, part of the allegiance to the system is internalized in each member. Therapy then is aimed at improving the quality and genuineness of dialogues that are possible between therapist and family members or among family members. This may lead to eventual separation and mature reinvolvement of members — for example, with marital partners.

COMMUNICATIONS THEORY AND DEPTH PSYCHOLOGY

It is a difficult, though necessary, task to bring the concepts of communications theory in connection with those of the depth psychology of relationships. One of the fundamental differences in approach is the premise of communications theory according to which the unit of interaction is the individual as an entity. He is in a relational context or field with one or several others and he "communicates" his intentions as well as reactions to the others.

Communications are composed of messages carrying easily identifiable content or denotational meaning and qualifying "metamessages." The latter convey communication about the communicated meaning as well as about the relationship between the participant persons.[14] Such implicit, qualifying messages nevertheless are assumed to "flow" *from* one person *to* another. In comparison, our concept of dialectical self-other delineation assumes a dual composition of the experience of selfhood in which some other is an inseparable counterpoint to the self. The risk of disturbed communications is loss of interpersonal confirmation through conflict, victimization, or slight; the risk of the disturbed self-other dialectic is unconscious fusion or merger of personalities with loss of even a chance for mutual confirmation.

Two examples may clarify the distinction between the two levels of relationships. The one is the well-known double-binding effect of the English formal response to persons being introduced to each other:

How do you do? It seems to express an interest directed by one person at another, but essentially it does not represent a question or request for information. Yet it confirms each individual at least to the extent of being addressed as a "you." Even an important person will interrupt his conversation when someone is being introduced and utter at least the pseudoquestion: How do you do? Thus, even if there is ambiguity in the communicated content, the context of two communicants as partners is distinctly retained.

To illustrate the other level, the one of distinctness versus fusion, I can think of a couple who presented themselves during treatment as two diagonally opposite personality types. The husband was reputed to be most repressive; he practically never showed his feelings, whereas the wife was overly expressive of emotions. This bizarre polarization of behavior was not only unanimously reported by all family members but it was evident to the therapists as well. All emotion noticeable in the parental couple seemed to manifest itself through the wife, while the husband appeared as the sole and exclusive spokesman of reason and control. They functioned as essentially two aspects of one whole human being, each aspect appearing as an exaggerated character type.

This situation, of course, was part of a family myth. On closer inspection it could be discovered that whenever the husband expressed some emotion, it was denied and distorted. However, the structure of this dialogue of interactions between husband and wife is worth exploring. On first approximation it would appear that these two people complement each other very well, due to their difference in style. In fact, at one time during courtship the prospect of such complementation may have been one of the attractions between the two. However, because of the consecutive fusion of their personality functioning, both partners have become symbiotically dependent on each other. Neither of the two would be a whole human being without vicariously living through the other. One could say that neither the unconditionally repressive nor the unconditionally expressive position belong to disparate selves trying to reach each other. One could assume that such fused personalities have a common "ego boundary" toward a third person — for example, the child of these two parents. The fact that the child can never get a whole human response from one parent alone contributes to an intrinsic symbiotic bond.

DOUBLE-BIND AS REGULATOR OF "CLOSENESS"

Double-binds were originally described as contributory mechanisms and parts of a familial hypothesis of schizophrenia.[1] In a later publication[2] the same authors claimed a much broadened role for double-binds which appear to be ubiquitous in a variety of human groups. From our point of view the latter statement seems to be more accurate. In fact, the painful shock experienced on the receiving end of a double-bind may be used as an important regulatory force in controlling overly demanding (e.g., dependent) relationships. The preceding assumption is one of several which may depict the double-bind as a weapon used for mastery. Quite typically, "seriously" courting men expect their women to use their sex appeal in double-binding ways and control the relationship thereby.

A defensive use is made of the double-bind when a parent applies this technique against the demands of the emotionally dependent and socially undefended young child. Initially the child can be considered as a "victim"; however, a certain amount of frustration is unavoidable as part of emotional growth, and the parent is supposed to be the regulator of the balance between gratifications and control. However, used repetitiously, his confusing communication enables the parent also to gratify his own immature possessive needs through making the child excessively dependent by being deprived of both trust and rational orientation in his surroundings. When exposed to confusing communications for years, eventually the child may give up his autonomy except for certain disorganized, unpredictable, periodical outbursts of rage or despair. In the interim the child learns to function as a participant, rather than victim, of the family system. He too will use the double-bind in regulating the other family members' demands.

INTERNAL VERSUS EXTERNAL RELATIONSHIP PATTERNS

One of the tempting oversimplifications in describing family therapy takes the form of an attempt at conceptually divesting here-and-now interactions from each participant's internal programming or internal relationship patterns. It seems as though the shift in methodology required for observing people in live interaction with their close family members would induce certain family therapists to abandon the entire existing framework of what we have learned from decades of individual therapy.

Individual psychotherapy and psychoanalysis oscillate between two dynamic process dimensions: evolving *intrapsychic* processes and overlapping realistic versus transference components of *relationship* attitudes of patients. Patient-therapist involvement is just as necessary a step there as freedom of self-reflective exploration. Without involvement there is no development of transference, and without freedom to explore the internal situation there is no chance of insight to be used for correcting transference-distorted relationship attitudes. Our key question is then: Is there an analogy between the dynamics of patient-therapist and close familial (intermember) relationships?

Central to this issue is the assumption that every interpersonal relationship is partly "programmed" by internal relational need configurations or "templates."[4] Regardless whether it is technically correct to designate one component of family relationship as *transference-based*, it is inevitable that, for instance, a grown-up son's attitude to his mother contains elements of his earliest attitudes. To the casual observer his infantile needs may be more or less masked by the reality of his grown-up dialogue with his mother. Furthermore, the reciprocal structure of the dialogue implies that each partner is made object of both "real" and "transferred" needs of the other. Experience with treatment of families has taught us to recognize manifestations of transferred, unconscious, childishly dependent or revengeful attitudes which some parents act out toward their children. Thus, on a deeper level, behind the facade of the visible parent-child relationship may lurk the hunger of the infantile core of the parents' personalities, each seeking a parent-like object. Consequently, it goes without saying that in family therapy the most important transference attitudes and distortions operate *between family members*, not between patient and therapist as in individual and group therapy. The current close relative is the most important reincarnation of the internalized significant objects of one's infantile past.

The concept of the internal patterning of relationship[e.g., ref.8] highlights by contrast the concept of mutual confirmation of persons. Confirmation of the other is based on the perception of the spontaneous acts of the other. A pure transference-based relationship would disconfirm the real other and handle him as though he were nothing but a screen for the projection of attributions required by the original needs of one's infantile core-personality.

MULTIPERSON CONSTRUCTS AND UNCONSCIOUSNESS

The transition from the treatment of one person to that of a family has raised many questions about relationship psychology and about the contributions of such psychology to the theory of personality and psychic structure. Although it is a massive historical fact that Freud formulated his ideas about unconscious psychic processes in connection with topographical and structural personality theories of disparate individuals, it has long been recognized that unconscious, irrational motivations can encompass more than one individual—for example, in "mass psychology."

The structurally unconscious requirements of fit between personalities, (e.g., between marital partners) have been a long-standing subject of interest for the students of human psychology. A psychoanalytic structural theory of fit between delinquent child and neurotic parent was developed by A. Johnson.[12] According to her theory of "superego lacunae," the child's action patterns are in an unconsciously dynamic equilibrium with certain deficiencies of the parent's superego structure. Thus, the theory conceives of a single superordinate structural principle regulating the motivations and actions of two persons at the same time. The child acts as though his parent's specific hidden need were his own need.

The Freudian concept of "unconscious" initially was a noun, emphatically denoting a reified agency of the topographically conceived realms of personality. Initially, the concept was also closely connected with the notion of instinct and its derivative deep motivations. In the later Freudian writings, "unconscious" becomes an adjective qualifying

a certain category of motivations, affects, and thought.[13] The concept
of configurational unconscious[3] is clearly distinguishable from unconscious content. Even communication-oriented authors use terms such
as "unconscious premises governing relationships" and "unconscious
rules of interaction."[14] In this paper, however, the concept "unconscious" is used in its dynamically determining or motivational sense
only.

Before attempting to extend the concept of unconscious motivations
to a multipersonal context, we should explore its implications for two
aspects of human psychology: experience and transactions. The basic
structural unit of experience is always the person, the experiencing
subject, whereas the unit of transactions is a dyadic process: the subject
acting toward or aiming at an object. Experience can be understood
by empathizing with the other's personal meanings; transaction is an
aspect of observable behavior. According to the *dialectical* principle
of psychic functioning,[4] the experience or sense of self implies the
unconsciously determined "ontic," use of an aspect of one or several
others as the self's delineating ground; for example, it may be easy for
a particular man to be masculine vis-a-vis a certain feminine woman.
The specific mechanisms responsible for this particular experience of
transactionally enhanced sex identity are, of course, configurationally
unconscious. The intrinsic mechanism of the other's meaning as my
self-delineating ground is largely transference-determined and outside
my awareness, even though I am aware of his or her actions. The
implicit confirmation operating between two persons is a two way
process, and I am even less aware of my own intrinsic meaning as self-
delineating ground for the other — that is, of the extent to which I
confirm or disconfirm the other by simply being or not being what I
am expected to be.

From the foregoing considerations it appears that one can distinguish
two types of confirmation or disconfirmation between relating partners: *direct and indirect*. Direct confirmation follows from what the
other *does*; indirect confirmation follows from what he *is*. For instance,
a man's sense of (masculine) identity can be confirmed by admiration
and disconfirmed by slight on the part of a woman, whether or not
she is particularly feminine. On the other hand, the presence of a

feminine woman confirms, and of an asexual woman disconfirms, his masculine identity regardless of what she is saying or doing.

Another level of unconscious motivational system shows itself in what has been described as *unconscious collusive patterns of transactions*. In considering this level, the unit of observation is not the biological individual, but a collective, shared aspect of experience and action patterns of people living in continued close relationships. The significance in any family of this level of multiperson motivations is proportionate to the degree of deficient differentiation of the family members as persons.

In observing a family, the therapist is bound to be struck by certain repetitious patterns of interactions. As he searches for the meaning of the family members' actions and reactions, first he has to listen to certain seemingly rational explanations, "family myths." With increasing knowledge of the family, however, the explanatory value of stated reasons fades out and deeper meanings have to be sought to explain the consistency with which family members cooperate in maintaining the structured coordination of the complicated action sequences. The family therapist has to find the invisible script that sustains the dynamic reason for detrimental action patterns.

The inexperienced therapist can be given a rule of thumb as the first step in search of the hidden meaning of family behavior: Reverse the meaning of the family myth! For example, if the mother blames the harshness of her husband for the daughter's disturbance, the therapist should explore the possibility that the woman may struggle with her envy because in her own childhood she did not have that amount of parental concern and guidance. Her deeper response to the paternal act of correcting is a wishful longing for proof of care. Or, when both parents complain about the irresponsibility of an adolescent, it is conceivable that the child is actually being "parentified" by them; that is, he is made to become a premature grown-up and is expected to take care of the parents in some respect. In one family the father described his 16-year-old, obese, and muscular schizophrenic son as a wild animal, even though, as it turned out, each night after falling asleep in a living room chair he was put to bed by the same son, as if the father were the child.

After having observed such explicit features of family systems as family myths, mystifications, and double-binds, the therapist may naturally wonder: Why do parents strive so hard to build up such confusing transactional systems, and why do children comply? Why do all members perform according to the rules of the game for most or all of their lives? In order to understand the reason for each participant's loyal support, we have to realize what the alternative to building up and maintaining a complex system of scapegoating, parentification, or other repetitious patterns of transaction would be. The alternative is individuation. Family members can choose between either investing their autonomous life goals with energy and rewarding other members for originality or creative intuition, *or*, conversely, consistently enforcing and rewarding allegiance to their never-changing system. Since the image of individuation and maturation implies eventual separation, it is understandable that parents who have been and still are unconsciously afraid of separation will build up family systems of stagnation and postponed individuation. Naturally, members of any family will have to work through the anxiety of prospective separation in order to grow emotionally. A common meeting ground of each individual member's tendency for the denial of past separations and desire for continued possession of one another can develop into an unconsciously *collusive system of postponed mourning and individuation.*[5] The term "mourning" is used here in a very broad connotation and it refers to a psychic process which is part of emotional growth of any sort insofar as growth involves losses through separation from familiar persons or enjoyable habits and patterns. Early bereavement experiences of parents are especially conducive to the family pattern of collusive postponement of individuation.

Haley's model of "error activated" self-corrective system[10] can be applied to the family system of collusively postponed individuation. Accordingly, the whole of individual anxieties adds up to an implicit "rule." As soon as any member invests his relationship interests on the outside, all other members begin to experience a painful loss. Any such action or intention would therefore amount to an "error" against the system and activate corrective measures on the part of the other members. The end effect is "concerted inaction" as far as spontaneous initiative is concerned. For each individual member the question of therapeutic change can be reduced to a preferential choice between two motivating forces: autonomous separateness versus compliance with the collusive system. In reality, family members may not be aware of the collusive nature of their patterns of behavior. If, for instance, the system is a scapegoating or pseudo-fighting type, the members may be aware of a need for more harmony only.

DIALOGUE

What emerges as an ideal model of relational psychology is the *dialogue*. This model of relating aims at mutual confirmation rather than exploitation of the participants. The implied mutuality of such relating does not have to be based only on satisfaction of particular instincts or needs. A sexual act, for example, may be mutually satisfying exchange of desires and experiences without necessarily contributing to the true personal confirmation of the participants. Generally speaking, any relationship based on one-sided or mutual disregard for the other as a person is incompatible with the dialogue.

I believe that the models of the complete and incomplete dialogue[6] form the units of a personally meaningful psychology of relationships. A capacity for *responding* and being open to the other's responses is the core of the genuine dialogue. It serves as a model of "healthy" functioning, aimed at developing those humanistic potentials of man that transcend a mere absence of illness. Dialogue is a means of growth and maturation in the social sense; it encompasses the processes of active assertion as well as interpersonal responsiveness and reactivity. It is a means of developing and maintaining selfhood through meeting the other, as well as having one's own needs met.

As a developmental process, the dialogue is based on the dialectical principle of "contrapuntal" harmony. For example, if a parent's actions represent the "melody" of masculinity, in response to this pattern the female child can develop her own melody of femininity. The first pattern induces the development of the second by antithesis instead of imitation of a model. Similarly, the symptomatic (e.g., schizophrenic or delinquent) child maintains an antithetical "harmony" with the parents and "well" children. This illustrates the dialogue as the shaper of identity, suggesting also that the behavior patterns of any individual are not limited by the repertoire of patterns exhibited by elders or other bearers of cultural tradition. The individual's creative potential enables him to develop his own "culture" of evolving reactive patterns, provided a meaningful self-other confirmation keeps the process in motion.

The dialogue as a transactional system is composed of an ongoing feedback of actions and reactions between relating persons. At any given moment the two persons can be considered as open systems, potentially modifiable by the partner and, in turn, by the self reacting to the partner. Thus, while the model describes the flow and process of a multiperson action system, it retains respect for individual goals and differentiation. It describes one person going toward another who in turn is approaching him at the same time.

The model of the dialogue encompasses the sum of two reciprocal object relationships, identity confirmations, need-gratifications, phenomenological and experiential encounters, communicational feedback, and game analytic patterns, though it is broader than any one of these basically useful part models.

FAMILY THERAPY AND THERAPIST

The relationship context of family therapy cannot be fully comprehended from our knowledge of the fundamentally different individual therapy situation. An adequate description of therapist-family interactions is limited by the availability of only a few additional conceptual frameworks—for example, theories of games and communications. An even greater theoretical challenge is presented by the complexity of subjective relationship experiences. What type of guidelines does the therapist have then in conducting family therapy?

Our school of family therapy maintains that even if much of therapeutic *leverage* can be based on the *game* aspects of the family therapy situation, the chief requirement of a genuine human exchange is an *empathic* ability on the part of the therapist. In many life situations, the cold, rational, efficiency oriented outlook gives different insights from those of the feeling human approach. The beginning family therapist is concerned about the multiplicity of simultaneous relationships which he has to develop with each family member. The experienced family therapist soon develops a sense of both the game aspect of his being cast in the role of an intermediary and also of the potential of his role as a facilitator of a genuine dialogue between family members. As he learns A's reaction to B and vice versa, he has both partners in his mind whenever he addresses either of the two. The therapist's empathic reconstruction of the dialogue between A and B becomes an implicit part of his dialogue with either one of them.

In the terms of technique the above attitude can be seen as a multidirectional partiality instead of only neutrality on the part of the therapist. As he stands for the positive elements of each participant's contribution to a mature dialogue, he also takes a position against the negative forces, mainly the individual and shared resistances in all members. The difficulty of this approach is that its goals lie beyond the possibility of a "cookbook-like" technical prescription. The guiding principles of this comprehensive and intensive family therapy derive from the mastery of the therapist's own life experiences, especially his own family relationships.

Intensive therapy of families[7] reveals covert aspects of individual and interpersonal dynamics just as intensive individual therapy uncovers hidden motivational trends. One may rightly ask the question whether at this time it is justifiable to subdivide the field of conjoint or unit family therapy approaches into intensive and supportive types. The meaning of the word "intensive" is complex and it has to be defined as it applies to family therapy. In a general, dictionary sense, "intensive" connotes application of force to specific areas or issues in a thorough, complete, or exhaustive manner. The term "intensive family therapy" refers to a rather ambitious goal: exploration aimed at significant and lasting change of the underlying individual and relationship patterns which manifest themselves in the specific symptom or symptoms of the disturbed family.

It is probable that currently available technical terms cannot adequately describe the requirements necessary for such therapy. It is perhaps easier to name certain approaches on the opposite end of the scale which, for lack of a better term, could be called *supportive* therapies. The goal of these therapies might be limited in a number of ways: by planned limitation of the duration of the therapy or limitation of the therapist's interest to certain phenomena — for example, to the quality of personal experience of family members, to the system or communication aspects of transactional processes, to the degree of efficiency or productiveness in work, school, etc.

Such limited approaches may intentionally ignore information relevant to certain areas of personality dynamics. Transactional and communicational schools of family therapy deemphasize interest in the connection between personal history and current functioning, internalized patterns of habitual relational distortions and misinterpretations, unconsciously determined resistance and defense mechanisms, etc. Conversely, other therapists may exclude the examination of important overt and covert aspects of interactional and transactional multiperson systems of communication. The ideal goal of intensive family therapy is comprehensive coverage resulting from exploration and meaningful integration of all significant factors that determine the pathological manifestations of the family members' relationships. The philosophy behind such ambitious goal is the belief that even if certain therapeutic shortcuts to effect change seem promising, only the thorough understanding of all major mechanisms of psychological change can form the basis for designing a rational therapeutic approach.

It follows from the foregoing that the training requirements for intensive conjoint family therapy ideally include a broad background in personality theory and its application in psychotherapy, communication and relational system concepts, and a type of personality, preferably with keen interest in people and close relationships. In other words, none of the current professional entities — psychiatry, psychology, social work, etc. — automatically qualify or disqualify the characterologically suitable person to practice family therapy. An additional specialized training with experienced family therapists and undergoing individual or family therapy experience may further help toward this goal.

CONCLUDING REMARKS

Conjoint or unit family therapy should give rise to a new psychology of relationships which will contribute significantly toward a comprehensive theory of motivation. At present, the theoretical guidelines used by therapists of whole families rely on various individual and group psychological frameworks. The writings of early family therapists (Ackerman, Bowen, Bateson, Jackson, Lidz, Fleck, Wynne, and Haley, among others) are especially valuable readings for the practicing family therapist. In the opinion of the present author the road toward a future comprehensive psychology of relationship leads through integration of the dual vantage points: subjective, internally felt experience and observable behavior.

The motivational field of the person-in-relationship is under the influence of three major kinds of determining influences: (1) *preinteraction patterning* of both partners' motivations, (2) one participant's reaction to what the person of the other *means* to him, and (3) one participant's reaction to what the other is *doing*. All of these influences are part of the unobservable core of a person's subjective experience, the content of which can only be inferred as a result of empathic identification with the observed person. On the other hand, his behavioral responses and the interactional feedback between what he is doing and what the other is doing are observable. At present the best we can do is an impressionistic, intuitive construction of each family as an idiosyncratic entity. The family therapist lacks a unitary language which would encompass all determinants of relationships.

Psychoanalysis and intensive psychotherapy of individuals usually assume arbitrarily that, for the purposes of therapy, behavior components can be minimized so that introspective exploration of marginally conscious subjective experience can be more fully explored. Whereas a certain amount of acting out cannot be eliminated from the individual-based therapy approach, the cues and responses of significant others, of course, can be completely excluded from the individual therapist's direct observation. Yet, since relationships are codetermined by both subjective experience and interpersonal feedback, in order to understand the motivational determinants of family relationships, we need an integrated model which encompasses factors from both realms. It has been proposed that such a model is the dialogue.

The practical implications of the multipersonal dialogue concept are fundamental for the orientation of the family therapist. It resolves the antithesis between individual and group or systems orientations by assuming that relationship of the two is mutually constitutive rather than exclusive. The dialectical framework assumes that the person is a product of a self-other antithesis and, in turn, only persons can interact with each other in a meaningful dialogue.

It would perhaps be easier for family therapists to assume dogmatic positions of either-or concerning individual or group-based, transactional, conceptual frameworks. It could readily be conceded that one is liable to feel lonely and vulnerable standing "in the middle." Yet viewed in a historical perspective only an integrated relationship theory can do justice to the conceptual demands posed by the "mutation" imposed upon psychiatry by conjoint family therapy.

ACKNOWLEDGMENT

The author is indebted to Mrs. Geraldine M. Spark for her contributions to the manuscript through significant suggestions and critical statements.

REFERENCES

1. Bateson, G., Jackson, D. D., Haley, J., & Weakland, J. H. Toward a theory of schizophrenia. *Behav. Sci. 1:* 251–264, 1956.
2. Bateson, G., Jackson, D. D., Haley, J., & Weakland, J. H. A note on the double bind—1962. *Family Process, 2:* 154–161, 1963.
3. Bellak, L. The unconscious. *Ann. N. Y. Acad. Sci. 76:* 1066–1097, 1959.
4. Boszormenyi-Nagy, I. A theory of relationships: Experience and transaction. In: *Intensive Family Therapy* (I. Boszormenyi-Nagy and J. L. Framo, Eds.). New York, Hoeber/Harper, 1965, pp. 305–319.
5. Boszormenyi-Nagy, I. The concept of change in conjoint family therapy. In: *Psychotherapy for the Whole Family* (A. S. Friedman et al., Eds.). New York, Springer, 1965, pp. 305–319.
6. Boszormenyi-Nagy, I. Relational modes and meaning. In: *Family Therapy and Disturbed Families* (G. Zuk and I. Boszormenyi-Nagy, Eds.). Palo Alto, Calif., Science and Behavior Books, 1967, pp. 58–73.

7. Boszormenyi-Nagy, I., & Framo, J. L. (Eds.). *Intensive Family Therapy.* New York, Hoeber/Harper, 1965.
8. Brodey, W. M. On the dynamics of narcissism. I. Externalization and early ego development. In: *Psychoanalytic Study of the Child.* New York, International Universities Press, 1965, pp. 165−193, Vol. XX.
9. Friedman, A. S., Boszormenyi-Nagy, I., Jungreis, J. E., Lincoln, G., Mitchell, H. E., Sonne, J. C., Speck, R. W., & Spivack, G. *Psychotherapy for the Whole Family.* New York, Springer, 1965.
10. Haley, J. The family of the schizophrenic: A model system. *J. Nerv. Ment. Dis.* *129:* 357–374, 1959.
11. Handel, G. Psychological study of whole families. *Psychol. Bull. 63:* 19–41, 1965.
12. Johnson, A. Sanctions for superego lacunae of adolescents. In: *Searchlights on Delinquency: New Psychoanalytic Studies* (K. R. Eissler, Ed.). New York, Int. Univ. Press, 1949, pp. 225–245.
13. Rapaport, D. Structure of psychoanalytic theory. *Psychol. Issues 2* (No. 6), 1960.
14. Watzlawick, P. *An Anthology of Human Communication.* Palo Alto, Calif., Science and Behavior Books, 1964, pp. 196–205.

6

Relational Modes and Meaning

A major goal of contextual therapy pertains to defining the motivational sources of close relationships, especially from the vantage point of the therapist. In this sense the meaning of relationship can be considered as a teleological, rather than linearly causal, determinant of relating. The present chapter completes and complements the conceptual explorations of my theoretical chapter in Intensive Family Therapy (Boszormenyi-Nagy, 1965). Determined also by each person's relational need templates, it follows that the subjective experience of one's personal identity is meaningful only in a relational, intrinsically dialectical context. This "ontic" dependence on the other partner is independent of the specifics of the relational needs of the partners. For example, two lovers may need each other on an ontological basis as self-constitutive objects for each other, in addition to the mutual fit between their specific emotional-spiritual need templates.

It follows that the arrested growth of the delinquent or psychotic child can make him a "useful" captive object for the ontic needs of the parent who may actually resent the child's troublesome behavior. Conversely, by accepting a negative self-identity, the child not only defines his self but also offers himself as an object to the parent. He is not just part of a molding context but also an indirect constituent of the parent's self. These considerations may help to explain certain aspects of incestuous or deeply ambivalent relating. The need for the other as a constitutive ground may outstrip the particular needs for sexual satisfaction.

The ensuing description of six relational modes introduces the concepts of symmetry and asymmetry as they culminate in the dialogue. The dialogue is not only a function of two individual persons but also the

79

condition of their existence. This chapter is an early attempt at an existentially tinged object-relations formulation of close relating.

Furthermore, letting the other delineate himself through the relationship contributes also to the other's existence and thus to his own ethical validation. This formulation of one's being an object for the other is thus a predecessor of the later concepts of loyalty, earning of entitlement and "self-validation." The most effective steps toward autonomous individuation lead through self-validation (Boszormenyi-Nagy & Krasner, 1986), that is, through responsible concern and relational accountability.

REFERENCES

Boszormenyi-Nagy, I. A theory of relationships: Experience and transaction. In I. Boszormenyi-Nagy & J. L. Framo (Eds.), *Intensive family therapy.* New York: Brunner/Mazel, 1965.

Boszormenyi-Nagy, I., & Krasner, B. *Between give and take.* New York: Brunner/Mazel, 1986.

The family therapist, more than any other psychotherapist, has to be concerned with the determinants and the meaning of relationships. Insofar as a relationship defines interactions as well as subjective feelings of identity, its meaning must be based on a dyadic model: the relating self and the other to whom the self is related. On the one hand, relating can be thought of as a form of observable behavior, but its true meaning can be inferred only from what we know of each relating person's private fiction about the meaning of the relationship with that particular other. This paper is concerned with the structures of subjective meaning in close relationships and the implications of these structures for personal identity.

A combative psychotic boy, who had been treated conjointly with his family for over a year, appeared especially aggressive toward his father in one of the sessions. Later in the same evening, his father could not control his own anger anymore and hit the boy for the first time since he grew up. For the observer during this session, the boy's behavior toward his father was that of a series of constantly threatening and belittling aggressive statements. As it turned out, however, the deep significance of this interaction and the subsequent beating was that it restructured the relational engagement between father and son: it proved to this boy of 220 pounds that his father cared, and consequently his sense of identity was subjectively defined as a child again. From a threatening sense of psychotic loss of identity, he managed to escape into a regressive but experientially meaningful identity.

Relating has an active and a passive aspect. The other is needed because I want to perceive him as the "ground" against which my person becomes distinguishable as a figure. I want to make him an object for myself as subject; I may want him as an object for my instinctual strivings, for my identity delineation, and for my security needs. In other words, being a self obliges me to express myself and I actually become an entity in the process of expressing myself to another entity. Sensory deprivation amounts to expressive deprivation; it is object deprivation as well as deprivation of the meaning of the self. The lonely person can only express himself by turning to the object of his fantasy

in daydream or hallucination, or to his own body through hypochondriac preoccupations that serve as internally available grounds for the
meaning of his self. The dialogue of the isolated or perceptually deprived person is truncated; its feedback components can come only
from such others as are internalized.

Although personal fictions and private meanings are essentially
inaccessible to direct observation, they can be inferred from overt
communication since they are context setters for what the person is
about to communicate in a given relationship. It is also true that the
structure of any given relationship tends to become itself a determinate
of matching self-fictions. For example, a young man may fall in love
with a girl because, though outside his awareness, the girl reminds him
of certain of his mother's features. Conversely, a real other can be
recruited to match an internal "relational need template" (Boszormenyi-
Nagy, 1965), e.g., in what is called "projection" or "transference" in
clinical usage.

Projection and transference are regarded, for our purposes, as examples of relational choice rather than mainly as distortions of person
perception. In fact, the so-called "nagging" wife may very well know,
for instance, that her husband has corrected his careless driving habits,
while she continues scolding him for his past and therefore potentially
present or future tendencies toward the same fault. Like the deluded
psychotic who "knows" the facts but is unable to correct his notions,
the meaning of this wife's self-delineation may be unconditionally linked
to her expressed relational need template: e.g., a husband who is a "bad
object." Consequently relational needs can be categorized according
to needs for (a) an object of one's drive and (b) an object of one's specific
need-configuration as a basis of self-delineation.*

The latter need can be called "ontic" dependence on a certain other.
By this is meant that my full self-meaning depends on a fitting other,
regardless of whether I am, in effect, dependent on the other. Thus,

---

*Ernest Jones (1953) cites Freud as having stated: "An intimate friend and a hated enemy have
always been indispensable to my emotional life; I have always been able to create them anew,
and not infrequently my childish ideal has been so closely approached that friend and enemy
have coincided in the same person" (p.10).

in order to experience myself as a leader, I need those who depend on me; as a healer, I need those who need my help. The essence of the relational complementation between any two persons lies in a "dialogue of needs" which guarantees that the relationship will not turn into a one-sided exploitation. Naturally, in addition to expecting certain attitudes, members of a family can manipulate one another to act in accordance with their private relational needs and expectations. Thus, the expectations of the various members are in competition for mastery.

This situation may be illustrated with a relationship based on two competing need templates: that of A for a "bad" object and that of B for a "good" object. For example, a masochistic man and a maturely heterosexual woman may discover, to their disappointment, that they cannot develop a working complementarity of roles. Each may try to "convert" the other by the assignment of fitting, expected object roles, yet neither is willing to oblige the other by actually conforming to the desired object role. If the couple don't break up, they can either continue their struggle, or the masochistically inclined partner will ultimately win because the resulting overall "badness" of their mutually frustrating relationship will provide a context that favors his object role assignment needs.

An important factor in relating is the formation of and the degree of completeness of a boundary between the relating partners. A self-other or ego boundary is often conceptualized as cognitive in nature, as exemplified in the infant's learning to distinguish between self and object. Perhaps it is easier to describe the affective and motivational ingredients of this boundary if we think of the child's learning the boundary between the two interdependent realms of "I" and "mine" rather than I and other. Cooley (1956) quotes Emerson's statement about friendship in what appears to be a similar emphasis on the value of the boundary between the self and the other: "Friendship requires that rare mean betwixt likeness and unlikeness that piques each with the presence of power and of consent in the other party. . . . Let him not cease an instant to be himself. The only joy I have in his being mine is that the *not mine is mine*. There must be very two before there can be very one" (p. 154).

Emerson's expression, "Let him not cease an instant to be himself" can be interpreted in a number of ways. On the one hand it certainly is a formulation of friendship or love that does not presume fusion or merger as its basis. On the other hand, he who remains himself and "not mine" in a sense will become mine nevertheless. That is, he will become mine, but not in the sense of a passive object of possession or a dependent appendage who lacks a will of his own. Or, to put this conflictual state of affairs in other words: I want the object of my friendship (possession) to remain a free agent (subject) of his own will.

A similar conflict is familiar to observers and therapists of families. The underlying ambivalent attitudes lead to the picture of contradictory messages which Bateson et al. (1956) named "double-bind." The conflicting wishes of possession and separateness can also lead to a vicarious fusion of motivations as exemplified by the phenomenon described as "superego lacunae" by Johnson (1949). In these cases the pattern of the child's acting-out is determined by the parent's superego configuration, as though the self-other boundary between parent and child were defective. Family therapy uncovers many other unconsciously collusive motivational systems which, in the extreme case, form what Bowen (1965) describes as "undifferentiated family ego mass."

Sartre, in his _Being and Nothingness_ (1956), develops a complex and sophisticated picture of the reciprocal conflict between lover and loved one. Each wants to possess the other as an ontological basis of his own existence, but wants to possess the other as a free agent rather than an automaton. In other words, both relating partners are a mixture of constitutive, active (subject) and constituted, passive (object) aspects, and each can say of the other with Emerson: "The not mine is mine." From the vantage point of his own experience, each can use the other as his constitutive object, by means of whom (and perhaps at the expense of whom) he can assert himself. He, in turn, can be used by the other as the latter's object or point of reference. One thing is certain as a consequence of the dialectic nature of personal experience: I need an other as the outside reference point or ground of my existence.

These rather abstract structural properties of the relationship experience are of considerable significance for the interpretation of certain clinical problems. For instance, when a woman complains that her husband lacks understanding, it is important to know whether she means that she misses his active inquisitive interest or his receptive availability and capacity to listen to her whenever she has something to say. Does she, perhaps, want a better harmony of the latter two processes in a well-functioning dialogue? Does she express a desire for a merger or fusion with the person of her husband?

Family members may question each other's capacity for loving. One may claim that the other uses the word "love" to mean selfish receiving while he himself means giving or give-and-take of emotional exchanges. Further, people's preferences may be divided between loving and being loved—between being the subject or the object of love.

It is unfortunate that the language of subjective relational experience is so inadequately developed. When a lover talks about loving or being loved, he knows he is describing very important subjective experiential differences. Such subjective relational meanings are the object of this paper, even though a more systematic language may appear to lack the desirable subjective experiential freshness.

Family pathology, or, perhaps more precisely, relational psychology, is badly in need of a comprehensive conceptual outlook capable of integrating our emerging knowledge of transactional or multiperson motivational systems with the individual-based outlook of classical Freudian personality theory. The subjective experience of one's personal identity is meaningful only in a dialectical, intrinsically dyadic context. On the other hand, the concept of a dyadic relationship cannot be restricted to the sphere of social action, particularly since Freud's structural theories have illuminated the great importance of intrapsychic relationships. By introducing the concept of superego as a quasi-personal, internal psychic representation, Freud established a relational framework as one of the most important intrapsychic structural dynamics. By means of the intrapsychic images of my parents, I carry the meaning of old relationships into my current relating to the other. This is the way he becomes meaningful to me. The other treats me the same way. In other words, my actions and attitudes toward the other will be determined by the constellation of my relational "need templates," a term I have used to describe certain aspects of internalized relationship orientations (Boszormenyi-Nagy, 1965).

To the extent that my need templates represent the core of my personality and my self is equal to the configuration of my relational need templates, I am what I need to make of other people. The fact that I have an emotional investment in seeing people fit my need templates (transference distortion) differentiates me from a camera, which has no need to project an image upon the objects it is directed at. Of course, I could not be a self if I were simply to register objects like a camera. Each person's identity evolves as a changing series of relational need templates. In this sense, we can think of the "regressed" psychotic as a person whose identity is composed of wishful constellations that we feel should properly characterize a child or at least the hidden and not the publicly observable tendencies of the grown-up.

Psychotically regressive need templates usually have an element of sensual specificity. A 17-year-old in-patient reported that she was constantly preoccupied with a desire to be held in the soft arms of a woman with soft breasts, and to be bottle-fed at the same time. Once she saw in a magazine an illustration of a woman psychiatrist holding a grown-up patient in her lap while the patient was being fed from a bottle. My patient was ecstatic about this picture and she pasted it in her scrapbook. Gradually, as the weeks passed, another daydream emerged as most meaningful; the fantasies pictured tall women who had to go through the torture of various humiliating treatments. Finally, she imagined the violent death of her parents and siblings in a fatal car accident. The two phases of this young woman's wishful imagery represented a transition from being a passive object to being an observer of what is done to others. These need templates, of course, can be analyzed according to their derivation from their instinctual roots. However, from the vantage point of relational meaning, they represent two distinct modes: in one, the self is the object; in the other, the tall women and the patient's family are the objects. The first of the two modes seems to be a more common structural property of wishful imagery of psychotic females. Several other patients had the wish to be held by their mother and one to be masturbated by her mother at the same time. A psychotic young man demanded that his mother sit at his bed and massage his jaw for hours because he claimed his jaw hurt him.

The reason for calling these primitive need expressions "relational" need configurations is complex. It is probable that they become fixated because they had a gratifying value at a certain earlier life phase, probably in early childhood. What is the most important single gratifying quality of these memories, however? As shown by the work of Harlow (1962) on monkeys, an inanimate, nonresponsive environment can produce an autistic-like monkey out of the experimental baby monkey. The lack of live monkey mothers resulted in growth that made the young adult's instinctual life disorganized, psychotic-like. Somewhat in the manner of psychotic humans, these young adult monkeys became incapable of sexual intimacy as well as motherhood. Whether the early life experience of our patients did actually contain an excess of loneliness or an exaggerated vulnerability for it, the wish configurations of being held and fed are reminiscent of the wishful components of loneliness and separation anxiety states. Their significance might very well lie in the reassuring effect of possessing someone who "responds."

Even though the response to the hungry and lonely infant's needs primarily means physical care and satisfaction of biological "instincts," no one could deny that the response yields a most significant psychological contribution as a byproduct. In the process of being taken care of, the infant obtains the first opportunity for ego-boundary formation: i.e., identity formation. Through her caring responsiveness, the mothering adult appears on the horizon as someone whom the child "has." The possession of predictable response on the adult's part leads to the development of "basic trust" (Erikson, 1959), the foundation of all later social functioning and identity.

The effect of having or possessing people is one of the most important known, experientially crucial factors in the etiology of a variety of psychiatric conditions. The loss of a parent, sibling, or child, or the birth of a child are among the most frequent "precipitating causes" of depressions, schizophrenic episodes, and so on. With the loss of a relationship goes part of our own self-delineation; with the loss of the ground, the definition of the figure is also lost, at least partly. It follows logically that family or other close relationships are constantly subject to opportunities and disappointments concerning deep object-possessive needs and expectations. In fact, much of the intrafamilial struggle cannot be adequately described in terms of conflict, love, hostility, and so on. The real struggle is to possess a secure ground for one's sense of selfhood—and that ground consists of the other.

The arrested social growth of the delinquent or psychotic child can make him a most useful and covertly rewarded "captive" object, although on an instrumental or practical level the child's behavior may represent pure nuisance for the parent (Boszormenyi-Nagy, 1962). Through his being and remaining a captive object, perhaps one unconsciously representing a parental introject of the parent, the child remains a delineating ground or object for the parent's self. Conversely, the child, by accepting a "negative ego identity" (Erikson, 1959) defines himself as an entity, at least as an object to the parent.

Recurrent acts of delinquency or other forms of negative identity choice are the clearest examples of a need for a certain *type* of identity at all costs. Even if the pragmatic or instrumental consequences of one's actions are detrimental, as long as one's identity delineation is contingent on a certain type of socially undesirable action, one will continue to act it out repetitiously. "Repetition compulsion" obtains a new explanation if we look at it as a manifestation of man's universal "need of symbolization": i.e., need for definable meaning (Langer, 1948, p. 32). Repeated actions help create the symbolic reference point of our autonomous self, whereas being the target of the actions of others can only define a nonautonomous self. The slave is a slave because he is depended on by his master while not being allowed to depend on his own right to possess another. In a dialectical, relational sense, autonomy is a paradox; it is an innerly sensed freedom achieved through dependence on those vis-à-vis whom we realize the assertion of our needs. As Rapaport (1958) points out, autonomy from the environment is a different concept from autonomy of the ego functions vis-à-vis the instincts.

The other or the others are antithetical and indirect *constituents* of the self, rather than merely its dichotomous, or moulding, context. I become defined as a parent when confronted by a child. As a child, I am implicitly confronted by a parent. If I were a closed existential system, my own parent-self could satisfy the self-delineation needs of my child-self. Of course, the notself-referents of my self can also be internalized, and, within limits, they can substitute for real, external others. It is the main assumption of this paper that it is essential to conceive of the self as arising vis-à-vis the antithetically complementing others, whether the other is a real person or an internalized replica like, for instance, the superego. This point of view has broad implications for the understanding of relational dynamics.

I would like to examine the vicissitudes of the choice of an other as context or ground in the self's struggle for its delineation or existence. For the sake of simplicity, this exploration will be mostly confined to two-person relationships.

Figure 6-1 represents six modes of relatedness, arranged in a hierarchic order.* The diagram is used chiefly to indicate the subjective symbolic structuring of the self's position in the various dyadic self-delineating relationships. This type of subjective symbolic structuring has to be distinguished from the concept of the unconscious fantasy. The former is a mode in which the figure-ground matching of two complementing relational positions is programmed; the latter are context-setting contents, viewed from the intrapsychic vantage point of one individual. Each consecutive step in the diagram represents a more satisfactory mode of relational self-delineation or boundary formation. Each segment of circle corresponds to a physical individual. Each broken line represents an ego boundary, achieved through a contraposition of self and other. This simple antithetical relationship is complicated by the circumstance that both self and other can be either subject or object, depending on the relative positions of the participants with regard to autonomy and assertive use of the relationship. The arrows indicate the directional and dynamic quality of the object-role assignment inherent in being a subject. The solid lines between subject and object imply available but not utilized relational "opportunities." The first two of the six relational modes are dyadic in structure, though they do not involve more than one physical person. The third mode is a nondialectical "intersubjective fusion" and does not lead to the formation of an ego boundary. The fourth and fifth modes represent asym-

---

*Reproduced with permission from *Intensive Family Therapy: Theoretical and Practical Aspects*, Boszormenyi-Nagy and Framo (Eds.), Hoeber Medical Division, Harper and Row, Inc., 1965. (Republished by Brunner/Mazel, New York, 1985.)

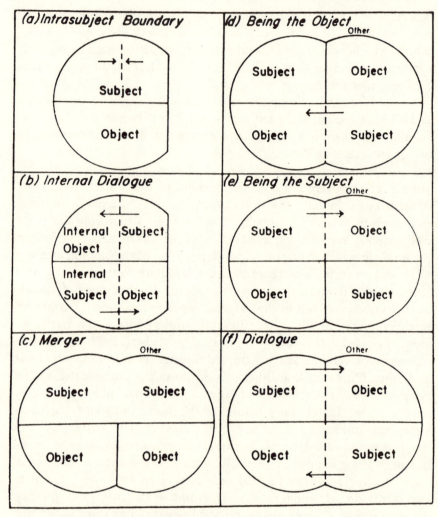

Figure 6-1. Six Relational Modes

metrically incomplete evolvements of dyadic relationships. The sixth mode symbolizes a potentially fully symmetrical social relationship that is qualitatively different from and more than the sum total of Modes (D) and (E). Experienced by both participants as a dialogue, the sixth mode is the basis of a working feedback system of mutuality and growth.

INTRASUBJECT BOUNDARY

This first drawing represents the least adequate form of self-delineation, which can appear for only short intervals as a defense against the threatened loss of a sense of self. Manneristic expressions such as: "I guess I don't feel like that" or "as I have so often said" are examples of these fictive splits between parts of the self. It is as though one part of the self were looking over the shoulder of the other. It is probable that some aspects of hypochondriac preoccupations are vested with this type of intrapsychic self-defining significance. The body and its functions are thereby partly experienced as aspects of the sensing subject, although in delusional forms of hypochondria they are experienced as objects (Szasz, 1957). Schizophrenic personality fragmentation can appear in the form of an unproductive intrapsychic quarrel of disparate selves that does not result in any enduring ego-boundaries.

INTERNAL DIALOGUE

The self is confronted here with the internalized others, the introjects. The internalized others may be regarded from the point of view of subject or object. A typical example of an internalized other is the superego. As subject, its message, the voice of conscience, can make one squirm and escape into a variety of "symptoms." Viewed as object, one can attempt to negotiate with one's conscience and even manage to bribe it occasionally. Intensive, enduring states of guilt represent typical examples of helpless exposure to a superego behaving as subject.

Hallucinations and delusions clearly have the structuring of an ego-internal object relatedness. In praising the reliability of his voices, one schizophrenic patient sounded like he was advertising the advantage of internal friendships over the less reliable external ones he encountered. We are all familiar with the variety of internal others we encounter during our dreams. In a systematic study on the direction of threat in dreams and direction of aggression in psychotics, Framo et al. (1962) demonstrated a correlation between two subject-object dimensions: patients who were the objects of threat in the manifest content of their dreams were more apt to make *others* objects of aggression through their actual behavior.

In summary, internal relationships differ from transitory intrapsychic boundary formations in that the former represent manifest motivational conflicts as the foundation of internal self-delineations. The impact of pangs of conscience or delusional convictions, for example, can lead to serious consequences. They can make a person pay a high cost for their endurance. One has to learn how to live with one's internal others just as with real others. In reality, every real interpersonal relationship is interwoven with internal relationships as reference points for meaning.

MERGER

This condition is partly responsible for the one described as confusion of relating with identifying. An area of primary identification is an area of lacking ego-boundaries. Certain members of a family, usually the mother and one or several children, may consciously think of themselves as one we-subject. Naturally, they can be a we-object, as when a mother has a tendency to react to any paternal discipline of the children as aggression against herself. In its more subtle motivational aspects, merger can be achieved through unconscious collusion or vicarious participation in the feelings or actions of the other. Recovering psychotic patients may be seen to shift from a preoccupation with delusional internal objects to a merger-like identification with the doctor or nurse. In a somewhat less conscious form, the person who loses his father through heart attack, can merge with him by having a lifelong disposition for medically unexplained cardiac pain. The fantasied pain has assumed the significance of a lasting tie with the deceased—a borrowed ego-boundary. It is probable furthermore, that a certain amount of merger with people who are important for us may be necessary for building up the experiential contents of the self as subject. In terms of families, shared "family myths" (Wynne et al., 1958) may represent a merger of several members vis-à-vis others who are represented through complementary roles or positions.

BEING THE OBJECT

The concept of object relationship implies a directional property; it hinges on A's capacity for making B his object as well as B's capacity for becoming an object vis-à-vis A as subject. Being a context for someone else's self-assertive or self-delineating projects can be preferable to being isolated from all meaningful ties with people. One may sense an implicit danger in such a passive role, however, and one can become exploited by, or a captive of, the other unless one insists on an equal chance for reciprocation.* In order to be accepted, adolescents often assume the role of the clown too willingly. It has been reported that prisoners who were kept in indefinite periods of total isolation recorded even periodic tortures as welcome evidence of their worth, at least in the role of the hated enemy. Children may willingly accept an assigned parent-like role that serves as an outlet for the transference needs of their parents. When the child grows up, however, such unilateral role exploitation may result in desperate, unconscious revenge motivations in the form of delinquent or psychotic behavior. As another example, many women sense deeply that the role of a wife and mother is essentially that of a martyr, and that to fulfill this martyr role, they must renounce their own personal ambitions and become merely a ground or context for the strivings of their husbands and children.

BEING THE SUBJECT

On this more accomplished relational level, the only significant missing element is a need for capacity for the empathic recognition by the subject of the other's needs for being a subject too. One participant may succeed in assigning the role of an object to the other, without giving due consideration to the other's autonomous existence. More

---

*Barnes (1959) quotes the cuckold from "The Baker's Wife" as a beautiful example of someone thinking of himself as a captive object: "How can I bake bread when I am busy being deceived?" (p. 57).

specifically, as *exclusive* subjects we avoid becoming a context for the other's self-delineating relationship needs, while we manage to "use" the other for our internal needs. Usually, the person is not fully aware of his tendency to assign object roles to others. A typical example of this tendency, especially if it is done by two or more people, is the phenomenon of scapegoating. The scapegoat is not given a chance to reciprocate and use the scapegoaters as objects for his own self-assertive strivings.

Some people are masters of using other persons' statements as a takeoff point for something completely different from what they wanted to say, thus totally overruling the meaning of the other's statements. Words can even be put into someone else's mouth without regard for the intention of the owner of the mouth. Transference "distortions" can be regarded as attempts at making the other a certain type of object. Being a subject can be considered as a relational mastery, but often a dubious one; it demands that the other exist for the one who is the subject.

DIALOGUE

The last diagram depicts a symmetrical and, therefore, a more stable relational mode than the preceding five. A prototype is the freely developing heterosexual involvement in which the more the male can realize his masculinity, the more he tends to offer the female a chance to play her counterrole fully. Perhaps here lies one of the explanations of the significance of the Oedipal conflict: in order to become a man, the boy must establish a role position in opposition to the mother, and not find a role in imitation of the father alone. Or, the doctor finds his role reinforced by the patient whose sickness makes him an object of the patient's needs. Many people, while seeming to ask for advice, ask only for a dialogue with someone. The give-and-take of an exchange of responses renders the decision-making process more secure.

A fascinating question about the dialogue is whether it can exist asymmetrically: i.e., fully from the reference point of one participant only, while the other experiences the dialogue merely as object. This may be possible if one partner does not or cannot assert his own autonomous needs while adapting himself to the role of a desired object of the other. In a decompensating marital pattern, for instance, the suspicious and malicious partner can produce a realistic suspiciousness in the other one in accordance with his or her own internal needs, creating thereby an emotional climate in which the other's needs for reciprocal admiration become irrelevant. Or the delinquent child by his self-destructive behavior may satisfy his parent's transferred infantile revenge needs vicariously, while the child cannot satisfy his own needs for a genuinely growth-promoting parent. Thus, while one party gets feedback fitting his needs, the other is incapable of extracting the same from the first one.

Family therapy offers a new vantage point for exploring the directional aspects of relational engagements. The family therapist can observe the specific ways in which a particular relationship may consist of two asymmetrical, partially internal dialogues. Yet one member's originally objectionable self-delineation needs and modes of relating may gradually find reinforcement through fitting him as object of the other member's needs. Therapeutic work with families requires new levels of analytic insight. Fundamental self-delineation needs express themselves through fixated, more or less archaic patterns of complementary behavior. A new type of behavior can be adopted only if it is capable of satisfying both persons' needs for self-demarcation. The simultaneous examination of both participants' undesirable subject and object roles may result in the uncovering of specific obstacles to the genuine dialogue.

According to the theory here presented, the dynamic structure of relationships is not to be founded on the fiction of individual persons as interacting entities. A more comprehensive view of relationships takes into account that a rhythmic oscillation of the dialogue is not only a function of the individual but a condition of his existence. As the philosopher Heinemann (1954) put it: "*Respondeo, ergo sum*" (I respond, therefore I exist).

The response structure of the dialogue can be considered as a communication system. It is important to study patterns of communication as expressions of meaning, but the essence of the relational dialogue is on a deeper layer than communications. It lies in the nature of the fundamental engagement of relational positions as part of each participant's striving for meaning.

My reason for such close consideration of certain modes of the relational process originates from the recognition of certain often-overlooked dialectic aspects of social motivations. What I chiefly wanted to convey is that certain structural properties of self-experiences in relating are important motivating principles in themselves.

Experience in observing people throughout the years has taught me to respect man's profound needs for being responded to in certain particular ways. To make people respond on our own terms seems to be at the bottom of the "game" of social life. In one sense, those people could be considered healthiest who are able to make the highest number of others respond willing to them on their own terms. Yet such other-directed explanations have failed to explain the subjective preferences that people manifest in their relational choices.

Some people prefer to sit alone with the inner voices of their past relationships; repeat sequences of (compulsive) acts according to some internal patterning; never assert themselves as differing from the other's point of view; or exploit every human encounter as an opportunity for hostile rather than trusting exchanges. Some of these people lead lonely lives. Others find partners who collude with them in building up "bad" relationships. In any case, people have deep motivations for maintaining their internal or external relational commitments, because these mean very much to them. One's self obtains meaning through relationships that mean much to it. Emotional growth, on the other hand, hinges on one's capacity for relinquishing nonworkable relational commitments and substituting workable new relationships. The process of exchanging one relationship for another depends on complex relational need configurations or templates in both participants.

In conclusion, I suggest that the concept of health in family therapy ought to be fashioned according to the criteria of the modes of relating I have tried to describe, and not according to values of reality, genitality, effectiveness, self-actualization, or related aims current in the individual-based writings on psychopathology. Emotional growth hinges on the quality and possibilities of the dialogue, realized within a context of mutually accepted autonomy. Existential freedom is a dialectical process; it is not love through merger. It is a capacity for symmetrical self-other delineation and continuous new resolutions of opposing positions in relationships.

REFERENCES

Barnes, H. E. *Humanistic existentialism; the literature of possibility.* Lincoln: Univer. of Nebraska Press, 1959.

Bateson, G., et al. Toward a theory of schizophrenia. *Behav. Sci.*, 1956, *1*, 251–264.

Boszormenyi-Nagy, I. The concept of schizophrenia from the perspective of family treatment. *Fam. Proc.* 1962, *1*, 103–113.

Boszormenyi-Nagy, I. A theory of relationships: experience and transaction. In I. Boszormenyi-Nagy & J. L. Framo (Eds.), *Intensive family therapy: theoretical and practical aspects.* New York: Harper and Row, 1965, pp. 33–86.

Bowen, M. Family psychotherapy with schizophrenia in the hospitals and in private practice. In I. Boszormenyi-Nagy & J. L. Framo (Eds.), *Intensive family therapy: theoretical and practical aspects.* New York: Harper and Row, 1965, pp. 213–243.

Cooley, C. H. *Human nature and the social order.* Glencoe, Ill.: Free Press, 1956.

Erikson, E. H. Identity and the life cycle; selected papers. *Psychol. Issues*, 1959, *1*, No. 1.

Framo, J. L., et al. A relationship between threat in the manifest content of dreams and active-passive behavior in psychotics. *J. abnorm. soc. Psychol.*, 1962, *65*, 41–47.

Harlow, H. F. Development of affection in primates. In E. L. Bliss (Ed.), *Roots of behavior: Genetics, instinct, and socialization in animal behavior.* New York: Harper, 1962, pp. 157–166.

Heinemann, F. *Existenzphilosophie lebendig order tot?* Stuttgart, Germany: W. Kohlhammer, 1954.

Johnson, A. Sanctions for superego lacunae of adolescents. In K. Eissler (Ed.), *Searchlights on delinquency: new psychoanalytic studies.* New York: Int. Univer. Press, 1949. pp. 225–245.

Jones, E. *The life and work of Sigmund Freud, Vol. I.* New York: Basic Books, 1953.

Langer, S. K. *Philosophy in a new key; a study in the symbolism of reason, rite and art.* Cambridge, Harvard University Press, 1942.

Rapaport, D. The theory of ego autonomy: a generalization. *Bull. Menninger Clin.* 1958, *22*, 13–35.

Sartre, J. P. *Being and nothingness; an essay on phenomenological ontology.* Translated by H. E. Barnes. New York: Philosophical Library, 1956.

Szasz, T. S. *Pain and pleasure; a study of bodily feelings.* New York: Basic Books, 1957.

Wynne, L. C., et al. Pseudo-mutuality in the family relations of schizophrenics. *Psychiatry*, 1958, *21*, 205–220.

7

Loyalty Implications of the Transference Model in Psychotherapy

This paper addresses the psychotherapist in general and the child therapist in particular.

For our purposes loyalty has to be defined as a triadic relational factor. Contextually, loyalty is a preferential relational option that is based on its object's earned merit; preference presumes an option to choose between two partners. Loyalty conflict is thus implicit in the concept of loyalty. Loyalty to one's parents is founded on the most substantial earned merit, and any later loyalty is subject to a conflict with our primary, filial loyalty. The teacher, the friend, the spouse or the therapist are all candidates for conflicting loyalties. Even the transference component of these secondary attachments represents disloyalty to the primary loyalty. Conversely, adherence to "pathology" may represent loyalty to one's family of origin, partly as renounced individuation and partly as rejection of extrafamilial help.

The professional offer of therapeutic help clearly intrudes into the family's primary loyalty context. The symptomatic child is often in an unbearably, self-contradictory family position. His physicial development pushes him toward individuation yet the parents' messages may endorse stagnation. Individuation is reacted to as estrangement rather

Mrs. Geraldine Spark, ACSW, was co-therapist of case material and co-architect of the conceptual analysis reported in this paper.

98

than as necessary differentiation. Even clinicians may confuse maturation in the context of relating with the need for physical separation. Regarding family-based therapy as an obstacle to the individuation of adolescents is another form of confusion.

Since family relationships are themselves embedded in a transference context, the therapist has to examine how that context is affected through the addition of therapeutic transference. This leads to the exploration of the parents' relationships with their own parents, both in their transference and current reality meaning.

A family's loyalty system may encompass each member's investment of sacrificed growth in return for tolerance of his regressive gratification and, more importantly, for his sense of earned merit. The child's active role in this is validated by the often observable solid contributions of even very young (aged two to four) children to family loyalty. The parentified child is an important link in the homeostasis of the pathogenic family system.

Its underlying loyalty model supports contextual therapy's strategic leverage that can utilize the transference situation for diminishing rather than increasing guilt over disloyalty. "How could you (the child) and I (the therapist) work as a team to help your family?" This is preferred to the formula: "How could I be a better substitute parent for you?"

This can, of course, be accomplished only if the therapist can afford to be genuinely concerned about helping all family members, whether or not they are seen in therapeutic sessions (multidirectional partiality). Subsequently the therapist will have to devote attention to all possible signs of the child's guilt over symptomatic improvement. In the end, paradoxically, concern about due filial accountability leads to the optimal degree of liberation from one's paralyzing overloyalties to the family. In today's formulation, through the earning of appropriate entitlement, the child gains freedom for growth and healthier patterns of relating. Specifically, the therapist's respect for the parent's loyalty to his parents will liberate the patient to express his critical reactions to the parents. The greatest obstacle to therapeutic progress resides in guilt-laden loyalty to one's parents. It is self-defeating to build the therapeutic goal on filial disloyalty.

The main concern of this paper is: Can the psychodynamic theoretical framework be expanded and integrated with the family systems orientation or are they mutually exclusive? It is assumed that the essence of family therapy lies in the therapist's commitment to all members of the family as his patients, rather than in any technical or strategic arrangement for and during the sessions. A further major concern is with the question of how to define the conceptual framework of multiperson system levels of motivations. I believe that such framework relies on the hierarchy of obligations and loyalties in any family. Ethical entanglements of our lives are a key dynamics. Furthermore, I suggest that pathology and resistance to change are codetermined on the system levels of loyalty and unconsciously collusive obligations, e.g., for retaining the "sick" role. More specifically, while transference and transferred "parentification" of the therapist are "technically" required for success, nonetheless they may lead to self-defeating mechanisms through implicit disloyalty to one's family of origin.

My theoretical position is identifiable as that of intensive family therapy.[1] As a family therapist, I treat many children, having the conviction that family members from age 1 to the 80s can and should be included in clinical work. However, for the last 12 of my 26 years as a therapist, I have not treated individuals in isolation from their family context.

We live in an era of open challenge to our social institutions and values. I believe a demand is being put on the so-called mental health professions to perform services which tend to make them appear as society's healer. The concern that mental health is on the way to becoming a prominent scapegoat for social ills of all sorts is justified. Our confusion in basic concepts could be too costly to tolerate.

I am convinced that it is important and urgent to improve the understanding between child psychiatrists and family therapists and that this task is being gradually accomplished.

An even more important task, however, is the systematic and comprehensive examination of the relationship between the individual-based or psychological outlook per se and the family or relation-based approach to dynamic theory and treatment. We have to find ways in which the mutual bias between enthusiastic innovators and the traditional purists can be reconciled through an integration and flexible expansion of our knowledge of the human condition.

There are widespread misunderstandings about the real issues that emerge from family or relational theory as contrasted with the individual approach. One of these is the belief that the relational approach focuses only on visible interactions and implies only a superficial interest in the structural aspects of individual family members. Another is the myth that the confidentiality of a one-to-one therapeutic relationship is sine qua non for therapeutic depth.

Throughout the years I have come to a conviction that the essence of the family therapy approach lies in a motivational and loyalty commitment aspect of the therapist-patient relationship. The fact that the therapist sees family members separately or conjointly is a dynamically much less relevant factor than his intention to be concerned with every family member's emotional well-being and growth. The main indication for family therapy resides in the therapist's capacity for "multidirectional partiality," i.e., his inner freedom to take turns in siding with one family member after another as his empathic understanding and the technical leverage require.

In this paper I am not trying to speak to the point of how the phenomena of transference differ under the condition of family therapy. Instead, I plan to ask the child psychotherapist to consider the merit of certain theoretical and strategic implications for individual, including residential, therapy of children. The essential point of my paper is not based on the "technical" premise that all family members are seen conjointly. Rather, I would like to focus on guilt over disloyalty to the family as a chief source of resistance to treatment and change.

Freud's monumental contribution of the concept of transference helped us to understand the patient's hidden structuralized personal commitments as they become externalized and displaced to the person of the therapist. In fact, the understanding of the patient's inclination to personalize a seemingly technical relationship became one of the main indicational criteria for undertaking psychoanalysis. I believe that the next logical step in expanding the scope of knowledge has to include the context of the patient's current close family relationships. We can ask ourselves the question: Do the patient's personal subjective commitments to the therapist have hidden family loyalty implications? Furthermore, if the answer is yes, we have to determine how important these loyalties are for therapeutic success.

Anna Freud, in her book *Normality and Pathology in Childhood*, remarks: "In periods of positive transference the parents often aggravate the loyalty conflict between analyst and parent which invariably arises in the child."[2(p48)] From the vantage point of the family therapist, it is of even greater significance to recognize that every step toward change or improvement impinges on the child's unconscious commitment to family loyalty. The mere establishment of a strong transference, whether positive or negative, constitutes a trigger of guilt over violation of unconscious family loyalty ties. Transference as an attempt at temporary adoption, aside from being an externalization of intrapsychic patterns, has to be antithetical to existing child-parent ties and should not be considered exclusively in the isolation of the therapeutic relationship.

Loyalty can mean many things, and I would like to define it for our purposes as one of the multiperson structuring forces which underlie relationship systems or networks. Multiperson relationships include but supersede the psychological organizations of their individual members. Using the language of systems theory, such organizations have a causal or motivational contribution of their own, just as water has different properties from the sum of the properties of hydrogen and oxygen.

It is well known that direct therapeutic work with the issues of relationship systems is extremely complex. Repetitious archaic patterns which are evoked in individual therapeutic transference neurosis and studied as if "in vitro" will have to be understood in an integrated pattern, interwoven with "real" interpersonal interactions. In an embittered marital feud both husband and wife lose perspective to the extent that they fight each other or the shadows of one another's internalized relational world. Classical psychodynamic theory has elucidated the conflicting forces of internal need configurations and the ego's attempts at mastering external reality.

The dynamic point of view pictures life as a process which takes place in a field of constantly changing forces. To change a personality in a certain direction has been the traditional frame of reference of individual psychotherapy. Transference phenomena, as A. Freud has put it,[2(p5)] have to be viewed as part of a "whole complicated network of drives, affects, object relations, ego apparatuses, ego functions and defenses, internalizations and ideals, with the mutual interdependencies between id and ego and the resultant defects of development, regressions, anxieties, compromise formations, and character distortions."

Some of the above concepts are individual-based, while others refer to dyadic relationships. The family therapist has to broaden his scope from dyads to larger relationship systems and to consider every member of the system from his own vantage point of the center of a universe.

In short, the therapist of families or relationships in general has to distinguish among three levels of relational systems: (1) purely intrapsychic (e.g., ego-superego, self and voice, self and imagined persecutor, etc.), (2) internal aspect of interpersonal (e.g., one's loyalty to a parent or mate), and (3) existential aspect of interpersonal (e.g., the fact of one's having or not having parents, siblings, etc.).

Relational phenomena which pertain mainly to one of these levels may interlock with and obfuscate phenomena or expectations on the other levels. Much confusion and irrelevant, unproductive struggle occurs between family members because of a lack of clarity or distinction even in the therapist's mind regarding on which relational level the essence of a problem lies.

Another illustration of the difference between relational phenonema on levels 2 and 3 would be the difference between talking about one's murderous, incestuous, etc., feelings towards one parent to (*a*) the therapist alone or (*b*) in the presence of the parent.

MULTIPERSON VS. ONE PERSON STRUCTURING OF MOTIVATIONS

One of the least constructive points of view in current writings about the family approach is the assumption of an either-or, mutually exclusive relationship between individual personality dynamics and multiperson relational or system dynamics. Certain authors talk of a "discontinuous break" between traditional psychodynamic theory and family or relational models of motivational theory.

My own outlook has been dominated by a search for a creative synthesis of mutually complementary and antithetical factors in evaluation of the total human situation. The fact that we have new and valuable information on the homeostatic regulatory laws of relationship systems, does not vitiate the validity of and the necessity for understanding the individual person as a level of motivational system.

The next major development in psychodynamic theory might very well be the description of the deep dynamic structuring of multiperson relationship systems. Such language will borrow a great deal from the essentially intraindividual and partially dyadic orientation of classical psychoanalytic theory. But it also will have to integrate the conceptual achievements of relationship theory and extend the usefulness of both frames of reference. Such theoretical extensions will, naturally, have to deal with those frontier concepts which will make the transition from individual to relationship system theory.

INDIVIDUATION AS
DIFFERENTIATION VS. ESTRANGEMENT

One of the myths frequently met among adherents of the traditional individual outlook pertains to the overvaluation of physical separation as a means of individuation. Not that I would argue with the value or necessity of certain marital separations, divorce, or of the adolescent's moving out when ready. What I question is the confusion of separation with differentiation as a means of maturation. Physically removing a schizoid young adult from his home, for instance, should not be expected to help as much towards his maturation as direct help with his dependent relationships as family therapy could accomplish.

Conversely, there is a widespread belief among professionals, or perhaps I should call it resistance, according to which treating the family members together would amount to the therapist's endorsing the family's everlasting symbiotic togetherness. If the therapist is experienced and properly trained, working on relationship dimensions in a conjoint meeting offers more hope for individuation than physical separation which may support the therapist's own illusion of emotional growth through avoidance of working through in relationships.

Confusion may arise from not distinguishing between individuation, i.e., "whether and from which point onward a child should cease to be considered as a product of and dependent on his family, and should be given the status of a separate entity, a psychic structure in its own right,"[2(p43)] and severing relationship ties. The former is a question of psychic boundary formation, whereas the second is often beclouded by a personal myth, based on some combinations of escape, denial, internalization of loyalty, or ostensibly hateful warfare.

The use of catch phrases like "he is old enough to move out of his parents' house" and "for some people it is better to have a divorce" may hide the therapist's own unresolved relationship with his family of origin. It depends on the therapist's capacity for dealing with his own family relationship whether he would devise a strategy for concrete help toward separation or a method for conjoint exploration and therapeutic confrontation in the case illustrated by the following excerpt from the husband's statement which he made in a first marital session:

It really doesn't matter to me doctor how my parents feel or what they do. I don't hold a grudge but the truth is they have never favored me. I started working at 12 and when I needed their help most, they didn't put up the money which would have kept me out of jail. Now I have a record and it keeps me from executive type jobs. For years I used to see my parents only once in six months. My trouble is a severe drinking problem. I love my wife but I don't come home from work until 2 to 3 AM. Actually, I have no emotion left for anybody. I sit in bars and drink to the point of unconsciousness. For the last two years I go to my mother's about twice a week. I only go there to help my father with things like insurance on his car, on his house, and things like that.

Some therapists would hear disinterest and distance in this man's description of his relationship with his parents; others, on the contrary, would be impressed by his paradoxical interest in visiting his parents twice a week as an emerging potential for exploring hidden loyalty ties.

INTERNAL VS. CONTEXTUAL CONFRONTATION

Whether it concerns a child or an adult, the relational theoretical point of view is adverse to the consideration of intrapsychic structures in isolation from the context of actual live relationships. The family therapist is not only curious about the effect of the relative's behavior on the patient, but he will extend the patient category to include the relative's own authentic personal outlook.

Freud expected the patient to have the capacity and courage to face his own internal psychic structures and internalized relationships. Relationship therapy also demands the courage to face up to the ghosts that reside in actual relationships. If I tell about you in your presence, you will observe my reactions and I will witness yours. What are the risks and potential gains for each family member in not only talking about one another but asserting their points of view in one another's presence?

Aside from dealing with one another's exposure of frightening or shameful experiences, it is obviously also true that the family members' collusively maintained pathological attitude is less likely to remain hidden if exposure is bilateral. Private and shared family myths are more likely to be revealed in the context of conjoint exploration. Unconscious vicarious gratifications in the other's destructive acts and covert manipulations of roles are apt to be uncovered in family therapy. The nature of the alliance between family and therapist is thus quite different from the traditional situation in which an individual is expected to confront his unconscious mental structures in the presence of a therapist.[3] The relatives not only become co-patients, but their interactions become directly observable rather than merely indirectly described and acted out through transference to and countertransference elicited in the therapist.

Experience has shown that a single conjoint session can reveal such striking, relevant pathogenic interactional patterns which could not be uncovered during months of separate, collateral individual therapy.

Many cases of schoolphobia attest to this. A 17-year-old girl was treated individually in one of the prominent training institutes as a psychotic. Two weeks after her transfer to the family therapy division, she and her stepfather revealed the existence of a half year of incestuous relationship. In subsequent family therapy the entire family of four made great progress and it was uncovered that the mother was in need of long-range therapy.

Before examining the transference aspects of the difference between the individual and the relational dynamic approaches, we have to consider a further expansion of our theoretical horizon. As our point of view progresses from relatively impersonal formulations of psychic mechanisms to subjective experience and meaning of exchanges among people, we have to consider not only psychological reactions, but also the ethical and existential entanglement of human lives. Concern and responsibility for one another is an important dimension inherent in every close relationship, even if it is a partially unconscious structural realm.

The therapist who wants to liberate the patient from his hidden binding concern for or guilt-laden loyalty to members of his family, while succeeding in removing certain manifestations of psychological guilt, may at the same time increase the patient's existential guilt. Buber[4] distinguished between guilt feelings and existential guilt. The latter obviously goes beyond psychology. It has to do with objective harm to the order and justice of the human world. If I really betrayed a friend or if my mother really feels that I damaged her body and existence, the reality of a disturbed order of the human world remains, whether I can get rid of certain guilt feelings or not. Such guilt can only be affected by action and existential rearrangement, if at all.

SYMPTOM AS LOYALTY

A key consideration of the deeper structuring of relationships concerns the role of "pathology" and "symptom" in the unconscious loyalty to one's family. Insofar as the pathogenic family system is supported by the regressive needs of all family members, the most loudly symptomatic member can be looked upon as a victim of his loyalty and of an unconscious shared agreement for not hurting any member through change in anyone. A child may cover up the parent's regressive needs by school phobia or a delinquent adolescent may try to balance a "yo-yo"-like marriage in which the parents take turns threatening to separate.

It is logical to assume, then, that the symptomatic member, most often a child, is made increasingly guilty as he undergoes symptomatic improvement. In a true existential sense, the more he improves his function, the more he is bound to harm the order of his human world. This is made even more true if his therapist promises confidentiality and a separate alliance; the familial betrayal becomes even more pronounced. Inasmuch as transference amounts to a trial and temporary adoption, its occurrence further magnifies the feelings of betrayal and becomes a source of psychological guilt in addition to the existential guilt inherent in symptomatic improvement.

For reason of completeness I have to add here that family therapy experience shows the strength and intrinsic healthiness of many an overtly symptomatic family member. His role is to bring outside attention and potential help to the entire system. He may be the only one who puts out action which can effectively lead to change. The big city gang member is one of the illustrations of this point, which also explains why so frequently the initially symptomatic, designated patient member has a better prognosis than the silently pathogenic parents or well siblings.

NEEDS VS. MERIT AS MOTIVES

The relational structuring of loyalty is only partially reducible to the existence of drives, hungers, and needs of individual members. The basic position of drive or instinct theory was based on a conflict or power model. Competitive struggle can exist between psychic systems or individuals. Yet, while I try to make the other an object of my drives, what happens to his needs to make me or someone else his object? What if competitively two of us make the same person an object of similar or different drives? What if I want to make you an object of affection and you want to make me an object of destruction? Freud's concepts of the primal horde, drive cathexis, penis envy, mastery by the ego, are illustrations of power oriented, energy-related constructs.

On the other hand, merit as a motivational concept has a multi-person structuring which is anchored in an ethical context. Whereas the ultimate reality of needs is in the nature of biological survival, the reality of merit is in the existential history of a group. As in families, in the history of nations or religious movements, the motivational determinative force of merit is immeasurable. Abraham's willingness to sacrifice his son in obedience to God served as the basis of the convenant which was believed to have pledged God's loyalty to his people. Christ's sacrifice revolutionized the merit of millions of subjected or condemned people for centuries. The self-sacrificing acts of a nation's heroes and the vile acts of their enemies determine the motivations of countless generations of young men who are born into an idiosyncratic merit context. According to Shakespeare, Romeo and Juliet were caught in an "ancient grudge" between families which can be buried only with the death of the "pair of star-crossed lovers."

The relational structure of loyalty encompasses the network of a merit-accounting of the history of a group. A child is born into a situation which is predetermined by the merit-accounting of previous generations. We all know cases in which a mother is determined to avoid exploiting her children the way she was exploited in childhood and in which, by the trick of unconscious motivation, she finds herself doing exactly what she hoped to avoid. The child gets caught in the parent's struggle for correcting an injustice and becomes himself a scapegoat for previous injustices.

TRANSFERENCE WITHIN THE FAMILY

In therapy, transference as a technical device is a means of changing a person's patterns of reacting. It is also a bridge between my habitual past reactions and my present or future ones. As I reexperience and act out repetitious past patterns toward the therapist, I can take a necessary distance from everyday interactions and begin to break up the repetitiousness of my pathological cycles.

The essence of transference is not a cool, objective cognitive experience. Nor is it chiefly a behavior modification process of the learning type. Instead, it is an emotionally charged, relational experience with the subjective excitement of promised fulfillment and the feared disappointment of a painfully familiar type.

As has been described, all of our emotionally significant relationships are embedded in a transference context, at least when transference is defined in a broader sense. As I fall in love with a woman, she may become a mother transference object to me. As my relationship with my boss gets personalized, chances are that I discover how I begin to reexperience some attitudes that I had toward my father, older brother, or grandfather as a child.

Beginning family therapists are soon struck with a different climate for therapeutic transference as they begin to see families rather than isolated individuals. The chief reason for this is the fact that family relationships themselves are embedded in a transference context and the family therapist can enter the ongoing transference relationship system rather than having to recreate it as a new relationship in the privacy of an exclusive therapist-patient work relationship. As the therapist gains access to the system of intensively charged deeper family relationships, he obtains a position which surely demands a specialized skill, but he also obtains new leverage, based on the mutuality of relationship involvements among family members.

Ever since Freud, psychoanalytic theoreticians have been curious about the individual determinants of a patient's capacity for developing intensive therapeutic transference. Such capacity in patients has long been viewed as a main condition for psychoanalytic treatment. More recently, attention has been paid to the instantaneous capacity of certain psychotic patients for symbiotic transference. The family therapist has to examine the multiperson system determinants of a person's intrafamilial transference involvements and his capacity for "transferring" relational attitudes from his family to outsiders.

The work of the analyst abstracts and condenses the exploration of repetitiously regressive relationship attitudes into the therapeutic relationship, hoping for the emergence of a technically accessible transference neurosis. The family therapist, on the other hand, is interested in the vicissitudes of the same tendencies *within* family relationships. I prefer to include members of the family of origin of both parents in any family I have in family treatment. Frequently, the parent-grandparent relationship becomes the focus of observations and target of possible intervention. Such parent-grandparent relationships are richly interspersed with feedback processes between so-called current reality and long suppressed or repressed early longings, disappointments, and their internal elaborations.

CLINICAL ILLUSTRATION

The family therapist postulates that regressive living and acting between family members constitutes one of the main aspects of the family's loyalty system. Each member's investment of sacrificed growth is repaid through the other members' tolerance of his regressive gratifications. Such subtle, partly unconscious interlocking between personal needs of members and idiosyncratic value system of the family builds up the context of familial intimacy. As individual psychotherapy or analysis redirects repetitious acting out through transference to the person of the therapist, the family's loyalty system becomes threatened. The threat is even greater when the patient is a child, because the child is usually sheltered in a more dependent position than are adult members.

One of the most enlightening learning experiences in the practice of family therapy pertains to the surprising amount of solid contribution of even very young children to family loyalty. The extremes of parental dependence on children can best be seen in cases of extreme parentification of children. Yet even if we disregard these extremes we may wonder which child doesn't get messages: "Never trust anyone but your mother" or "Your mother is your only real friend," either explicitly or implicitly.

The case of a 10-year-old boy and his family may be illustrative of many similar situations. I was consulting with the staff of a private residential school in their effort to broaden their psycho-analytic, individual treatment model in which the boy was seen by a psychotherapist whereas his mother had long-distance tele-phone conversations with a social worker.

The child's presenting problem was an irritating retardation of motoric performance combined with an obsessive focusing on detail. The life of the family was revolving around his slow re-sponses. The parents reported that it took the boy hours to go to bed, meals were taken extremely slowly, and the boy could hesitate for a long time in deciding on which side of the closet to hang his shirt. It was easy to see the family's despair over this behavior and wish for a change, at least on a conscious level.

Psychological testing revealed good intelligence and the boy's motoric system was found to be well-coordinated. His 7-year-old sister was a very quick, vivacious child. Unfortunately, no data were collected on the contributions of the apparently well sibling member of the pathogenic family system. I shall omit the descrip-tion of the intrapsychic dynamics of this boy and focus on rela-tional factors rather heavily to make my point stand out more clearly.

The workers assigned to this case reported that the parents were intellectually active but emotionally rather detached people. The father was a chemistry professor and the mother, who had wanted to become a social worker, ended up studying sociology. The mother once was hospitalized for psychiatric reasons for three weeks and had subsequent neuropsychiatric treatment for a while. She was desperately determined to regard her child's problem as essentially an organic one and she recalled having been trauma-tized in a clinic where, as she alleged, attempts had been made to make her feel like a "rotten mother." She did not like to talk about her family of origin, which she had years earlier left behind in another city. She stated that she would see her cold, "neurotic" parents once or twice a year. Her relationship with her parents was superficial; she could not be spontaneous with them. She claimed she did not trust professionals either. All she wanted was help with her son's slowness. Yet, paradoxically, she would talk once a week up to an hour on the telephone with the social worker from a distance of almost 400 miles.

The workers had the impression that the child's father was an extremely aloof and passive parent and that his only assertion manifested itself in his final insistence on sending the boy to a residential school. Although there was little reported about the father's role in the pathogenic family system, it was easy to postulate that the parents in this isolated nuclear family did not have much reason for vitality of human relationship. Thus, the stage was set for a subtle parentification of the children.

The therapist of this boy stated that the marked slowness of the child's behavior was also exhibited in the school and that there had been only one situation in which it seemed to be almost completely absent. This happened during an excursion in a house outside the school's realm where the boy took his meal at a normal pace. They also reported an interesting observation. On the occasion of a school excursion the boy appeared to be enjoying himself greatly. When his family visited several months later, he made them drive through the same itinerary as the school wagon had gone, in the hope of conveying a similarly happy experience to his family. The therapist added that the boy could also recall that he had done likewise on a number of occasions at home: e.g., he made his parents drive through the same route as he and his uncle had driven earlier in a happy mood.

The child's capacity for giving to his parents was a striking feature, considering the lack of personal warmth in their own relationships. To view a child whose symptoms demonstrate a devouring oral demandingness and tiring anal obsessiveness as a family healer certainly appears paradoxical. Yet, at the minimum, we can assume that the parents were able to use their child's symptoms as an escape from dealing with their own unresolved problems with their families of origin. Furthermore, on an existential level, the child's misdirected life energies could revitalize the stale marital relationship. The sick child provided an agenda around which the parents' weak identity can crystallize.

A more specific gratification inherent in parentification consists of the parents' utilizing the child as a possession for the purpose of unconscious undoing of early object deprivation experiences of their own. Early deprivation, as we know, can lead to a never resolvable need for symbiotic clinging, with no capacity developed for individuation and separation. The more the child is caught in his own symptomatology, the longer the period of implicit possessive gratification for the parent. The parent can defend himself against insight into such inverse dependence on his child's pathology, for instance, by a rigid insistence on the organic nature of the condition. It was reported that this mother had been preoccupied with viewing her child as organically damaged from the first few months of his life. The social worker reported that most of their long conversations on the telephone pertained to arguments whether the child's condition was organic or not.

On a deeper level, the child's behavior revealed a great extent of concern for his parents. Through covert messages it must have been conveyed to him that even though his symptoms irritated his family, his illness may prevent his mother from facing her own depression, loneliness, and hurt feelings. We have found that, in cases in which a parent's previous psychosis or conflicts are never openly revealed to a child, the child nonetheless has a corresponding anxiety which makes him respond with a déjà vu type familiarity to the belated communication of the secret fact.

Had this been a case of actual family treatment, one would have obtained a more complete picture of all family members' involvement in the emotional system. Typically, the therapist would gain access to the pathological and pathogenic features of the parents' marriage. It was known already that insistence on institutionalization was what appeared to be the first act of assertive position-taking on the part of the distant, inactive father. The significant contribution of the "well sibling" could not even be touched on in the present setting.

If we assume then that the homeostasis of the pathogenic system is regulated by loyalty-bound regression and arrest of development, we can expect the child's guilt to increase to the extent he lets his parents down, so to speak. Leaving them behind to struggle alone at home already borders on disloyalty; if in addition he would improve symptomatically, it could amount to psychological treason. Guilt over his familial loyalty is not simply a regressive fixation, anchored in an internalized situation; it is, rather, validated by interpersonal reality of the parents' own messages. To keep his guilt down and, also, to protect his parents, the child has to appease the system by (1) preserving his symptom and (2) trying to help his parents through sharing with them everything he can enjoy in life. Thus, it would be unrealistic to expect the child to progress too far in the face of actual disloyalty and a mounting guilt feeling over it.

This model seemed to be at some variance with the traditional model of the school's therapy team. They were aiming their strategy at hoping to have the child invest the therapist with sufficient transference to gradually undo his fixated patterns so that, with the therapist's guidance, he could begin to acquire new patterns of behavior. As they pointed out, this happens in a great number of residential treatment cases, although it is often reported that the effect may not last too long beyond the time of discharge when the family's influence seems to manage to reverse the therapeutic change. It is as if the transference parent's (the therapist) approval were antithetical to the real parents' needs and wishes.

As a family therapist I felt an intense frustration over the lack of the availability of the parents in this setting where they would come to visit only four times a year. How can I as a consultant suggest methods to affect the system under the circumstances? Once again I noticed the severe handicap that institutionalization can place on the family approach.

Yet the logic of our loyalty model supports a possible use of the transference situation in a manner which is aimed to diminish the guilt caused by the patient's disloyalty to his family of origin. What if the strategic motto then were "How could you and I, the therapist, work as a team to help your family?" instead of "How could I be a better substitute parent, so that you can use me for growing up emotionally?" If the first formula is followed through in practice, the therapist can, by listening to the child's own description of his daily experience, design ways in which the child can help his family and in turn be permanently helped. What is required is the therapist's genuine capacity for being interested and concerned in helping all the other family members, each as his own patient. The means then can be developed, even though the contacts between child and family may be limited (e.g., visits, phone calls, correspondence).

More specifically, it would follow that the therapist has to obtain clues for ways in which the child could help the parents. The child actually may be surprisingly aware of such possibilities and eager to discuss them with someone who is willing to recognize his role as a desperately eager family healer. In such instances it is easy for the therapist to offer an alliance for developing strategies for more effective help for the family. In cases in which the child is not aware of his leverage as a potential family healer, the therapist first has to explore and verify what the child's own notions are regarding his family role, and encourage the child's thinking by giving recognition to the hidden loyalty aspects of his concern about his family. Using his own role and the meaning of therapy in this manner, the therapist can considerably diminish the loyalty conflict implicit in the child transference-determined devotion to him.

In considering the above strategic formula for therapy, naturally I do not want to underestimate the goal of increasing the autonomy and functional effectiveness of the individual patient. However, whereas in the traditional individual approach the goal is accomplished chiefly via the transference relationship to the therapist and by learning of new patterns, I suggest an additional dimension of exploration: the loyalty implications of both transference investment and subsequent symptomatic change. This would require that the therapist include in his field of vision and concern the vicissitudes of the loyalty investment of all family members as a major dynamic determinant for the patient's capacity for lasting growth.

In summary, the therapist of families is not satisfied with the theoretical and technical view that the therapeutic transference should be considered in isolation from loyalty commitments within the patient's family. Consequently, it is natural for a family therapist to encourage new avenues for involvement among family members. Working with such an open relational system gives the therapist far more leverage than would a consideration of the transference relationship in "pure culture," as it were.

The traditional view of isolating the therapeutic transference investments from family loyalties implicitly assumed a liberation of the child from repetitious feedback chains of family interaction. The exclusive, confidential alliance between therapist and patient implies a formula: with my help you may defeat your pathogenic forces, your repetition compulsion and, (especially if the patient is a child) the influences of your pathogenic family environment. If, however, the therapist includes into his design family loyalty as one of the system determinants of repetition compulsion, by the same logic he will have to include the relatives' interests in his contract for therapeutic alliance. All family members will then have to receive help in order to maximize the potential for change in everyone. I for one have learned not to trust the signs of a child's or an adolescent's angry wish to emancipate through abandoning his anxious, constraining, guilt-provoking, "parentifying," or "infantilizing" parents. I prefer to search for the underlying antithetical guilt-laden loyalty and to consider the structure of the paralyzing existential guilt which follows disloyalty to the system. In summary, I cannot fully understand the structure of the guilt laden loyalty without knowing and being concerned for all members of the relationship system.

REFERENCES

1. Boszormenyi-Nagy, I., & Framo, J. L. *Intensive Family Therapy*. New York, Harper & Row Publishers Inc, 1965.
2. Freud, A. *Normality and Pathology in Childhood*. New York, International Universities Press, 1965.
3. Boszormenyi-Nagy, I., & Spark, G. M. *Invisible Loyalties*. New York, Harper & Row Publishers Inc, 1973.
4. Buber, M. Guilt and guilt feelings. *Psychiatry, 20*, 114–129, 1957.

8

How I Became
a Family Therapist

This brief paper highlights the connections between a conviction of the effectiveness of the relational (family) therapy approach, including commitment to the good of all family members, and the personal needs of the therapist. It reflects the relatively isolated, lonely position of family therapists among their fellow professionals, even in the early 1970s.

There must be several overt and covert reasons why I ended up doing family therapy fourteen years after I had started my work as an individual psychotherapist. I could list a number of pertinent reasons as they come to my mind.

If I make a more focused effort to answer the question, however, it appears to me that it was a genuine conviction about doing more relevant and hopeful work which caused my initial conversion.

Whatever my deeper personality reasons may be for choosing the approach to psychotherapy through family relations, ultimately I could not have made the complete switch without a *conviction about the effectiveness* of the approach. As professionals, our group could not have survived without a commitment to the principles of causal or rational treatment as it evolves from scientific medicine.

My conviction about doing a more causally relevant and therefore a better job of treatment through the family even as far as the designated patient is concerned pre-dated my subsequently growing conviction about the treatment needs of all other family members. Today I do relationship-based treatment whenever it is feasible because I consider it "scientifically" the most rational treatment for the "patient" as well as for all others involved in his important relationships.

It is difficult for me to make a comparative evaluation of my personal qualities and family experiences as distinguished from those of other people. On a somewhat deeper level, I must have wanted to fight the dark forces which captivate us in pathological relationship patterns. It was a challenge to meet with and fight these forces in what seemed to be an open battlefield.

As to changes in myself, I think as a result of family therapy work I have become more secure in human relationships—but also more demanding, I am afraid. Many things that I would have accepted in the past as satisfactory responses appear now to me as phony or lacking openness.

In my practice I have greatly lost my valuation of secrecy and confidentiality as important therapeutic factors. I also have, I believe, a better understanding of what an individual is: patterns of action rather than patterns of conceptualization or reflections on experience.

I have experienced a greater separation from colleagues who have not made the transition to the relational approach. Their concepts are painfully incomplete for explaining the phenomena I am dealing with.

I believe I cannot help but apply my learning of relational patterns to my own family relationships in my everyday living. I have sharper frustrations and deeper satisfactions as a result.

9

Ethical and Practical
Implications of Intergenerational
Family Therapy

In this article the contextual approach is still referred to as "intergenerational family therapy." Through its secondary title, Invisible Loyalties *was the first book designated as intergenerational family therapy. However, the ethical dimension of therapy is explicitly stressed here when the family members' active search for justice is regarded as, potentially, a good prognostic sign. Therapeutic goals are then to be integrated into a balanced multipersonal and even multigenerational context of loyalty, fairness and mutuality.*

The therapist's responsibility and commitment, rather than specific scientific or technical criteria, define any family or relational therapy. In this the therapist is guided mainly by the factual nature of balances of justice and injustice in intergenerational relationships, balances which determine the offspring's capacity for trust. Subsequently, my current emphasis on consequences surfaces here through therapeutic concern about the most critical aspect of a genuine dialogue—our responsibility for our actions.

Pathogenic overloyalty, like excessive family loyalty expectations, is described as a source of pathology. Yet causal considerations contribute less to the indicational rationale of family therapy than do relational leverages for change. To mobilize these leverages the therapist has to be committed to the welfare of all family members; moreover, the therapist's task is to design action patterns which will benefit all members. The newly found balance of reciprocal fairness will obviate substitutive patterns of relational mastery through avoidance. In this, rather than suggesting a unilaterally self-denying altruism, the contextual intergenerational family therapist suggests a search for a dialectic balance of receiving through giving.

Abstract. Family therapy and its basis — relationship theory — constitute a new outlook rather than another method for psychotherapy. The new outlook originates as much from a state of bankruptcy of the value base of traditional psychotherapy as from the accumulating experience of therapists who work with whole families as relational gestalts.

The essence of family therapy itself lies in the therapist's commitment to all members of the family relationship system. In the advocacy model of individual psychotherapy the offering of confidential alliance to one family member implicitly denies the right for the other members and their aspirations to be considered by the therapist, even when the "patient" behaves in a patently exploitative manner toward the other.

The realization that when close relationships end, they can become intermittently mutually exploitative, leads the family therapist to a reciprocally balanced commitment, based on "multidirectional partiality," empathizing with now one, then another family member, according to the issue at hand. Rather than refusing to concern himself with the members' convictions about exploitation, the therapist should welcome the family members' active search for justice as a potentially good prognostic sign. Not every family has a capacity for facing and working through the difficult, value-laden implications of close relationships.

This reorientation toward the dynamics of balance versus imbalance in relationships radically alters the values and goals of psychotherapy, whether members are treated individually or conjointly. As a result, traditional, non-dialectical psychotherapeutic values of assertiveness, adjustment, effectiveness, genital competence, increased consciousness through insight, self-actualization, health, etc., become limited goals which have to be integrated into a balanced multipersonal and even multigenerational context of loyalty, fairness, and mutuality. Facing the multigenerational ledgers of obligations and designing corresponding action strategies become the deeper dimensions of intergenerational family therapy.

It is the revaluation of the merits of instinct, pleasure, self-actualization and power models that builds the bridge toward the social systems model of psychotherapy in general and family therapy in particular. Instead of being a congeries of discrete, simultaneously struggling, self-assertive individuals, the social network emerges then as a system held together by visible and invisible loyalties and put under strain by inevitable structural exploitativeness.

Aside from its profound effect on therapeutic goals, the shift in value orientation has fundamental implications for community mental health practices and a wide variety of social functions. To mention only one example, law and court functions obtain a thoroughly different meaning when viewed in the light of the recently discovered, unconsciously collusive relational structures, instead of the traditional individual based framework.

Ultimately, relationship theory and intergenerational family therapy will offer a renewed definition of both health and prevention in the field of mental function.

By asking a family therapist to define what psychotherapy is, it appears that the organizers of our Congress have opened the door for radical departures from the traditional definition. In an era which questions the social value of psychotherapy, and in which some believe the traditional family is becoming extinct, it seems appropriate to explore whether the family approach has a new ethical base to offer for reexamining the psychological and societal premises for psychotherapy.

FAMILY SYSTEM AS A LEDGER OF ACCOUNTS

For the purposes of intergenerational family theory the term family should first be defined as an ongoing social system, not merely a single nuclear family. It is based on an invisible ledger of structured expectations concerning the integrity underlying observable interactions. Because of their existential interwovenness, family members remain personally accountable for both benefits received and injuries inflicted. Ultimately, they cannot avoid facing the balance sheets of fairness of their exchanges. Such a ledger of transgenerational accountability has been the concern of insightful thinkers ever since the writing of the Hebrew Bible as well as the great playwrighting of Ancient Greece. The intergenerationally oriented family therapist has the privilege of witnessing the hidden script of a family's destiny as it emerges from minor denials to tragedies of everyday magnitude. The outcome of the drama can rebalance or further upset the ethical balance of relational accounts. For example, overt or even covert exploitation of a child by its parents, if maintained unilaterally, can undermine the child's base of trust and belief in human justice to such an extent that, upon becoming a parent, the new adult will be "programmed" to start his relationship with his child with an already overencumbered balance sheet. He is actually entitled to make the rest of the world accountable to repay his damages. The invisible script that follows from such a ledger of intergenerational reciprocity sets the stage for many so-called "emotional distortions", manifested in close relationships: projective distortion, parentification, scapegoating, idealization, etc.

It has been customary to view family therapy as merely another method of treatment. The question of specific indications is often raised: Should this schizoid adolescent be treated by individual or family therapy?

Assuming that a more comprehensive knowledge of the patient's relational world can only be helpful, I suggest that the essence of the family or relational approach to psychotherapy lies in the scope of the therapist's responsibility and commitment, rather than in any technical criterion. As the family therapist "contracts" for the care of an entire family, he negotiates from an ethical position entirely different from that of the individual therapist, who forms a confidential alliance with one member while remaining uncommitted and unaccountable to the other members. In contrast, as his contract expects him to refrain from siding with one member or from prejudicially overlooking this member's unfairness to the others, the family therapist is drawn into a role similar to that of a judge who cannot help but consider the balance of reciprocal fairness in human interactions. It is mainly for this reason that the conclusions of this presentation can neither be obtained from nor contradicted through individual practice. The family therapist can temporarily avoid his intrinsic role expectation of "multi-directional partiality" by focusing his attention on the here-and-now, visible interactions and power ploys that fill out the days and hours of any human group. But in so doing, the "interactionalist" family therapist is likely to miss the very dynamic that determines the motivational patterning of long-term, ongoing, multigenerational systems of relationships. How then can motivation be defined on a new multiperson, system level?

ETHICS AND THE THERAPY OF MULTIPERSON SYSTEMS

Somewhat paradoxically, the family relational approach poses a serious challenge to the notion that it is psychology that forms the basis of psychotherapeutic intervention. By this I mean, if psychology is defined as the study of the properties of one human mind, or one person's behavior, experience and underlying motivations, then psychological theory by itself constitutes an incomplete base for understanding the regulatory forces which govern healthy or pathological functioning in individual members. I postulate that the psychological forces themselves are determined rather by the factual nature of balances of justice and injustice in intergenerational family relationships. For example, the actual fact of the exploitation of a child affects not only the child's psychology but it becomes a determinant in the ongoing relationship among family members surrounding the child, including his future children and grandchildren. Their capacity for trust, satisfaction, and reality testing will be affected. The individual's so-called developmental psychology is molded in accordance with the fluctuating balance of human integrity in the dealings of his important others.

It is very important for us to also recognize that the time has come to end the pseudo-scientific myth of the desirability of a valueless manner of thinking, as has been customary in contemporary social science and psychotherapy. Furthermore, if psychotherapists are change-agents or catalysts, they cannot deny any longer that they have to define that which should be changed. In fact, the family therapist raises even the question: Who should change? Very frequently it turns out in the course of therapy that it is one of the "well" members who needs the most help.

I do not believe that every family therapist can adopt the intergenerational approach. Resistance to adopting the approach originates mainly from the intrinsic demand that its practitioner face the embedment of family relations in a context of ethical responsibility. Unprotected by the disguises of an "interactionalist" curiosity for here-and-now events, or unilateral confidential alliance with one individual member for his psychological cure, or alleging to be a valueless agent of behavioral change, the intergenerational family therapist has to face the most difficult aspect of a genuine dialogue: our responsibility for our actions and our responsibility for also holding the others responsible in their dealings with each other and ourselves.

It is true then that the individual is not responsible for, yet bound by those aspects of the system which derive from the multigenerational ledger of justice. Actually, children can often be devoted to the task of balancing the ledger to the point of placing its cause above their individual goals in life. As Shakespeare states in the prologue to *Romeo and Juliet*: "A pair of star-cross'd lovers take their life; Whose misadventured pitious overthrows, Do with their death bury their parents' strife."

Yet, familial loyalty has its positive, mutually gratifying aspects. A devoted and concerned readiness of small children to volunteer to try to rebalance their parents' unhappiness over their parents' own self-destructive patterns of behavior, is one of the most moving observations that family therapists are liable to make. Familial or filial loyalty is thus not based on the power model of enforcement, like a slave's loyalty to the master. It is based, instead, on spontaneous caring and concern and on the fundamental primary obligation of repaying with gratitude to those who gave us our lives. Gratitude is a frightening aspect of relationship: it can be used for exploitation. In fact, certain parents do manipulate children's loyalty in such a way that it can far outstrip the extent of benefits the child actually has received from the parents. Real exploitation of children is always based on a manipulation of their loyalty, and almost never on a mere successful power contest.

SYMPTOM AND PATHOGENIC LOYALTY

The extension of the dynamics of reciprocal fairness into the question of psychic health and illness underlines the importance of pathogenic loyalty in what leads to individual psychopathology. If we assume that family systems are held together by loyalty, it follows that even self-destructive behavior, like delinquency, drug addiction, psychosis, and other forms of "symptoms" may be maintained in compliance with family loyalty expectations. In fact, I suggest that in understanding the basic dynamic of family systems, one of the principal tasks of the family therapist is to seek out the hidden, invisible loyalty aspects of allegedly objectionable, rejecting or rejected behavior on the part of family members. He has to ask himself the question repeatedly: in what way may this member's seemingly pathological behavior assure his continued availability for the family of origin?

The spread of focus from individual through marital to intergenerational system levels of problems can be briefly illustrated by a typical marital therapy situation:

A young couple in their mid-twenties came into therapy, essentially upon the initiative of the wife. She was rather desperate, almost suicidally unhappy over the failure of their marriage. She complained that her husband had hardly any sexual interest in her. She described that their personal relationship oscillated between long, painful, periods of silence and destructively hostile arguments. She was the only child of intelligent, serious and overly concerned parents.

The husband readily admitted that there was hardly any sexual activity between him and his wife. He attributed this circumstance to his wife's tendency for having cutting, hostile moods, which would completely demotivate him from sexually approaching her. He claimed that these moods developed as a result of long, daily conversations between her and her mother. These conversations became especially intensified during the past year in which the couple decided to move to California in the hope of having a "life of their own."

For a number of weeks the wife kept on refusing to acknowledge the importance of the long evening conversations between herself and her mother as having anything to do with the couple's sexual problems. First, she defended the open, emotionally sincere style of communications of her family against the repressive and indirectly expressive style of her husband's family. Gradually, however, she began to talk about the way in which she would get hurt in the long talks with her mother. A recurrent theme of these conversations was that the mother would insist on proving that the daughter had been neglectful or lacking concern towards her parents, for example, by not preparing meals for her sick mother. In one instance, the mother's sickness consisted of a questionable back pain of several days' duration which did not make her bedridden. The well-to-do mother had obviously many options to obtain pain help instead of expecting her married daughter to leave her husband's company in the evening. The young wife added that, as a rule, such quarrels with her mother would not stop until she would admit her guilt as an ungrateful daughter.

Actually it was a good prognostic sign that this family of an only child handled loyalty expectations with such explicitness, rather than through subtle innuendo and manipulations. In many families the recognition of similar loyalty conflicts is made extremely difficult by complex layers of denial, double messages, and the intensive scapegoating of outside persons. An open confrontation with loyalty expectations was made easier in our case by the fact that this young couple were still childless. In many families children become the most suitable means for avoidance and displacement maneuvers, since the ethical obligation to minister to small children may temporarily silence the conflicting loyalty expectations emanating from the families of origin. The battle of loyalty conflicts then goes underground, so to speak.

It is always risky to try to summarize the complex rationale of a form of therapy in a brief space— *Boszormenyi-Nagy and Spark* (1973). The foregoing clinical illustration can be used only to highlight a few aspects of the therapeutic rationale of intergenerational family therapy. First, in contrast with individual psychotherapy, no family therapist would regard the earlier mentioned young woman's psyche as a finite realm of causation, and responsibility as an agent of change. The family therapist would regard her relationship with her parents as an important leverage for change, rather than merely of developmental or historical significance.

Nor will the intergenerational family therapist accept the limited framework of marital couple therapy. In his view the conflict of loyalties is anchored in both families of origin and in the marriage. All three systems should be utilized for maximum benefit in the difficult task of resolving conflicts through rebalancing loyalties. In implementing this strategy, the intergenerational family therapist holds up the grandparents' welfare as part of his primary therapeutic goals. Finding a suitable way of repaying her filial gratitude will not only directly help the young adult, but will also satisfy her parents' legitimate needs for receiving affection from their grown-up child.

Specifically, the intergenerational family therapist will not consider the older generation as merely an interfering agent, a tool for helping the young nuclear family, or a source of interference. He will regard the ethical balance of the relationships of all family members from the point of view of his commitment to all of them as his "patients". The intergenerational family therapist will consider the *real* obligations of the emancipating daughter in our case to be concerned about the feelings of loss occurring in her parents. The therapist's sympathy will be extended to both the suffering young wife and her painfully grieving parents. He knows that avoidance of the reality of the obligation to repay benefits received will tend to be extremely costly to this young woman. Her loyalties to her family of origin would then go underground and could invisibly pervade and undermine her commitment to both marriage and motherhood.

THERAPEUTIC RATIONALE

What is then the intergenerational family therapist's therapeutic strategy? First, I would like to state what this strategy is not. The intergenerational therapist is not symptom or behavioral oriented. He does not assume by implication that basic decency and gratitude of children toward their parents is reducible to an error in learning which should be removed by relearning. Nor is he interested in chiefly accomplishing insight into the genetic and remotely conscious areas of the psychology of his patient. Like the young woman referred to earlier, his patients may be conscious of the painful guilt-inducing reality of their not being able to repay gratitude to their parents. One reason for this may lie, for instance, in a mother's inability to accept and receive repayment. What the "patient" may need help with, is to enable her mother to receive the repayment and, thereby, in turn, to become liberated herself for a warmly loving and giving partnership in her marriage and for a devoted motherhood later. Therapeutic strategy then is based on an action design rather than on mere cognitive gains through increased consciousness or on unloading of emotions through increased expressiveness. The suffering subject of a loyalty conflict has to be helped to find appropriate action patterns through which the object of loyalty can be effectively helped or repayed without pathological, self-destructive, symptomatic or sick patterns of behavior. In distinction from the concept of "working through" in individual psychotherapy or analysis, the welfare of all members is considered in designing the action patterns. Instead of simply trying to eliminate the pathological obligation from his patient's mind, the intergenerational family therapist will help her to face the implications of her realistically unrequited obligations. Such confrontation should never be considered completed until it can be converted into designs for appropriate and successful *relational* strategies, the goal of which is restoration of a balanced reciprocity of fairness. The newly found balance will enable each participant to relinquish substitutive patterns of relational mastery through avoidance.

Many times the real obstacle for such strategy lies in the past of the grandparent. As a carrier of an overencumbered familial ethical ledger, she may be in no position to ever settle the account between herself and her child. Just as the grandparent was kept in arrears regarding the chance of repayment to her parent, she in turn will be inclined to keep her child in arrears. Another obstacle might lie in the parent's justifiable disdain and resentment for his parent. Often it is difficult to maintain an attitude of fairness toward a parent who is persistently manipulative and exploitative through arousal of guilt.

An important strategic leverage for intergenerational therapy lies in the exploration of the grandparent's past. The uncovering of circumstances which used to exploit the grandparent in her own childhood, may rearrange her own account and help reestablish a fair exchange between herself and her child. Subsequently, it will help her child to exonerate his parent through learning about the latter's human dignity and suffering.

In summary, the essence of intergenerational family therapy lies in an ethical or justice orientation. In contrast with individual therapy, it does not offer exclusive alliance with any member at the expense of its concern for other members of the same relationship system. It does not assume that one member can lastingly benefit from effective, successful power manipulation through a complete disregard for the other member's interest. Advocacy is thus extended from one individual or a couple to the entire system of relationships. Similarly, expectation of change is also extended to include every member of the relationship system. Whether he comes to family therapy sessions conjointly or remains absent, each member has to be both considered in his own rights and alerted to his responsibilities for improving his side of the balance of reciprocity. However, rather than suggesting a unilaterally giving, self-denying altruism, the intergenerational family therapist suggests a dialectic balance of receiving through giving.

Many observers of the American scene allege that psychodynamic psychotherapy is on its way out. After decades of undeniable contributions, the dynamic individual approach has shown what appears to be its limitations. If it is true, other, currently popular varieties on the theme of individual psychotherapy, such as behavior therapy, encounter and sensitivity programs, traditional group therapy, are also to face relative disillusionment in the not too distant future. Similarly affected will be the many community mental health programs, most of which are based on a mixture of individual psychodynamic with "valueless" sociological theoretical assumptions.

The systematic thinking-through of the implications of intergenerational family therapy should, however, not only help to point up the areas of relative bankruptcy in the individual dynamic model. It should, instead, offer an opportunity for the extension of the therapeutic framework by integrating individual insights with the systemic, intergenerational orientation into a holistic approach. Such integrated framework holds exciting possibilities for the redefinition of such basic concepts as health, pathology, prevention, as well as individual legal rights and perhaps eventually even of certain basic notions of international relations. Hopefully, the intergenerational family systems approach will contribute to the discovery by governmental, religious, etc. agencies, that we can no longer afford the cost of continued dodging of responsibility for preventive planning.

REFERENCE

Boszormenyi-Nagy, I., & Spark, G. M. *Invisible loyalties: Reciprocity in intergenerational family therapy.* New York, Harper and Row, 1973.

10

Behavioral Change Through Family Change

In the tradition of individual therapy, change as a goal concept has to be anchored in what is defined as illness or pathology. Family therapy requires a radical departure from this approach. By caring about all family members, the family therapist contributes to a broadening of individual focus psychotherapy and theory rather than its invalidation. It should be noted that one person's dynamic of need configuration constitutes the other's "external reality." Furthermore, individual therapists should examine critically the implicit hypothesis that a person's health interests are automatically coterminous with those of his or her family members.

Simultaneous therapeutic accountability for the good of several persons in relationship with one another creates the need for concern with relational ethics. "Desirable" change becomes uncertain when considering whose vantage point should determine the desirability of behavior or of change. Conversely, all individual therapies, at least implicitly, must confine their contract to an individual-defined goal. This is true of an approach as diverse as classical behavioral therapy. From the point of view of a dialectical understanding of relationships, reward and pain as motivators are too simplistic to explain the complexity of close, existentially interlocking relationships.

The invisible "establishment of collusive postponement of mourning" illustrates the complex intertwining between apparent benefit and essential victimization. It is not always possible to distinguish clearly between the essential creditor and the seeming creditor. Can the parent's "emotional cost of living" be reduced at the expense of a consecutive long-range cost increase for the child?

Contextual therapy is, of course, explicitly resource-based. What are relational resources? Personal availability is one. The prospect of a constructive handling of legacy expectations is another. The family's reason and rationality is still another resource. The extent of available accountability in a family leads to an atmosphere of trustworthiness — yet another leverage. Courage for initiative, honesty and commitment to relationships all represent therapeutic resources. Concern about the existential-ethical aspects of resources requires a humanistic therapeutic attitude, which includes concern for the good of posterity.

Traditionally, the goal of psychotherapy, or therapy in general, originates from the wish to eliminate illness. Physical health is then defined "objectively" from the vantage point of one individual: the absence of processes or outcomes detrimental to the biological welfare of the organism, or, conversely, the optimum potential functional state of the given organism at the given age. Psychopathology, defined as one form of illness, fits into this individual (medical or psychological) model. Consequently, the traditional goal definitions of psychotherapy were confined to changes aimed at the improved functional health, i.e., diminished symptomatology, unhappiness, or psychopathology of one individual.

The perspective of the family therapist is so radically different from the perspective of the individual therapist that it requires a careful definition of what the concept of change connotes in one case and in the other. The field of family therapy is concerned not merely with a new technique but with a new understanding of the causes and meaning of human behavior on a variety of levels. Although this point has been made repeatedly in the literature, it has been often stated that family therapy lacks consistent ideological cohesiveness.

Family therapy approaches are often perceived as being essentially "discontinuous" in their departure from the individual basis of psychological description and understanding. The main characteristic of "systems puristic" family therapy approaches is often criticized as impersonally manipulative, in relative disregard for any individual family member's discrete psychological needs. The fact remains, however, that no mature therapist can ignore human concern, empathy, and consideration of other persons' needs, which constitute vital elements of close relationships. In reality, relationship theory underlying family therapy should broaden rather than invalidate individual personality theory.

The psychological or individual framework should not be rejected or replaced but, if transcended, included. Each family member's individual health aspirations become components of the therapeutic contract. Psychodynamic knowledge about motivational conflicts, projection, self destructive tendencies, etc., continue to be vitally useful areas of knowledge for the relational or family therapist. However, each person's "outside reality" is not relegated to a nondynamic random sequence of impersonal facts but is seen as the dynamic interlocking of all relating partners' needs. One person's dynamic need configurations constitute part of the other's outside reality and vice versa. Furthermore, the understructure of the "external reality" of each family member includes suprapersonal regulatory dynamic forces.

Another area in which spelling out the premises of dialectic intergenerational family therapy leads to a useful distinction is the relevance of human values for behavior change. The great social ethical issue of all times is the balance between egalitarian, democratic concern for everybody's welfare as contrasted with the Nietzschean world of conquest by the powerful, rugged individualism, subjection of the weak or disadvantaged and, ultimately, genocide. The egalitarian concept of everyone's right to the pursuit of optimal physical and emotional health is founded on social justice and equitability. It is based on the premise that one person's health interests are coterminous with those of any other person. Thus, while it is in the interest of A's life goals that, for example, his coronary attacks be prevented from recurring, it is assumed that this goal does not infringe on B's aspirations for a healthfully effective life of his own. To carry it one step further, if A is B's slave (or useful resource person), it becomes B's selfish goal to keep A optimally healthful and effective.

As we make the transition from the notion of "health" to that of "desirable change," the importance of ethical value issues becomes increasingly obvious. What is desirable, for instance, from the vantage point of the exploiter is usually not desirable from the viewpoint of the exploited one. It is a common observation that, inadvertently, people can have a neurotic investment in the self-defeating "symptomatology" of their spouse or child. A mother's security may collapse at the point when her school-phobic son returns to school, and she may request psychiatric hospitalization for herself. What then is the desirable goal from the vantage points of (a) the mother's therapist, (b) the son's therapist, or (c) the family therapist respectively? Furthermore, beyond the complexities of adversary positions, is it possible to integrate them into a mutually satisfactory shared therapeutic strategy?

The widespread notion that psychic (behavioral) function and human values should be considered in separation from one another is untenable, false, and "pathogenic"—both individually and socially. The criteria of both malfunction and desirable change have inevitable value connotations. To ignore or deny these connotations would lead to further confusion and mystification of the public in an era of already existing value confusion. Our age has experienced frightening examples of large-scale political change-makers whose seductively phrased ethical premises turned out to be consistent with genocide and absolute subjugation of the justice and freedom of millions. Effective electronic mass indoctrination of children and adults into either a valueless or a destructive value orientation can produce amorphous or directional destructiveness respectively between the members of one social group or toward outsiders. The view of family therapists is inevitably affected by their observation of striking examples of both selfless devotion and callous exploitation.

I realize that a broader than behavioral concept of change is liable to exact a considerable cost on the part of the therapist. A simple behavioral concept of change appears to provide a safer basis for therapeutic contract; all your patient wants is to lose weight and you are the one to teach him or her how to achieve this goal. Such a deceptively simple model does away with all notions of human conflict, destructiveness, exploitation, selfishness, and even resistance to treatment.

By contrast, therapy defined as a thoroughgoing evaluation of the life goals of patients, aimed at helping them to reexamine their accounts and to find liberation through balanced interpersonal fairness, sounds threatening to many people—as if concern with deeper "ethical" issues implies too costly an intrusion into a patient's life.

Yet, obviously, as soon as we consider the welfare of more than one human life, we enter the field of competition, interlocking complementary and noncomplementary needs, hunger for trust and confidence, concern and loyalty, disappointment, exploitation of the other one's trust, betrayal of confidence, revenge, forgiveness, guilt over disloyalty, insensitivity to guilt of harming others, etc. If we simplistically assume that each family member struggles to influence the other in the direction of "desirable behavior," the question still arises: from whose vantage point should the therapist determine the desirability of behavior? Human life is thus inseparable from its relational ethical context. *

I strongly advise therapists to be interested in whole human lives, not just in behavioral modification. The essential goals of any therapist as behavior modifier and of the one to be modified by him or her lie, of course, beyond the technical realm of simply "how to do it." There is diversity between the goals of the two individuals and also between the various levels of aspirations within each individual. As a rather shockingly awakening example of unidimensionally therapist-defined goals of behavior change, I have seen occasions of successful "reinforcement" by therapists of the patients' independence, autonomy and self-actualization in disregard for the built-in, "abnormal" over-devotedness of the patients to their families of origin. In a number of cases, admirably successful "separation" was followed by suicide or even suicide-murder. The escalating guilt over filial disloyalty was not dealt with, and it backfired.

In essence, this chapter challenges the nondialectical concept of the individual as a self-contained goal for self-actualization. (See also Boszormenyi-Nagy and Spark, 1.) Attempts will be made to expand the realm of dynamic depth psychology into an existentially/ethically grounded theory of relationships. The relevance of such relational dynamics will be examined here as a basis for psychotherapy in general and for family therapy in particular. Finally, it will be suggested that family therapy and its relational conceptual understructure offer a far-reaching leverage for the coordinative strategy of all types of psychotherapy, for strategies of prevention, and for a relational definition of the model of "healthy" behavior. Accordingly, individual-based therapeutic strategies will have to be coordinated with the comprehensive relational understanding suggested here.

---

*The term "ethical" is not used here to designate any particular religiocultural code of behavioral prescriptions. Instead it connotes an intrinsic dynamic property of human relationship according to which each party to the relationship is inherently accountable to the other for the existential impact they mutually exert on one another.

THE DIALECTICAL ASPECTS OF RELATIONSHIP THEORY

One of the characteristics of twentieth century thought is its departure from an orientation toward fixed, thing-like entities as the discrete elements of its world view. The replacement of the assumption of absolute facts by a consideration of the process-like vicissitudes of relative determinants represents a shift toward an increasingly dialectical view of reality. Even if direct evidence of a causal link between Hegel's early 19th century dialectical philosophy and the dawn of non-Newtonian physics is questionable, Einstein's theory of relativity is logically consistent with the dialectical world view. Furthermore, the relational humanism of Martin Buber (2), introduces the dialectic view of man as being unthinkable without his being party to a dialogue with another.

On the other hand, the conceptual revolution of the 20th century has hardly reached the everyday philosophy of contemporary Western man and his social institutions. The elaborations of modern psychological theories have continued to confirm the view of the individual as a self-contained universe. Selfish disregard for the interests and needs of others has been elevated from vice to scientific object and political myth, the latter disguised as unconditional liberty. Resistance to the conceptual challenge posed by a dialectical view of understanding goes, hand-in-hand, with resistance to the recognition of the importance of a reexamination of ethical priorities.

Returning to the therapeutically significant question of what constitutes "desirable change," therapists have to consider the long-range "cost" of current function vis-à-vis their own or their patients' notions about desirable change. By recognizing that human function is deeply determined and substantially programmed by invisible interpersonal accountabilities and family loyalties (Boszormenyi-Nagy and Spark, 1), therapists have to learn to critically reevaluate the dominant myth of our Western civilization. They will find that the dynamic understructure of close relationships is at variance with the idealized images of both the absolute autonomy of the fully grown-up adult and the individual's total separation from the family of origin. They will also find it necessary to redefine the relational significance of both standard assumptions about human life aspirations: (a) heterosexual gratification as the ultimate basis of marriage and (b) simple criteria of power and success as need-satisfaction. Concurrently, the practitioners' own life-long investment in the values of their cultural myths will have to be examined as possible causes of their resistance to recognizing the structuring significance of deep-dynamic relational ledgers. Furthermore, some of the therapists' genuine conflicts in their own close relationships will have to be confronted and integrated into a balanced multilateral view of relational goals.

The relationship between individual and relational (family) therapy strategies raises the question of indications. Usually, the question is posed in the form of assuming that the family approach should define a special basis for indication. This is based on the unspoken premise that individual-based therapy is the generally applicable or baseline form of psychotherapy and, therefore, that the relationally-based approach needs a special justification. Yet, conversely, we have postulated that the broadening of understanding, humanistic concern and therapeutic contract with all persons prospectively affected by the intervention is *never* contraindicated.

In accordance with our thesis the question should be reversed, based on the premise that what is always indicated is a broad-based, combined—i.e., relationally *plus* individually grounded—understanding of dynamic processes. Thereafter, the question needs to be asked: What are the *risks* of a narrowly defined *individual-based* therapeutic strategy? More specifically, the cause should be shown why the extended understanding and increased leverage for change, implicit in the relational approach, should be ignored. It may be accurate to say that the only contraindication to a broader understanding and concern lies in the available therapist's own personal limitations for facing the existential/ethical issues involved in close human relationships.

Of course, it should be the right of all therapists to choose the limits of their own approach, and to function within their own recognized preferences and competence. This is all that can honestly be expected of them. No one should be obligated to perform professional work which will cause depression, lost sleep, or psychosomatic illness. Nor would it be fair to expose clients to techniques inadequately mastered

by a therapist. Even if surgery is the treatment of choice for appendi-
citis, it would not be fair to put the knife in the hands of a well-meaning
dilettante, self-proclaimed surgeon, regardless of how pressing the
symptoms of the patient may appear.

FROM INDIVIDUAL
TO RELATIONAL CONCEPTS OF CHANGE

Individual concepts of "desirable change" as the goal of therapy
originate from the traditional medical framework of health and illness.
Health is a one-dimensional construct; it is the ideal antithesis of illness.
Illness in a physical sense is a fault in the machinery of the body: it
interferes with effective function and longevity. All individual concepts
of physical or mental health therefore relate to effectiveness, power,
success, and enjoyment of effectiveness. Their ethical premise is that
man is committed to his own good in an isolation from the goal of
others.

Such otherwise radically different therapeutic approaches as psychoanalysis and classical behavioral therapy still converge in their individual-defined goal of the desirable change: health, effective function,
and freedom from symptoms. Although their definitions of need-configurations clearly differentiate the two theories, both are basically
confined to a need-satisfaction or pleasure-principle type of goal. Both
classical psychoanalysis and classical behavioral therapy aim their
change-inducing strategies at the success and psychological satisfaction of one individual. Both approaches confine the formation of the
therapeutic contract to one symptomatic individual and the therapist.
Changes in the patient's close relatives are considered incidental and
assumed to be automatically advantageous to those others. Both approaches would refer the treatment of coincidentally occurring symptoms in a relative to what should become separate, *de novo* treatment
contracts.

First, the notion of discrete individual personality change, allegedly
occurring outside the context of relational change, requires investigation. Since long-term relationships obviously require a mutuality of

need satisfactions, the restriction of clinical contractual interest to the need-satisfactions of one person amounts to an advocacy for the advantages of ignorance. It is as if the denial of the interlocking mutuality of human need satisfactions would result in a "clearer," more manageable task.

Yet it is obvious that as people become more effective in the pursuit of their need-satisfaction, to the same extent they become more capable of making others the objects of their needs for security, dependence, trust, stimulation, etc. Consequently, any change in the capacity of one person to use the other as a need-satisfying object naturally affects the balance of need-satisfactions the other can achieve for him- or herself. Relationally-based dynamic understanding and therapeutic strategy are therefore clearly based on the premise that man is committed to the good of his relationship system.

It is logical to assume that in order to maintain a fair balance, as one's capacity for need-satisfaction increases, one's concern for the other's needs should also grow. Unless one is capable of including such concern for the mutuality of one's relationships, one is likely to fail in all of one's long-term attachments. Thus, the systemic dynamic principle of multipersonal change coincides with the attitude of ethical openness to concern, caring, and trust as interlocking dynamic determinants of relationships. In long-term, close (e.g., parent-child) relationships, it is inconceivable that the fate of the other's needs could remain completely indifferent to the self. Emotional investment, of course, can take both positive and negative forms. Sacrificial devotion and passionate anger are both based on intensive involvement.

At this point it is important to recall that the concept of ethics underlying our further explorations is by no means synonymous with any particular system of moral regulation. On the contrary, the broad humanistic base of a genuinely relational ethic will inevitably challenge and test the priority schemes of particular traditional moral codes. In my view, dogmatic concepts of good or bad will have to be replaced by the dialectical notion of the consideration of both sides of any relationship. The relational solution is a classical Hegelian one: out of a simultaneous synthetic consideration of the two antithetical sides of any relationship, the conflict between reciprocal need gratification efforts has to be transcended and resolved into an equilibrium of fairness, tolerance, concern, trust, and reliability — mutually needed for the survival of the relationship.

The implications of the dynamic significance of such an ethical point of view are hard to overestimate; yet its adoption as therapeutic rationale exacts considerable emotional cost from most therapists. It requires that the therapist set the traditional Western efficiency, power, and reward orientations to values at a critical distance. Moreover, it is only human to resist the adoption of the ethical balance point of view, since its acceptance calls for increased accountability, a seeming cost-increase in relationships. Furthermore, the criticism has often been raised whether an ethical point of view will rigidly impose the therapist's own moral code upon the family. Of course, nothing is further from the truth. On the contrary. On closer examination, the customary, "value-free" professional orientation can turn out to be rigidly value-based.

The allegedly value-neutral therapist can be deeply committed to the desirability of "separation" from previous, especially seemingly unsatisfactory, relationships. Often, in supporting the ideal of separation, the professional can lose sight of the personal interests of all parties involved. Predictably, the majority of contemporary therapists would almost automatically endorse what they perceive as adversary interests of a young family member against the "possessive" influence of the parent, for example, by unconditionally supporting the notion of "separation" of young adults. By contrast, dialectical relational therapists will tend to reduce the seeming adversary positions of close relatives into a mutuality of genuine interests. They have learned that both parent and child would pay with significant lasting guilt for an ultimate "victory" of one over the other. Furthermore, by a simultaneous consideration of the mutuality of fairness from both sides, therapists become liberated from their own rigidly biased side-taking position and are ultimately rewarded by an increased satisfaction in their professional work.

Even if some of these basic resistances can be overcome, a considerable complexity of levels has to be understood before the dialectical ethical principle can be translated into pragmatic, strategic thinking.

On this level of sophistication, the simple notions of reward and pain as motivators could hardly explain the complexity of close, existentially interlocking relationships. For example, the seeming beneficiary of unilateral generosity becomes, on a deeper level, through accruing indebtedness to the partner a helpless captive of a sense of irrepayable obligation, indebtedness, and worthless selfishness. The self-denying giver becomes the ultimate taker in every long-term, close relationship.

A 27-year-old man was diagnosed as having an incurable illness. He was faced with the prospect of losing both his life and the young woman he was planning to marry within a year. However, his fiancee did not desert him. Despite all advice from her family, the young woman persisted in the relationship and went through the wedding as planned. Moreover, she did so in the face of warnings from several of her husband's physicians that not only was his prognosis for life very guarded but in case of survival he would lose his male fertility.

As it turned out, the young man survived the operation and did indeed become infertile. From the vantage point of his own needs, first and foremost, he had to face the threat to his own life and the continued fears of recurrence of his illness for years after the operation. Needless to say, his wife's uncommon integrity and devotion helped him in his struggles with anxiety. Thus, from his point of view the marriage was a highly need-satisfying relationship; he became the beneficiary of his wife's noble integrity. Considered from the wife's vantage point, the relationship could be regarded as sacrifical, unilaterally unsatisfying, or even self-defeating. Although her husband could not be blamed for his illness, for the subsequent atmosphere of anxiety, or for his ultimate infertility, all three circumstances tended to deprive his wife. Yet the young woman disclaimed credit for any unusual act of integrity and stated that she had simply acted on her great love for her fiance.

Therapeutic exploration some twenty years later revealed that the husband did not feel that he was obligated to his wife. The prevalent explanation in his mind was that, in the main, he had been preoccupied with the threat to his life which he had gradually overcome through the years. Thus he saw himself unfairly victimized by fate rather than as the cause of his wife's unhappiness. He was not aware of his wife's being frustrated because she could not bear her own child. His wife had kept reassuring him by asserting that she had never wanted a natural child and that she was perfectly satisfied with having a child through adoption.

Upon further investigation, it turned out that the wife's attitudes to all of her relationships and to the world as a whole were based on sacrifical devotion and self-denial. The question could then be raised: Is her unselfishness itself a form of selfishness? Was her choice of mate essentially a need-gratifying one? Does the beneficiary of her unconditional devotion have to become the carrier of a sense of accountability, guilt, intrinsic selfishness, even inferiority? Furthermore, is it possible that the husband pays part of the accumulating cost of the wife's martyr-like, over-devoted attitude vis-à-vis all of her relationships?

A technical illustration of the relational dialectical point of view results in the practice of inducing children to reveal the secrets of their families. While the measure can lead to a desirable change on a communication-transactional level, it may turn out to be costly for the child in terms of betraying filial loyalty. As a matter of fact, the more the therapist tries to side with the child against the parents and the more he or she counts on the child's cooperative contribution to the therapeutic strategy, the more likely is the child to be entrapped in filial disloyalty.

The foregoing has direct practical implications for the individual approach to psychotherapy. The traditional individual contract for psychotherapy follows from the medical model of illness and health; it disregards the unplanned consequences of the intervention for persons whose lives are closely interlocked with that of the "patient." This is consistent with the traditional medical notion of the therapeutic contract being between the doctor and the patient for the benefit of the patient. Procedures that emphasize the individual-based privacy, confidentiality, and legal accountability of such contract all tend to imply its exclusiveness and possibly its adversary character vis-à-vis the claims and interests of all other persons.

Only occasionally has the literature on traditional individual based therapeutic procedures considered the importance of the potential conflicts between professional and familial *loyalties*. When considered, it usually surfaces in the form of strategies designed for the obstructionistic or otherwise resistant attitudes of the relatives whose behavior could otherwise hamper the treatment goals. In the relational or family therapy context, patient-relative and patient-therapist loyalty conflicts have to emerge as dynamic leverages of the greatest practical significance (Boszormenyi-Nagy, 3).

Recent insights into the nature of the dynamics of close and especially intergenerational (parent-child), relationships have emphasized mutual accountability and invisible loyalties as crucial motivational determinants (Boszormenyi-Nagy and Spark, 1). Detailed demonstration of the relevance of such invisible interpersonal mechanisms to behavioral change will have to become the object of further careful study. It can be envisaged that the demonstration of such hidden relational mechanisms will meet difficulties similar to those encountered in past efforts aimed at the documentation and proof of the existence of unconscious "Freudian" mechanisms as determinants of visible human behavior. The ubiquitous psychic defensive tendencies of avoidance, denial, reversal into the opposite, etc., on the part of each participant individual will make the demonstration of such invisible relational determinants even more difficult. As in the case of searching for "scientific" evidence for unconscious psychological determinants, it is impossible to prove the connection between invisible relational "ledgers" of accountability and overt behavior except through the therapeutic effectiveness of strategies based on the knowledge of such underlying dynamic motivational forces.

There is no space to develop here the full theory of deep relational structures as manifested through the "merit ledger" and "intergenerational legacy." However, it is of the utmost importance to stress that the essence of these mechanisms is *not psychological*. Loyalty to personal and familial legacies is not merely a question of each family member's superego psychology. The existential structure of the legacy is a primary given which preceded the psychological adaptation of the offspring and, in fact, of subsequent, not-yet-born generations. The circumstances, for instance, in which the mother's relatives were wiped out in concentration camps, or in which three or four preceding siblings died of physical illnesses, or in which a mentally retarded sibling was born have their existential structure independently of anybody's psychological processes. Conversely, such existential structural determinants affect each individual family member's psychic organization as specific, structured outside realities, i.e., external expectations. The varying ways in which all family members share responsibility vis-à-vis the fulfillment of their legacies create the vicissitudes which make such reality a dynamic determinative force.

A more detailed knowledge of the depth structure of family relationships would picture each family member as partner to an oscillating balance sheet of inputs and withdrawals. The nature of the balances is a three-dimensional one. For example, at the same time that the "delinquent" adolescent withdraws from the family's shared accounts, he or she can be repaying heavily on another level as being the last one to leave the home. Sacrifice of one's own success and psychosomatic health may amount to alternating "currencies" by which invisible "pathological" repayment can be made.

THE RELATIONAL OUTLOOK AND PREMISES FOR CHANGE "TECHNIQUES"

The relational outlook to therapy and change has to take two major considerations into account. First, the contract between the therapist and the patient or the family has to be broadened to a point of view of "multidirectional partiality" and empathy. Second, the therapeutic task, i.e., the realm of phenomena to be changed, has to be broadened to include a fuller understanding of the deep existential grounding of close relationships.

As mentioned earlier in this chapter, the individual definition of psychotherapeutic contract is predicated on the therapist's offering to the patient both expert technical performance and a deep alliance, both to the exclusion of the interests of the members of the patient's family. As described elsewhere in detail (Boszormenyi-Nagy and Spark, 1), the overcoming of such benevolent professional bias and partiality is the most decisive step in becoming a family therapist. The term "multi-directional partiality" was coined to capture the essence of this therapeutic stance.

In addition to overcoming the natural limitations of the basic individual definition of the therapeutic contract, most psychotherapists have to learn to transcend their intrinsic bias for siding with the child against the parents. In choosing their profession, most psychotherapists are influenced by their emotional commitment to the cause of the suffering, "emotionally disturbed" individual. At the core of their empathy with the suffering child-self of any prospective client lies the memory of the therapists' own suffering. In their marginally conscious desire to share the "techniques" of mastery of their own childhood suffering, most psychotherapists implicitly scapegoat the patient's family of origin. In assigning the role of causation of detrimental developmental influences to the patient's parents, and in nobly fighting the cause of the patient's liberation, therapists may easily overlook their own hidden psychic benefit, derived from the intrinsic exoneration of their own parents at the expense of the patient's family of origin. An act of invisible loyalty to one's ambivalently protected parents is a frequently overlooked major dynamic cause of deep existential conflict in therapists themselves, too.

In order to comprehend all major relevant dimensions of both change and resistance to change, therapists have to transcend not only the behavioral but also the psychological limitations of their conceptual armamentarium. In considering behavior change, it is essential to define the premises of that which does change or fails to change. While overfocusing on the need for visible behavioral change, therapists may lose sight of the reasons for malfunction.

Behavior changes deemed desirable from the change-agent's viewpoint can be induced by threats, rewards, suggestions, and hypnosis. Such change may attest to the power and the skill of the professional, without necessarily reflecting the patient's motivational aims. In order for the behavioral change to become a part of the spontaneous self of the patient, it has to become syntonic with, or at least neutral to, the spontaneous motivational tendencies of the patient. If behavior change and basic motivations are in conflict, the change will eventually be

rejected like an incompatible surgical transplant. Experienced intergenerational therapists have learned to balance the conflicting motivational aspects, each on its respective dynamic level, so that their therapeutic impact will have spontaneous endorsement on the part of all
or most family members, and a chance to endure.

A couple in their mid-twenties came to the office for help with
their marital problems. Although he has better than average intelligence, the husband holds a rather undemanding job. Drug addiction of several years' duration has made his job security even
more tenuous. At home he spends most of the time sleeping, and
sexual contact between the spouses has dwindled to near nothing.
The husband freely admits that he is not doing his share of household chores. Both spouses recognize that although they would like
to have children, they are far from capable of planning a family.

The husband is the only son of possessively anxious parents,
who have the habit of dropping in on the young couple, unan-
nounced, many times during the week. He has been unable to say
"no" to his parents' intrusive initiatives. His parents also insist
on paying many of his expenses while they completely refuse to
accept anything he or his wife offers to them in return. In the
continuous argument between the spouses, each seems to be
defending his or her own family of origin. It seems that the
husband has been tied closely to his parents by a never-repayable,
shapeless, total obligation. In an attempt to avoid facing both his
failure of adult assertion and his guilt over escalating indebtedness
to his "devoted and helpful" parents, the husband has inflicted
an unfair burden of unilateral adult responsibility upon his wife.
His own irresponsibility and absenteeism as a husband are the
chief means whereby he "parentifies" her.

For several months the couple attended a couples' group program. The emphasis there was on giving tasks, utilization of paradoxical injunctions and improvement of communications. Yet,
in the long run, nothing changed as a result of this effort. In my
view, lack of significant change in such cases is often associated
with lack of therapeutic consideration of the relevant relational
understructures. The ethical-existential roots of this couple's marital problems have been deeply anchored in the nuclear family

context of the husband, coupled with the collusive pattern of marital transactions contributed by a wife who has undeniable martyr-like inclinations. Simple inducement of a "more mature" behavior on the part of the spouses could lead into further imbalance, intensifying the husband's sense of guilt over filial disloyalty in the face of his "pathological" overloyal relationship with his parents. The question for the therapist then is not to choose whether to work behaviorally or in terms of a deep relational strategy, but in what way a therapeutic strategy can be designed to liberate this young couple from both the symptoms of marital failure and the destructive legacy of overcommitment to their respective families of origin.

In order to design their therapeutic strategies, dialectical relational therapists need a comprehensive evaluation of the balance of the relational determinants exemplified in the foregoing clinical vignette. This would include the dimensions of the husband's individual psychopathology marital evaluation, evaluation of the husband's relationship to his family of origin, assessment of spouse-team collaboration regarding relationships with both families of origin, the evaluation of the intergenerational legacies of obligation in each family of origin, and the assessment of the prospective parenting team relationship of the spouse if children are ever to be born to this nuclear family. In order to indicate the interlocking complexities of relational dimensions to be considered, Figure 10-1 is presented.

The peaks A, B, and C represent three closely related individuals, for example, grandparent, parent, and child. By analogy they can be considered to represent three icebergs, each showing one-tenth of its mass above the symbolical water level, represented by the line between Zones I and II. If the navigator's vision could be extended to cover all of Zone II, he still could not tell whether he is dealing with three separate icebergs or three peaks of a single huge iceblock. Conversely, the observer who could only have information about Zone III, could not tell whether the peak consists of 1, 2, 3, or more separate entities. He would be dealing with one apparently continuous ice-slab.

The figure symbolizes the three essential levels of relational dynamics and therapy:

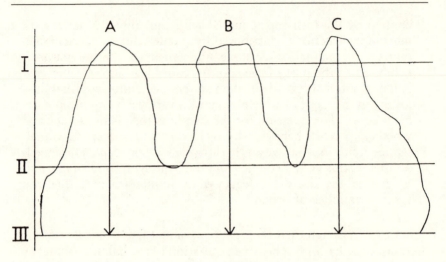

Figure 10-1.

Zone I is the realm of visible behavior and overt inter-individual interaction. Most pertinent functions are conscious in the interacting individuals, through not necessarily so. This is the realm in which the outside observer can notice both malfunction and its change to improved function. Easily recallable or observable shared knowledge or customs are also located in this realm. Customs and habits characteristic of a certain religious or ethnic background, if manifestly practiced, are also located in Zone 1.

Zone II comprises the covert, although not necessarily unconscious, part of inter-individual interactions or transactions between closely related persons. A shared secret may be conscious for the participants but not visible to the outsider. The vertical arrows within each peak designate the dimension of intrapersonal surface versus depth. This is a psychological dimension: inside the individual there is a realm of consciousness and, on the opposite, a realm of continually decreasing consciousness to the point where dynamic psychological exchanges are distinctly unconscious. However, Zone II contains not only individual psychological characteristics and attitudes but systemic properties of person-to-person relationships. Genuine dialogue between two individuals can build up trust in each and a relational atmosphere of trustworthiness and balance of justice between the two of them. The existence of concern connects the needs of both: it is in my interests to consider your needs, if I want to stay in close relationship with you. The resulting systemic ledger of give-and-take determines the fluctuating balance of inter-individual obligations, and is distinctly different from the psychological responses of each individual to the state of their relationship. Guilt may or may not be registered in each individual, though not necessarily in proportion to the extent of the factual imbalance in the pattern of give-and-take between them.

Essentially, *Zone III* is the realm of the deep understructure of close relationships. Whereas each individual represented by a peak is positioned at a certain location relative to the understructure, none of them determines the relationship of the other two individuals to the common understructure, which is determined, so to speak, by fate or by the special destiny of their birth. The importance of Zone III is relatively negligible in casual peer relationships but crucial in existentially interlocking—e.g., intergenerational—relationships.

DIMENSIONS OF THE DYNAMIC UNDERSTRUCTURE OF RELATIONSHIPS

It is important to indicate five major dynamic dimensions, though space does not permit a full elaboration of a theory of deep relational understructures.

(A) Legacy

This dimension could be called the transgenerational call for existential obligations. The basic existential/ethical obligations derive from the generative, enabling significance of parent-child relationships. For example, regardless of whether the parent enjoyed or regretted becoming a parent, the child's existence is irrevocably owed to the parent. Particular burdens that the parent had to carry—exceptional fears of childbirth, damage to the mother's body, for example—contribute to additional primary ethical claims of the parent on the child. Both family ancestry and religio-ethnic background can assume the appearance of creditors toward new members who are the recipients of life and of patterns of survival. However, the ethical demand characteristic of the legacy has to be clearly differentiated from the transmission of patterns through transgenerational learning. The outcome of (B) and (D) feeds into the legacy of the next generations.

(B) Existential Vicissitudes

Not every family has to survive under excessive degrees of extenuating circumstances. Yet, in certain families most members were wiped out by the holocaust. In other families several consecutive generations lost their mothers at an early age. Early death of several siblings or the birth of a brain-damaged sibling can constitute rapid escalation of overweighted legacies which calls for an existential rebalancing of the unfair destiny of the family and its members.

(C) The Ledger

The mutually quantitative, balance-like nature of the fluctuations of give-and-take in human relationships can best be described in terms analogous to those of financial transactions. Not only are there ledgers to be balanced between members regarding fair equitability of give-and-take, but each member can be perceived as a potential debtor vis-à-vis the legacy of the family. The measure of mutual indebtedness is not given by the criteria of an outside, "objective" justice, but has meaning only between persons in relationship. Nonetheless its reality exists, and can be uncovered only through a multilateral consideration of merits from all the vantage points of all participants. Most of the time the fluctuation of positive or negative balances on the ledger is not conscious in the minds of family members. The ledger becomes significant at points at which stagnant, fixed imbalance develops, usually reinforced by denial and avoidance. An especially damaging imbalance can be created in children by the parents' non-receiving attitudes, which can make the child's obligation toward the parents unrepayable, amorphously global and all-encompassing.

(D) Acts of Collusive Commitment

Concerted actions on the part of all family members, both in response to expectations of the legacy and in fair consideration of each other's interests, contribute to the survival and further elaboration of the deep understructure of relationships. An illustration of such action is the collusive postponement of mourning (Boszormenyi-Nagy, 4). In this act every participant is a contributor to the collusive act and also a seeming beneficiary of the shared intention to spare everybody from pain. Such acts naturally contribute to the "invisible establishment" (see under E) of a stagnant, inadequately balanced "overencumbered" relationship system. Consequently, all family members become obligated to share the detriment arising out of the resultant pathogenic, stagnant imbalance of relationships.

(E) Invisible Establishment

The invisible establishment is based on a quasi-political set of rules of operation, which are the resulting reified products of the total build-up of the loyalty expectations of a family. Its nature is inert, static, and possibly stagnant. The invisible establishment has no primary ethical claim; its dynamic characteristic is activated whenever it opposes attempts at free individuation or acts of disloyalty to the family. It places the individual in a passive recipient or accepting role unless the individual member appears to be disloyally assertive. The invisible establishment prescribes specific rules of operation; for example, in the case of collusive postponement of mourning, it may expect certain specific behaviors and prohibit others. Members may consistently avoid certain important subjects of discussion, aiding each other also in the perpetration of a conspiracy against clarity, meaning, and individuation. In my view, Stierlin's (5) important concept of parent-induced "delegation" represents dynamic processes belonging mainly to this category.

The foregoing brief description of depth relational structures only indicates the complexities of invisible dynamic configurations which constitute the context of psychopathology and therapeutic strategy. It shows also the important limitations of the conceptual frameworks of both individual (psychological) dynamic theory and transactional-interactional systemic formulations. If we are to arrive at a broad-based theory of therapy and behavioral change, both thought models have to be considered and integrated.

That a specific relational mechanism of existential vicissitudes of destiny of family events is able to program long-range determinants of behavioral patterns was outlined in a recent exploration of the family background of Hitler (Boszormenyi-Nagy, 6).

THE RELATIONAL DEFINITIONS
OF CHANGE-INDUCEMENT STRATEGIES

The criteria of therapeutic change are usually considered from the vantage points of either subjective psychological experience or observable individual behavior. Although both of these dimensions of change are important for family therapists, they learn in the course of their work that the most significant leverages both for behavioral change and for resistance to behavioral change lie in the dynamics of close relationships. Consequently, our definition of change also has to be a relational one, its smallest unit being balance between at least two people, rather than the psychology of any given individual.

The majority of contemporary psychotherapists probably would tend to overlook the dialectical implications of the risk of encouraging filial disloyalty while endorsing a young adult person's "individuation" or "separation." Even if such therapists are able to avoid the pitfall of "countertransference acting out" based on their own unrecognized conflicts about filial loyalty, many a young adult's "pathological" over-devotion needs a sophisticated relational approach for behavioral changes to prevail. Traditional uncovering individual therapy usually reveals that patients are ambivalently tied to their (introjected) parents through hidden and disowned ambivalent attitudes. Subsequently, it is a common therapeutic expectation that patients own up to their ambivalent feelings, try to understand the roots of these feelings, accept them, and become adjusted to at least a partial separation from the family of origin. As a result of such "insight" into and "working through" needed separation, it is hoped that the patients' overt behavior will obtain the best chance for a lasting change. From our vantage point, however, even while visible progress is being made toward functional autonomy, it should be examined to see if it is confined to the patients' acceptance of their negative filial attitudes as the end-point of therapeutic relational goals. If so, the patients are likely to end up with an increase of conscious or unconscious guilt over disloyalty, even though they may learn that their loyalty is excessive and pathologically reinforced. Guilt over existential disloyalty is capable of undermining patients' behavioral gains and, in the long run, it can lead to self-destructive "backlash" motivations.

Transactionally based, "puristic" family therapy approaches can also suffer from a lack of dialectical relational sophistication. Transactionally oriented family therapists frequently emphasize the "here-and-now" significance of what appears to be an inter-member competition for *power*. They suggest that the more clinically experienced therapists are, the more accurately they can perceive and describe the manipulative communicational-behavioral binds. Subsequently, therapists are advised to design "paradoxical" or other behavioral techniques for unscrambling the power arrangement and, hopefully, for liberating the victimized family members from the tight holds of such power schemes. It is apparent that the traditional individual approach and the transactional, power-oriented "systemic" family approach have much in common, in that they both disregard the loyalty-based invisible under-structures of relationships.

The dialectical relational outlook provides an extension of the understanding of the change-inducing implications of one of Freud's great discoveries: the phenomenon of *transference*. Traditional psychoanalytic theory appropriately assumes that a primary, quasi-familial investment of the person of the therapist on the part of the patient is a requirement for thoroughgoing therapeutic change. Much of psychoanalytic literature unnecessarily confines the therapeutic significance of this important relational event to the therapist-patient relationship. As a matter of fact, in their clinical practice, many experienced analysts, especially child therapists, give practical recognition to the fact that the intensification of the therapist-patient relationship occurs in a live dynamic equilibrium with the patient's commitments to other close relationships.

Of particular practical significance are the loyalty implications of the transference phenomenon for change, regardless of whether they are considered in individual or in family therapy (Boszormenyi-Nagy, 3). In short, it can be assumed that the symptom or pathological behavior can be partially determined by the patient's loyalty to the family of origin. Naturally, the more destructive and self-destructive the symptom is, the more paradoxical this reasoning seems to be. Paradoxically, also, at the point when therapeutic success leads to the motivational reorientation of patients, reinforced by the transference wish to please the substitute parent-like figure through progress towards health, autonomy, and growth, they also become intrinsically disloyal to the "pathogenic" expectations of their own families. The more positive the transference, the greater the risk of filial disloyalty. This consideration has far-reaching strategic implications (Boszormenyi-Nagy and Spark, 1). It necessitates techniques which restructure the therapeutic goals and avenues in such a manner that patients will not have to incur significant disloyalty as the price of change toward a healthier function.

Naturally, family therapists have to deal with the collective convergence of parallel dynamic configurations anchored in all members of the families they are treating. Given the specifics of a certain familial legacy, they may expect a certain amount of "pathological" behavior. In addition, in order to minimize inter-member controversy and suffering, family members owe each other loyalty of collusive mutual commitment. Family therapists have to acquire sensitivity to the intergenerational and inter-member ledgers of merits and obligations. Through life experience of their own and through their professional experience they have to learn the principal ways in which family members can actively rebalance merit ledgers so that they are not left with the helpless feelings of pessimism, despair, and inactivity. Conversely, they have to learn about patterns which reinforce captive indebtedness and lock members into irreversible exploitation. Naturally, the cost of imbalance is both existential and psychological, and the two factors have to be considered in separation. For example, if it is discovered that a wife has a hereditary illness, possibly a malignant one, it becomes a complex question to determine whether she is more the victim or more the one who, though unintentionally, inflicts both damage and pain on her husband and children. The existential balance of such situations does not result from the feelings, thoughts, wishes, and other psychological characteristics of these individuals. On the contrary, their feeling reactions and thoughts are secondary to the basic existential/ethical configuration. Aware only of having been unfairly victimized by destiny, the hereditarily ill wife may overlook the fact that, nonetheless, she has become indebted to her husband for staying by her, never bringing up the subject, handling all the exigencies, and remaining sexually loyal to her.

If therapists who want to induce "desirable behavioral change" lack a sensitivity to the underlying deep issues, they will at best manage to patch up the condition temporarily while remaining ignorant of deep-rooted ethical issues. For instance, a therapist might want to have the essential creditor make further concessions to the seeming creditor. The foregoing example illustrates the relevance of deep existential structures to the question of enduring change, and the limitation of simple interactional or transactional definitions of change often used even by sensitive and complexly humane therapists: " . . . families must change their ways of functioning so they will not nurture harmful modes of interaction and perpetuate ineffective or damaging models of behavior from one generation to the next" (Satir, Stachowiak, and Taschman, 7, p. 11).

An even more important practical consideration follows from the recognition of the connection between the notions of existential/ethical ledger and behavior change. Doubtlessly, valuable effort has been spent on developing simple behavioral reinforcement-based models of the management of close relationships. Readers of these contributions can benefit from the wisdom of behavioral "techniques" which can lead to smoother function and mutual inducement of more gratifying behavior. However, insofar as such behavioral models of intervention are limited to the individual-anchored notions of need gratification and power, such techniques may encourage the active avoidance of the ethical/existential meaning of relational action. Moreover, while learning techniques for the smooth inducement of "desirable behavior" on the part of, for example, the child may aid the latter's useful socialization, it may also lead to symbiotic, lifelong enslavement of the child. The subsequent short-term rewards and penalties do not account for the total "cost" of any change of behavior. The following "Skinnerian" citation should illustrate the foregoing point: "Much seemingly complex human behavior can be understood in terms of a person's efforts to maximize rewards and to minimize pain" (Patterson, 8, p. 9). If the parent's "emotional cost of living" is reduced at the expense of a consecutive long-range cost increase for the child, the apparent behavioral improvement formula is more antitherapeutic than therapeutic.

According to classical psychoanalytic theory, therapeutic effort should ultimately be aimed at changing the patient's pattern of defenses. Once that is accomplished, the actual change of manifest behavior requires minimal or no therapeutic guidance. Parallel reasoning could be applied to the relational theory of therapeutic "mechanisms." Accordingly, the attitude of responsibly facing the ledger is the step most intensively defended against by family members. Progress toward a decreasingly resistant facing of the ethical/existential implications of a relationship amounts to facing the costs of responsibility, accountability, and guilt over unfair exploitativeness of relationships. Once the family members can afford to confront the balance of their accountabilities, their inner satisfaction over the evolving, more genuine, relatedness will be the "rewarding" determinant of their visible behavioral change.

What Buber defined as the genuine "I-Thou dialogue" (Friedman, 9) is implicit in the systemic notion of the ledger of merits and of balances of give-and-take. A simple additive summation of all family members' needs would not ever lead to the dialectical concept of the ethical/existential ledger. It could only lead to power competition and coalition models of understanding. Only through the dialectic of the genuine mutuality of needs, of A's concern about B's needs, can we arrive at the concept of the ethical existential ledger, according to which no concerned relative can gain by the "success" of exploitative mastery over the other members of the family.

It is essential for the family therapist to develop a multilateral or multidirectional view of partiality in order to overcome a common bias shared by all traditional individual psychotherapies, i.e., finding the thing or person that is "wrong." The culprits assumed to have such pathogenic influences are numerous. *Developmental* theories stress the detrimental characteristics that can lead to faulty development: critical periods for imprinting, early deprivation, parental inadequacies, lack of object constancy, among others. Another group of pathogenic circumstances may be defined as *medical* limitations: brain damage, hereditary conditions, defective intelligence, and metabolic diseases. A third category of detrimental causative circumstances is designated as the realm of *intrapsychic*, usually unconscious, conflict. The proper correction of this condition usually is conceived in terms of long-term classical individual therapy or psychoanalysis aided by transference toward the therapist, with the resulting insight and gradual rearrangement of behavior. A fourth category of "wrongs" is ascribed to the notion of *faulty learning*. Accordingly, in the course of their early or current life experience, patients have acquired nonadaptational, nonrewarding, and noneffective ways of coping with life situations. The habit of having learned wrong patterns is supposed to prevent the individual from a self-correction of the error, as it were, and from adopting new ways of coping. Systematic attempts at reconditioning would be the procedure of choice according to this therapeutic orientation.

In contrast with goals aimed at changing pathology in individual family members, the basic strategies of relational therapy are aimed at the utilization of available relational *resources*. *Personal availability* of the other person is naturally the baseline of relational resources. The early loss of one's parents or spouse amounts to a drastic loss of primary resources. The so-called "empty nest" syndrome refers to the difficulty of parents at the time when their children have left the home. On the other hand, death and permanent separation of any kind usually bring out the hidden resources which have resided in the otherwise ambivalently accepted relationship with the lost one. The relatively fortunate configuration of the familial *legacy* constitutes a resource in comparison with the detrimental legacy of another family. The availability of the degree of *reason* and *rationality* in certain families is a great resource aiding the development of the personalities of the children, in contrast with families in which impulsive, chaotic, bizarrely motivated interaction is the rule. The extent of *accountability* prevailing in a given family determines the degree of one of the most important relational resources available. In certain families, members know that, despite a seeming distance, they can count on one another in case of a genuine need. In other families, accountability pertains to fairness in the handling of business matters, to the exclusion of concern for the personal emotional needs of other members. One of the most significant relational resources, of course, is the availability of basic trust, i.e., an *atmosphere of trustworthiness*. As family members get used to seeing one another as trustworthy, children acquire the building material for the fundamental stage of personality development: basic trust (Erickson, 10). The degree of *courage* for initiative, honesty, commitment to relationships and to action characterizes certain families and constitutes a major relational resource for the offspring.

The concept of *relational stagnation* (Boszormenyi-Nagy and Spark, 1, Chapter 5) leads to the consideration of forms of negative resources in relationship systems. Relational stagnation connotes much more than fixed repetitive patterns of behavior. Its essence lies in a fixed imbalance in the ethical/existential ledger of relationships, connected with an enduring avoidance of facing the imbalance. For a variety of reasons, the natural self-correcting relational processes of families do not seem to work either intergenerationally or between members of the same generation.

Space does not permit the description of the main manifestations of relational stagnation. Basic unrelatedness, symbiotic clinging, undifferentiated ego mass (Bowen, 11), negative loyalty (Boszormenyi-Nagy and Spark, 1) are some of its more frequently found forms.

GUIDELINES FOR INTERVENTION

A brief summarization of the principles of the therapeutic rationale of dialectical intergenerational family therapy and its application to relationally-based individual therapy helps to clarify the question of family-based behavioral change. A more complete outline of the rationale of this therapeutic approach is found in *Invisible Loyalties* (Boszormenyi-Nagy and Spark, 1). Since the essence of the approach is anchored in the depth dynamic of relationships, its practice requires more than "technical competence." The persistently active, guiding attitude of this type of therapy cannot be sustained without the therapist having a deep-going conviction about the validity of the fundamental premises of the approach. A capacity for facing and dealing with the ethical aspects of human relationships can only be acquired at the cost of the therapist's willingness to apply the same premises to the exploration of his or her own relationships. Such personally worked-through conviction is a requirement for the successful application of dialectical relational therapy. As Wynne (12) has pointed out, the personal competence of the therapist is a major part of the indicational criteria for the undertaking of family therapy.

Implicitly, the therapist's insistence on relationally based or family therapy by itself constitutes an extension of concern for the multi-laterality of the family members' need-configurations. The offering of such simultaneous concern for the conflicting needs and interests of all family members is founded on the therapist's capacity for a corresponding humanistic ethical stance rather than on particular indicational criteria of a given family. This is an extremely significant, often overlooked point. The therapist's offer of simultaneous concern for the balance of fairness in relationships is thus *a priori* and not dependent on diagnostic criteria, the family's awareness of shared problems, or the particularities of feelings and hidden motivations in family members. The essential definition of family or relational therapy lies, therefore, in the therapist's capacity for transcending the ethical limitations of the traditional individual psychotherapeutic contract.

The foregoing basic rule of relational therapy is anchored in the principle of *conjunction*. Accordingly, regardless of the outside criteria of interactional behavior, the therapist should assume that close relationships are the greatest potential resource for trust, security, and personal fulfillment. In fact, the more a relationship is presented in negative terms, or even its very existence denied, the more likely it is that the basic assets of close relationships are not being utilized. According to such relational dialectic principle, the overtly or ambivalently angry son's attitudes toward his family of origin should be explored not only from the point of view of the psychological roots of his anger, but also from the perspective of his underlying concern for his family. Like the passionately angry rejected lover, the frustrated family member has an underlying core of concern, wish for love, and desire for giving. By the same principle, the therapist should point out to the childishly fighting, divorcing parents that their children are the major parties affected by their decision. The principle of conjunction implies that the therapist should have no fear of alienating the parents by directing attention to their children. In other words, the assumption that the fundamental interests of parents could be genuinely adversary to those of their children is always false. The widespread professional notion that adolescents or young adults have to be helped to "separate" and "cut" their relationships with their families of origin as the price of their capacity for peer involvements, for the establishment of their proper social life, and for their eventual new nuclear family is unfounded but consistent with the cultural ideology of the last two centuries of Western civilization, according to which individuals should be helped to untangle themselves from all power schemes of manipulatively controlling authorities—kings, bishops, lords, fathers, teachers, presidents, and policemen are automatically suspect. This political attitude is then associated with the valid discovery of behavioral science that children are usually most critically victimized by their own families of origin. It is to be expected that by allying themselves with their patients, therapists tend to form an implicit alliance against the patients' families of origin.

It is easy, for instance, to see patients as the deprived, inhibited, wounded children of their families of origin, who need someone to parent them so that they can grow up into more wholesome human beings. Taking the option of such unidirectional professional partiality would be automatically adversary to the alternative option: siding with the patients' parents as potentially deprived and injured children in their own families of origin. The advantage of the intergenerational approach is that it encourages the therapists to put themselves in the role of their patients' children and, by the same logic, to look critically at their patients, from the vantage point of the patients' parents. Through such a dialectically balanced multi-intergenerational position of siding with the parent and child side of each relationship, the adversary point of view dissolves into a new synthesis. The application of the conjunctive principle helps to discover the leverages of hidden resources contained in intergenerational relationships and provides the maximum psychotherapeutic leverage available.

Although the leverage of intergenerational dynamics leads to the most advantageous elicitation of information ("history") about the family, the main therapeutic goal is not knowledge or insight but a responsible, active attitude of facing the ledger of merits and obligations. Therapists have to train themselves to make the transition from a primarily psychological orientation to one of recognizing ethical balances. This is made difficult by the family members' tendency toward denying the ethical/existential ledger and by the weightiness of the implications of the ethical ledger, when confronted.

An attractive young woman underwent severe strain and a transitory guilt-laden depression following the death of her father, who was suffering from cancer. An uncommonly painful scene took place at the father's burial at which time the family, including the mother, openly blamed this daughter for ingratitude and disloyalty. The accusation was based on the fact that the young woman did not remain with her dying father during his last five weeks of terminal illness, while he was hospitalized. However, further exploration revealed that the only family member who had given thorough nursing care to the ailing father was this daughter. She performed the duty as if it were both for herself and for her mother, who could not stand the stress of these months. Only at the point when she felt physically and emotionally depleted did she arrange for her father's hospitalization and her own return to the city where her fiancé was living. The young woman refrained from becoming a counter-accuser of her mother by not using her good ground as a bludgeon, and was thus able to utilize this leverage for a constructive reexamination of the life-long distance which existed in her relationship with her mother.

Relationally enlightened therapists need a combination of courage, commitment to fairness, skill, and compassion as they approach the dramatic situations in which, for example, a mother's hidden complicity in a father-daughter incest has to be examined. Similarly, standing up for the right of an adopted child to learn about and meet with his or her natural parent requires significant courage and conviction on the part of therapists. The underlying deep ethical balances on the interpersonal ledger constitute the premises and regulate the prospects of lasting individual or transactional behavioral change. Being able to therapeutically utilize this deep dimension of relationships, rather than merely follow the "technical" rule of "seeing family members together," is the real criterion of family-based therapy. Naturally, there are special conditions for which it is almost mandatory to actually deal with more than one family member—for example, if one member has suicidal inclinations.

In their concern about liberating all family members from the relational ties of "captivity," therapists are faced with several types of binds. They have to design their strategies in the knowledge of the nature of the familial legacy, the expectations of the invisible establishment of the family, the true state of the merit ledger between the members, and the characteristics of each member's internalized ledger (superego). This can only be accomplished if the therapists are able to assume the attitude of multidirectional partiality. Much harm has been done in the past by therapeutic attitudes that lead to labeling mothers or grandmothers as detrimental influences only in need of exclusion. The multidirectionally partial therapist has to be sensitive to the alternate aspect of any family member's being either on the overdrawn or the overpaid side of the merit account of relationships.

Dialectical intergenerational therapy requires a fundamentally active orientation. Unceasingly, regardless of the state of the ledger in which a particular individual finds himself or herself the therapist should seek and encourage active, courageous strategies rather than passive contemplation, commiseration, or mere insight into feelings.

A mother of two teenage children was seen in an exploratory interview. She had spent a number of years in psychiatric hospitals for periodic depressions with greatly regressive symptomatology.

She had two unsuccessful marriages and was living in marked social isolation. The exploration of the merit ledger of her family of origin revealed that she has been used primarily as the parentified child in a family in which the parents' continuous, hopelessly unresolvable conflict placed the children in a "split loyalty" situation. This term indicates a situation in which children are repeatedly being recruited to side with one parent against the other and vice versa. Consequently, they can never be loyal to both parents at the same time. In such families not only are the conditions for the development of basic trust missing but the "legacy" of the helplessness of the parents' marriage places the children in a structural expectation of automatic "parentification" (Boszormenyi-Nagy and Spark, 1). For example, as an adolescent girl, this daughter was the first person, including mother, to whom father had revealed his decision to get a divorce. Her comment eloquently described her situation during the subsequent years: "I'd be home and I'd be hearing things about my father, and I'd go down to my father, and I'd be hearing things about my mother."

The legacy of such a split loyalty situation burdens the child with an unresolvable, heavy expectation and it can cripple one of the offspring—to the extent of serious suicide attempts in the foregoing case. According to the conjunctive principle of therapeutic strategy, such a person should be encouraged to find an active attitude of exploring the relational roots and origins of her parents' basic humanity, rather than "cutting" off her relationship with her family of origin. Such encouragement is contrary to the usual professional attitude. However, the ultimate relational economy of the conjunctive strategy can actually reduce the number of serious suicide attempts made by relationally trapped individuals. This is consistent with the general clinical experience that the more individuals are "cornered" in their basic life aspirations, the more necessary it is to regard their symptoms in the context of the depth aspects of their personality and their close relationships.

The required attitude of multidirectional partiality can be just as taxing on therapists as on the family members. The therapists have to be able to absorb the cost of their own abrogation of the scapegoating of the patients' parents. Moreover, resisting the hidden "psychic economic gain" of scapegoating the patients' rather than their own parents presents a challenge to the balances in the therapists' own familial merit ledger. In summary, the essence of the relational (family) approach is not a conjoint "technique" that excludes communicational, behavior modification, game analytical, or individual-based psychological techniques. The relational approach presumes a deep respect for all relevant factors rather than opting for "short-cuts."

A regard for the complexities of the interlocking ethical reciprocities must be a common denominator of most family therapists' professional choice, even though there are variations in the capacity to spell out their premises in sufficiently dialectical terms.

Concerning the therapeutic impact of the relational approach, change is not the ultimate criterion. In accordance with the conjunctive therapeutic principle of its strategies, dialectical intergenerational therapy utilizes the leverage of unused relational resources. The goal includes — but does not require — desirable change. At a minimum the baseline of the goal spectrum is a situation in which the therapist avoids an artificial disjunctive intrusion — one that could jeopardize relational resources.

In essence, the ethical/existential, conjunctive ideology of dialectical intergenerational therapy raises the ethical question of basic therapeutic goal: change in whose interest? In accordance with the thesis that no family member's cost of relational accountability should be diminished at the expense of increased costs to any other member, it becomes evident that the desirability of change has to be evaluated from every member's vantage point. This includes the deceased parents, the family "legacy," and, even more significantly from a preventive perspective, the yet unborn child. Thus, dialectical intergenerational therapy emerges as an implicit strategy for the future, with its ultimate value residing in prevention — the most desirable "change" imaginable.

ADDENDUM QUERIES

I

Dr. Burton: All psychotherapeutic approaches which follow Freud are more or less dependent upon an unyielding devotion to or love of the patients and their irrationalities — at least in point of some limited time parameter, which is the course of treatment. The patients challenge to determine the limits of such trust, and will yield their therapy and growth if dissatisfied with the results of their challenge. How, therefore, do family therapy approaches satisfy this requisite of patient-therapist belongingness in more than a pro forma or theoretical way? Is there not a danger that no one will gain from therapy?

Dr. Boszormenyi-Nagy: Perhaps my answer somewhat restructures the premises of your question. I respond to your question mainly in terms of its challenge to my extension of the therapeutic contract from one patient to all relating family members.

If the individual therapeutic contract and its consecutive "love-affair" (transference-countertransference) necessitates that therapists actively disregard the welfare of all those affected by their intervention, its very definition is not only arbitrary but deceptive. Therapy cannot itself create or invalidate existential/ethical interdependence, births, parenting, filial gratitudes, and ingratitude. The latter are, instead, constituents of the ethical/existential ledger created by the genetic interlocking between the generations. Subsequently, the options of parental abandonment, infanticide, cruel filial ingratitude and parenticide are costly but permissible ones. They may cause psychological maladjustment, psychosomatic illness, alienation, and large-scale social disintegration.

It is paradoxical to talk about the "danger" of extending genuine concern to all those affected by therapeutic intervention. In reality, there is much more danger in accepting an individual or even marital definition of therapeutic contract, and base its success entirely on the welfare of the contracting adults. Their children, absent and under-represented, often tend to be the ones who pay the highest cost. According to the basic principles of intergenerational family therapy (see also *Invisible Loyalties*, 1), children have to be considered as the main contractors of therapeutic work affecting their parents. In the long run, divorce often means an exciting and liberating, though disappointing, game for the adult participants. For the children, their parents' divorce may mean the end of the trustworthiness of their world.

In summary, the "danger" of the extension of the strict individual therapeutic contract exists only for those who expect an exploitative unilateral gain from therapy.

II

Dr. Burton: Your chapter seems to reify the family in an almost Old Testament way. By this I mean that the Judaic Covenant with Yaweh seems to come through as a sacrosanct family covenant which is tampered with only at great peril. Yet family breakups and divorce occur in the millions, new interpersonal arrangements are made, and the world goes on. Are there then specially sensitized or delegated families who may or may not be representative of the rank and file?

Dr. Boszormenyi-Nagy: I would like to stress the distinction between reification and the existence of invisible, denied, underlying dynamic forces. I would like to emphasize also the interhuman rather than religious connotation of obligation ledgers. Human history shows that religious notions of obligation to the Godhead can be used to bypass and avoid interhuman accountability. Adherence to reciprocity of fairness is, in my view, the opposite of authoritarianism.

Even if the notion of accountability sounds old-fashioned or boring, in the long run nobody can benefit from denial of interhuman accountability. Usually, such denial is the foundation of the multitudinous manifestations of "relational stagnation" (*Invisible Loyalties*, 1). The large number of divorces is a perfect example of the fatal strength of invisible loyalty obligations, amounting to unwitting testimony to overtly and consciously denied, invisible filial loyalty.

III

Dr. Burton: Your emphasis on the ethical and existential aspects of psychotherapy is refreshing since most healers prefer to disregard these dimensions of their work. But the question arises as to whether your emphasis on family intactness and equilibrium is not itself a value, and one which goes counter to modern developmental trends. Is successful psychotherapy that which maintains the dimensions of the family — its substance — and permits society to continue, or is the treatment successful when perhaps one or two family members make a brilliant or original contribution to mankind. Whose values are being served?

Dr. Boszormenyi-Nagy: Relational accountability is indeed an ethical issue which should take high priority if society is to prevail. Yet its underlying dynamic relational premise—a reciprocal balance of fairness—is not only a value. In terms of the classical Freudian dimensions of ego, id, superego, and external reality, it can be ascribed to the realm of dynamic relational reality. What in the classical theory was conceived as a relatively nondynamic "external reality" of the person consists relationally of the highly dynamic id, ego and, superego configurations of persons he or she is closely related with.

It is true that a mutual consideration of one another's welfare is to some degree contrary to the modern ethos of Western civilization, ever since the early 19th century utilitarians tried to equate the ethical issues of right and wrong with the sensual issues of pleasure and pain. The limits of such thinking begin to show in what appears to be the threatened disintegration of our civilization. Reciprocal human accountability has often been abandoned in the aristocratic belief that brilliant individual contributions can justify the exploitation of others. From the winner's point of view, slaveholding, genocide, and pollution of the other nation's river are excusable. Selective disregard for the others has often been justified in the name of an allegedly sympathetic Godhead, sacrosanctity of racial or religious superiority, etc. In families, the mentally retarded, the helpless child, or the aged can be exploited in the name of utilitarian necessity. I maintain that the best guarantee against overtly or covertly exploitative ideologies lies in the principle of reciprocal fairness and concern.

IV

Dr. Burton: It is not clear from your chapter whether you are giving up the pleasure principle for some family ego principle. Does personal pleasure (id) come only when the family is requited? Or is it that for our patients pleasure comes basically through the family or with family permission?

Dr. Boszormenyi-Nagy: The notion of pleasure or of pleasure principle is a typically individual one. These concepts belong to a different systemic realm than the relational concepts of reciprocity, justice, fairness, ledger, etc. If pleasure means an overall long-range satisfaction with one's life, it has to transcend the notions of "id," as Freud himself recognized when he alleged that his reality principle is identical with a long-range, economical pleasure principle. Most specifically, as individuals liberate themselves from an unnecessary amount of stagnant, invisible, unrequited obligations, they are bound to obtain more satisfaction from their personal lives.

V

Dr. Burton: Would you comment on children (and families) raised in kibbutzim, which several independent observers have recently claimed as perhaps a new mode of family or mental health? Are such children (and families) indeed less neurotic than those in the United States?

Dr. Boszormenyi-Nagy: The high emphasis of our civilization on the desirability of the nuclear family pattern of living certainly does not increase the available resources badly needed by young parents. Careful attention has to be given to all possibilities which reconstitute supporting structures around the modern nuclear family. The kibbutz experiment is one of many which try to remodel the social support systems around the nuclear family. With appropriate modifications accounting for cultural and historic specifics, the kibbutz and similar social undertakings are worth exploring in terms of their possible contribution to strengthening the integrity of social relationships throughout the "civilized" world.

REFERENCES

1. Boszormenyi-Nagy, I., & Spark, G. *Invisible Loyalties: Reciprocity in Intergenerational Family Therapy*. New York: Hoeber-Harper, 1973.
2. Buber, M.: *I and Thou*. New York: Charles Scribner's Sons, 1958.
3. Boszormenyi-Nagy, I. Loyalty implications of the transference model in psychotherapy. *Arch. Gen. Psychiat.*, 27, 374–380, 1972.

4. Boszormenyi-Nagy, I. The concept of change in conjoint family therapy. In Friedman, A. S., et al. *Psychotherapy for the Whole Family*. New York: Springer, 1965, pp. 305–319.
5. Stierlin, H. *Separating Parents and Adolescents*. New York: Quadrangle, 1974.
6. Boszormenyi-Nagy, I. Comments on Helm Stierlin's "Hitler as the bound delegate of his mother." *Hist. of Childhood Quart.: The J. Psychohistory, 3*(4), 500–505, 1976.
7. Satir, V., Stachowiak, I., & Taschman, H. A. *Helping Families to Change*. New York: Jason Aronson, 1975.
8. Patterson, G. R. *Families. Application of Social Learning to Family Life*. Champaign: Research Press, 1975.
9. Friedman, M. S. *Martin Buber: The Life of Dialogue*. New York: Harper & Bros., 1960.
10. Erikson, E. H. Identity and the life cycle. *Psychol. Issues, 1*, 1, 1959.
11. Bowen, M. Family therapy with schizophrenia in the hospital and in private practice. In I. Boszormenyi-Nagy & J. L. Framo (Eds.), *Intensive Family Therapy*. New York: Hoeber-Harper, 1965.
12. Wynne, L. C. Some indications and counterindications for exploratory family therapy. In I. Boszormenyi-Nagy & J. L. Framo (Eds.), *Intensive Family Therapy*. New York: Hoeber-Harper, 1965.

11

Comments on Helm Stierlin's "Hitler as the Bound Delegate of his Mother" in History of Childhood Quarterly

This commentary on Stierlin's article about Hitler's family is a brief example of the broader, societal applications of the contextual approach. Contextual principles of legacy and merit-ledger are to be applied here to loyalty-based ethnic groups, as well as to Hitler's family role. Stierlin's concept of delegation implies psychological-transactional dimensions, whereas my legacy concept is based chiefly on the factual and merit dimensions. Delegations derive from one's parents' needs, whereas legacies result from one's total existential context.

Hitler's drive for excessive achievement is seen through illustrations of legacies of survivorship, ancestral shame, split loyalty, and fusion. As a logical exercise, speculations are offered in this article concerning prospective prevention of the development of excessive legacy expectations in any young person. Naturally, the historical factors of Germany's post-World War I climate have to be considered in any serious attempt at explaining the ascendance of Hitler's power.

From here, even further implications are explored, based on an analogy between the merit-ledgers of family loyalties and those of larger loyalty-defined (e.g., ethnic, religious or national) groups. Although no therapist role can be cast into the international scene, it is intriguing to transpose the model of multidirected partiality into a prospective international forum. Is it true that if there were an agency for the documentation of each nonself-governing ethnic group's claim to entitlement, at least some of the desperate effort currently flowing into terroristic attention-seeking behavior could be channeled into developing each side's argument? It is a fact that no international forum exists now that is constituted to hear the pleas of nonself-governing groups. By the stated intention of its designers, the 1945 Charter of the United Nations avoided this far-reaching "democratization" of the proposed international order. In this regard the world order falls far short of Woodrow Wilson's dreams about a League of Nations that would serve the justice of nations and not only the justice of governments. In summary, the contextual approach leads to a reevaluation of psychohistorical hypotheses according to the consequences of unchanneled group loyalties.

There have been numerous reductionistic attempts at explaining historic events with the help of constructs developed on the basis of the psychology of the individual. Complex intertwining of economic, cognitive and systemic communicational factors were then equated with notions of sexual or aggressive drives, guilt feelings, projections, etc. Such personification of large scale multiperson systemic events is unsatisfactory even though the contribution to social events of psychological factors on the individual level is undeniable.

Another question pertains to the understanding of the deeper dynamics of large human (social) systems as contrasted with overt, mechanistically understandable societal determinants. Large human systems have their intrinsic dynamic laws of evolution, growth and decay. It is in this realm that the evolving field of family relational therapy and theory can offer a distinctly novel contribution to the understanding of large scale phenomena. Whereas psychological explanation is anchored in the personal and subjectively unique experience and vantage point of each of us as individuals, systemic relational theory of families conceivably handles a multiperson domain analogous to large scale social systems. Consequently, the family approach is bound to shift from the ethics of personal effectiveness to the ethics of mutual concern and coexistence.

A third issue concerns the discrete and unique causal contribution to historic events of any single leader. Does the leader create the societal trend or is the leader fitting into the call of his time? Again, the understanding of the "psychology" of the leader in the context of his family relational system seems to offer a solid and comprehensive ground for the analysis of the fit between his personal leadership and large-scale expectations of his social group.

Helm Stierlin can rely on a combination of backgrounds and orientations to use in his study of Hitler. As a family therapist of unique theoretical penetration, he is qualified to interpret the familial historical material available on Hitler which may have created an inescapable legacy for the son of an upward mobile lower class Austrian family, especially in view of the unique tragedy of his mother's having lost four of her six children at a very young age. History knows many survivors of tragically extinguished families or nations who then had to excel in order to make up for the lost chances of those wiped out by unjust destiny.

As a psychoanalyst, the author can talk with relevant specificity and detail about the psychological implications of some of Hitler's known behaviors. Also, the author can rely on his depth understanding of psycho-dynamics in his task to postulate in what way did Hitler as an individual internalize the legacies of his family and eventually translate them into the kind of adult motivational configuration which made him a leader of millions of citizens, many of whom with higher educational accomplishments than his own.

Finally, having been thoroughly trained in Hegelian (and general) philosophy, Stierlin has the breadth of thinking to transcend the "technical" limitations of and contradictions between the "scientific" outlooks of psychology, communications theory, and European history.

My own emphases regarding the subject matter as well as the material here presented have to be placed in an overall agreement with most of Stierlin's arguments. Therefore, I will present some of my own thoughts as complementary rather than contradictory to the main conclusions of Stierlin's article.

More specifically, I would like to see the opportunity of a family relational and psychohistorical analysis of Hitler as a historic figure for the illustration of my notion of every family's "invisible establishment." Whereas the visible establishment of a family can be seen through physical, behavioral and overt psychological manifestations of the members, the invisible establishment continues from generation to generation via devotion, expectations, legacies and ledgers of merit (see also Boszormenyi-Nagy and Spark, 1973). The process of delegation thus originates both from the systemic deep dynamic core of intergenerational relationships and from the person-to-person obligation ledgers developing between a particular parent and her or his child.

In this general sense it appears to me that Hitler's legacy of excessive achievement came from the following factors in addition to the one originating from his mother's personal "delegating" influence:

1) The Legacy of Survivorship

The most significant single factor leading to the deep existential "call" to excellence may lie in the fact that 4 of Adolf's 5 full siblings died at an early age. The indebtedness of the survivor to all those who were not given a chance to achieve becomes magnified many times. Guilt of survival and the pressures of an unique existential opportunity join their forces to drive the survivor to superhuman strength and commitments. Thus, the invisible establishment or systemic relational dynamic factor of his siblings' premature deaths constitute a legacy that does not originate from any person's "psychic" motivations.

2) The Legacy of Ancestral Shame

Through his deeply ingrained loyalty and obligation every child is burdened with the task of exonerating and explaining the "shady" aspects of his family background. In my experience the most difficult facets a child has to deal with in his past are the shame of their parents' and ancestors' lives.

It is never easy to evaluate the intensity of shame experienced by a person. Shame has its own psychology, of course, but it is essentially anchored in the existential reality of those persons whose acts the person includes in his own shame and also in the value standards of outsiders. By one definition (Boszormenyi-Nagy and Spark, 1973), persons whose acts can cause shame in me are the ones whom I include within the boundary of my loyalty commitments: my family, my nation, my race, my co-religionists, etc.

It appears from the historical data cited by Stierlin that one of Hitler's legacies had to do with undoing the shame of his family of origin. The sexual and occupational value system of the middle class status which Hitler's father seemed to have acquired is in sharp contrast with that of the marginal lower class existence of his background. Hitler's "hard working" parents established themselves in the lower echelons of burgeois respectability against a background of poverty, illegitimate births, name change, uncertainty of origins and the shadow of an illegitimate "liaison" between the two of them while Hitler's mother had been a maidservant in his father's household from her age 15 to the death of the second wife 9 years later. The more painful the shame of his origin, the more thoroughly invisible the child's mission gets in order to prove the family's worth through superhuman effort and momentous achievements. In summary, I propose that the "mechanism" of undoing intrinsic family shame may represent at least as powerful a restitutive motivation for the child as that of revenging an allegedly incompetent or perhaps irresponsible doctor's detrimental practices which may have contributed to his mother's premature death due to cancer.

3) The Legacy of Split Loyalty

In my experience a circumstance which can be called "split loyalty expectation" can be the most painful and devastating to the child's autonomous life potential. Whereas I consider loyalty obligations to one's family of origin constituting the irreplaceable sources of basic trust primary and life sustaining, an ominous constellation of relational dynamic can interfere with the very formation of primary loyalty. Specifically, this develops if each parent expects the child to be loyal against and to the exclusion of the child's loyalty to the other parent. Under the circumstances the child is constantly caught in the existential dilemma of failing to achieve the same goal to which he is constantly driven by parental personal expectation on the one side and by guilt of omission and imputed betrayal on the other. By its own intrinsic unfulfillability, the invisible legacy of split loyalty expectations can "delegate" the child to a superhuman effort at unifying the rest of the family, all of his national or religious group, or even humanity.

4) The Legacy of Loyalty: Fusion

A substitutive extension of one's deceased parents into the totality of one's nation represents a promising option for the child's sustained efforts at fulfilling his legacy-defined mission, even though through a re-direction of efforts. The hurt and shame of the family of origin can thus still be redeemed through a symbolic fusion, in Hitler's case of the Nazi definition of a super-race of Nordic Germans, with the family.

No trace of split loyalty is tolerated then in the monolithic tyranny of "Ein Volk, ein Reich, ein Fuehrer" (One people, one empire, one leader). Germany becomes for Hitler then not just the symbolic mother but the representative of all personages of his ancestry to whom he, the lone survivor of his mother's first five children, owes limitless loyalty. The "humiliation" of Germany in World War I could fittingly reinforce the fusion between family and country for Hitler.

5) Immunity to Guilt as an Aspect of the Legacy

The particularities of superego formation determine the individual's susceptibility to guilt of one kind or another. Earlier (1962) I described a particular imbalance of superego function, the "counterautonomous" superego. This configuration dovetails with the relational structure of excessive, invisible familial loyalty expectations. The more excessive the demand, the more the superego becomes polarized toward guilt over autonomous pursuits of any kind. In its extreme, marriage, procreation and loyal commitment to the grandchild generation might represent the ultimate of primary disloyalty to the grandparent generation. The more self-sacrificial than the offspring's counterautonomous loyalty, the less sensitive he may become to being unfair to outsiders. Insofar as all ambivalent hostility to one's ancestors becomes denied and displaced upon outsiders, one can even score gains in primary loyalty by sparing the ancestors and victimizing the outsiders. Naturally, from a systemic point of view, as already Freud indicated, the superego of the individual stands also for the value expectations (legacies) of one's ancestry.

Conversely, the counterautonomous tendencies of his superego would not permit the person to develop an enjoyment in play, sex or personal gains of any sort. This may explain Hitler's failure in his efforts at any bourgeois career, his puritanical life habits, his lack of sustained sexual companionship of any kind, and avoidance of parenthood.

All of this leads us to the recognition of the limits of every explanation of complex human events. Even more limited are the options for purposeful strategies aimed at social prevention. Stierlin's concept of delegation and the concept of systemic balances (ledgers) of merit

(Boszormenyi-Nagy and Spark, 1973) perhaps offer a conceptual avenue toward preventive strategies. The greatest wrongdoer in history may develop out of the unjustly overburdened child, whose devotion could go either into noble goals of humanitarian activism or cruel, absolutistic exploitation of others or even genocide.

A first order practical question then is: how to recognize the characteristics of children who suffer from excessive, unbalanceable legacies of their past? How to know the criteria of overburdening legacies which arise not only from the persons of the parents but also from the invisible (tragic) establishment of families? What are the first signs of immunity to guilt shown in families?

A subsequent question would pertain to avenues of channeling existing overcharged commitments of children back into the family system for appropriate re-balancing and, gradually, toward a sense of sound and merited autonomy.

Before this can be done though, a new language has to be developed to parsimoniously describe the configurations of both personal and contextual (loyalty) obligations of children. As I have implied, this language has to transcend psychology and has to comprise existential-ethical balances of merit. Hitler's existence can be seen as conceived in an overloaded context of ethical imbalance, under the shadow of the three deceased siblings. A satisfactory relational therapeutic strategy could thus be built on the understanding of the ways in which young Hitler could have learned to be available to his parents, as well as to the hurt justice of the family's invisible establishment in order to re-balance his indebtedness and his escalating need for higher and higher degrees of superhuman (and inhuman) effectiveness in order to redress the injustice of his family's tragedy.

At this point it is necessary to extend the same conceptual framework into large-scale socio-historical perspectives. As I stated in the beginning, no leader could be fully understandable without a meaningful reconstruction of the particular stage of historical process which interweaves with the deeper dynamics of the leader's personal life characteristics. Is the merit ledger of larger loyalty-defined groups (nations, religious, racial, etc. minorities) analogous to the ledger of familial loyalties? If so, are there criteria of intergroup balances of merit and fairness which should be recognized and openly dealt with, rather than denied and avoided? Would humanity benefit then from a forum which would begin to define the criteria of justice and injustice in the dealings of nations and minorities? Would such clarity of criteria help toward separating out national tendencies aimed at justifiable redress from those aimed at power-motivated, imperialistic over-compensations, causing new injustice on the other side, in never ceasing confusion of historical justice with scapegoating, possessiveness and power-driven vindictiveness? Would the clear definition of such criteria lead humanity to the development of a more just structure of international organization than the current United Nations charter permits? Could the governments of nations tolerate the articulation of the claims for justice made by all human loyalty groups, or will our civilization be sacrificed to a blind struggle between imperialistic governments and an increasing "terroristic" activity of all groups whose injustice cannot be heard at any forum other than the military and police headquarters of absolutistic governments? Can there be a new progressive intellectualism developed in our youth which can be liberated from the fallacy of a world organization to be built on the notions of individual human rights as pretext for denying group rights to all minorities?

In conclusion, I would like to emphasize the seminal contributions of Helm Stierlin, who through this article and his book on Hitler achieved an integration of several discrete points of view regarding our understanding of man. By applying a well thought-through relational theory to the explanation of one of the most disturbing historical phenomena of modern times, the author opened the door to a courageous humanism which could serve as a preventive principle for the future. Finally, Stierlin's authentic scholarship and profound familiarity with both psychoanalysis and Hegelian dialectic cannot fail to stimulate the thoughtful reader to re-examine Freud's ingenious psychological system with a view toward expansion into the broader vistas of systemic theory.

REFERENCE

Boszormenyi-Nagy, I. The concept of schizophrenia from the perspective of family treatment. *Family Process, 1,* 103–113, 1962.

12

Clinical and Legal Issues in the Family Therapy Record

[This paper was written with Neal Gansheroff, M.D. (Senior Author), and John Matrullo, J.D.]

In the entire literature on family therapy it is rare to find articles about record keeping. This is unfortunate because family-based record keeping would have implications not only for therapy and legal procedure, but also could benefit immeasurably our entire health care system. This article is written from a generalized family therapy perspective but its principles are compatible with the contextual growth.

The good family therapy record contains information about each member as a person and about their mutual positions regarding conflicts and supportive availability. Comments are needed to describe the therapeutic stance and its limitations. Legally and ethically, care should be taken to prevent unnecessary or harmful revelations about any family member, regardless of whether or not that member was attending the sessions.

The authors present guidelines for writing family therapy records that are not only clinically meaningful but also not unnecessarily damaging to a member of the family or the therapist in case the records are subpoenaed. They suggest that when deciding what to include in the record, the therapist should remember that those in treatment are both individuals and members of the family. They also recommend that a patient's right to privacy be safeguarded by omitting potentially damaging or embarrassing material from the record.

In writing a family therapy record, the therapist must strike a delicate balance between including enough information to make the material clinically meaningful and useful and avoiding, as much as possible, the inclusion of material that may be legally damaging, shameful, or embarrassing to individual members of the family. When he makes an entry, the therapist should remember that the record may not always be left untouched in the file drawer. It may be needed by another therapist for continuity of care or used to satisfy accreditation standards. Or it may be subpoenaed as evidence in a malpractice or divorce suit or in a child-custody case.

The family psychiatry department of the Eastern Pennsylvania Psychiatric Institute recently revised its format for keeping family charts and established guidelines for writing the charts. Those guidelines emphasize the need for therapists to consider four main, somewhat overlapping, aspects when writing records: hospital accreditation standards, clinical aspects, legal aspects, and respect for patients' privacy.

Therapists working in centers accredited by the Joint Commission on Accreditation of Hospitals must pay special attention to the commission's standards for writing medical records. Every two years the commission inspects those hospitals, including their medical records. If the records are considered completely unacceptable, hospitals can lose, and in fact some have lost, their accreditation. The standards are contained in the *Accreditation Manual for Psychiatric Facilities* and require, among other things, that "The medical record shall contain sufficient information to identify the patient clearly, to justify the diagnosis, to delineate the treatment plan, and to document the results accurately."*

CLINICAL ASPECTS

Many therapists who may be quite adept at writing a meaningful, high-quality record for an individual patient have major difficulties organizing and satisfactorily recording the wealth of complex, inter-related data obtained in treating an entire family. It is one thing to write a record on a single patient; it is quite another to write one about two adults, usually parents, and possibly several children that portrays each as an individual and yet conveys their complex nuclear- and extended-family relationships. If the records are to be meaningful, both individual and family data must be recorded.

Two basic questions should be asked to determine if the records will aid in the clinical management of the case and in a possible legal defense: does the chart tell what is happening in the family, and does it justify a particular therapeutic or administrative decision?† As an il-lustration of such a justification, take the case of a therapist who, in the initial sessions, is faced with parents who want to focus only on their symptomatic child. He elects to postpone intensively exploring their marital relationship until later in therapy. He explains in the record that only a minimal marital history was obtained thus far because he felt that therapy might be jeopardized if that area were opened before the resistant parents were ready to discuss it.

Specific guidelines for family charts, as well as formats in which to include clinical material, have been established for the department's recently revised initial family report, progress notes, and closing sum-mary. The formats were designed to be broad enough to be used by most therapists, even those with diverse orientations. Nevertheless,

---

*Accreditation Council for Psychiatric Facilities, *Accreditation Manual for Psychiatric Facilities*, Joint Commission on Accreditation of Hospitals, Chicago, 1972.
†D. H. Mills, "Hidden Legal Dangers of the Hospital Chart," *Hospital Medicine*, Vol. 1, October 1965, pp. 34–35.

since any formats or guidelines will reflect, to some degree, the viewpoints of those who developed them, there may be some criticisms. The formats and guidelines are not intended to be the final word on family records, but rather elements that can be modified as new ideas are introduced and experience in using them is gained.

Initial family report. This report should contain the name of the family and of the therapist and the dates of the sessions. Under the heading "identifying information," the names and ages of all family members should be given, as well as their occupations, presenting problems, and source of referral. The next section is "history of presenting problem," followed by, unless the material is included elsewhere, one on "marital and family history."

Under the heading "characterization of family members," there should be pertinent information about race, religion, nationality, socioeconomic status, developmental history of each member, the parents' families of origin and current relationships with them, and personality descriptions of each member in therapy. Under the heading "observations of family system" the therapist should record what goes on in the sessions, both verbally and nonverbally, between family members and between the family and the therapist. Main issues and themes should also be recorded here, as well as feelings evoked in the therapist.

A section on "dynamics and treatment plan" should include the therapist's understanding of each member, of the family system, and of how the presenting difficulties came about. Psychodynamics, societal, hereditary, and constitutional factors should also be included. The proposed type of treatment—for example, weekly family therapy or chemotherapy—and goals should be stated. Here the therapist may also give a prognosis.

Progress notes. These reports should state what is happening with the family relationships as well as with the individual family members in terms of important events in their lives and their emotional states. It should also include dates of therapy sessions, who attended them, how the members interacted, what was discussed, and the therapeutic approaches used.

Closing summary. This brief summary of the entire case should include an identification of the family members, the presenting problem, the treatment process, the outcome for the family as a whole and for each of the members, the reasons for termination, and the disposition. The date of the initial and final sessions or contact should also be included.

The essence of these formats is that people are individuals in their own right who significantly affect and are affected by their family members. Thus the formats provide for including valuable information about subjective experience and individual psychodynamics as well as a description of the family's systemic relationships.

LEGAL ASPECTS

Some therapists think of a clinical record as being used solely for clinical purposes. They should realize, however, that any member of the family may at any time become involved in a legal action. Divorce proceedings, child-custody disputes, and certain other civil as well as criminal cases may arise during or after family therapy. In some instances the records may be subpoenaed.

What protection do therapists and patients have against having the records opened in court? It is the physician's or psychologist's ethical duty to keep confidential the information he has obtained about a patient in his professional capacity. In almost every state, such information is privileged and thus may not be disclosed in a legal proceeding without the patient's consent. A few states have extended the privilege to psychiatric social workers as well as physicians and psychologists.

Regardless of the professional degree of the family therapist or whether he is protected by privileged-communication laws, family therapy and family-based record-keeping raise very special problems and legal issues. Privilege and confidentiality are affected by the type of legal case involved and by the sheer fact that more than one person is involved in the therapy. For example, a husband and wife go to a therapist for marital therapy. One later sues the other for divorce. One raises the issue of mental condition in either the claim or the defense. Most state courts would consider privilege to have been waived. But what if the other party did not want that information to be brought up?

Should one member of the patient-family have the right to waive the privilege to the detriment of other members of the family who may either still be in therapy or simply want their communications with the therapist to remain confidential? That issue has not yet been directly addressed by case law or statute. An argument could be made that the patient is the entire family unit and that each member must waive the privilege before the records can be examined. Although that argument may be used successfully in a divorce case,*† its chances of success in a child-custody case are slim because the court's primary concern is for the best interest of the child. Massachusetts law, in fact, explicitly denies privilege to any therapist in any child-custody case in which either party raises the mental condition of the other party.

In sum, a general principle of law is that the court has a right to every person's evidence. The psychotherapist privilege is a justifiable exception but is strictly construed and is itself exception-laden. Most important, current law as it relates to family therapy, and records in particular, is at best unsettled. According to Slovenko, the test of relevancy—not privilege—governs the right to nondisclosure.** Thus a therapist-family communication is best protected from disclosure by showing that the communication would have no relevance to the issues in the case.

Therefore, the therapist should be cautious about what information he includes in the records. For example, the admission by a husband that he is coming to family therapy sessions to make his case stronger in an anticipated child-custody struggle might best be omitted from the record. If it is mentioned at all, the reference should be a vague one such as "Motivations for therapy were discussed." Certainly incriminating or conclusive statements such as "The wife is an unfit parent" should be avoided. How detailed the records should be will depend upon the setting in which the therapist works, the family problem being treated, and the type of litigation that could arise.

Ellis v. Ellis, 472 S.W. 2d 741 (Tenn. App. 1971).
†*Simrin v. Simrin*, 233 Cal. App. 2d 90, 43 Cal. Rptr. 376.
**R. Slovenko, *Psychiatry and Law*, Little, Brown, Boston, 1973, p. 67.

As a final precaution, each adult family member should be asked to sign an agreement that he understands that all of the communications are confidential and that the therapist will not disclose any communication unless all participating members join in the waiver. If each member does sign a release, the therapist must make sure that he did so knowingly and intelligently. But until the legislatures and the courts recognize the need for an absolute privilege for family therapists, this type of written agreement will provide very little protection in the event records are subpoenaed.

The lack of an adequate privilege law for family therapists has led some therapists to question whether they should keep any records at all. To be sure, accurate records are the therapist's best defense against a malpractice suit.* Perhaps more important, accurate records ensure continuity of care. Nevertheless, many private practitioners keep no charts except the customary record of appointments and billings; others risk perjury by keeping two sets, one to be turned over in case of subpoena and the other for treatment.

PATIENT'S PRIVACY

In the course of an evaluation or therapy, patients may reveal various intimate aspects of their own or their relatives' past or current life. They generally do so with the belief that the information will be used by the therapist to help them and will not be passed on to others except in certain situations related to their treatment. To safeguard the patient's right to privacy, we recommend that certain damaging or embarrassing material not be written in the chart. Such material may include the details of sexual difficulties or an extramarital affair. In deciding how much, if any, of such private material should be included, the therapist should balance the need to have complete, useful records against the patients' right to privacy.

The more private the material is, the stronger must be the clinical

---

*Mills, *op. cit.*

reason for writing about it. We have found that an adequate description of the therapy process can be given without including details of exceedingly shameful or damaging material. It is more important to be clear about the strategy and management of the therapy than to be detailed about private matters.

13

Contextual Therapy: Therapeutic Leverages in Mobilizing Trust

This is the first paper with the name "Contextual Therapy" in its title. Already in Invisible Loyalties *(1973) the last chapter was entitled "contextual guidelines," yet the approach as a whole was called "intergenerational family therapy." The starting point for this therapy is an ethical redefinition of the relational context. This is the first publication that deals with the four dimensions of relational determinants: facts, needs, transactions and merit. This clustering of relational factors resulted from years of search for an inclusive scheme of a mutually nonreduceable minimum number of clusters of independent relational and therapeutic factors. Thus, the four dimensions constitute a framework for the integration of a wide variety of therapeutic techniques under the umbrella of dimension four.*

There is a major philosophical-practice question: Can therapy fulfill its mandate in a world of disintegrating trustworthiness and credibility? In a world of decreasing commitment to communities and marriages, therapy should not become a technology for forcibly changing people, nor should the family be targeted as "pathological." In a cold world of tough economic competitiveness, the mother's care for the helpless infant remains the last reserve of trustworthiness. Contextual therapy aims at the goal of eliciting the trust resources of close relationships.

The contextual therapist views himself in a pluralistic therapeutic contractual ethic. Its guideline assumes that the fastest way to achieve

The author acknowledges suggestions made by Dr. Barbara R. Krasner in the revision of the final format of this paper.

191

a secure hold over the essential dynamics of a relational system is a catalytic one: eliciting every family member's responsible review of his or her side of mutual entitlements and indebtednesses. This review includes the very young or yet unborn offspring, since the consequences of the quality of parenting have a direct impact on the quality of the lives in the following generation. The therapist's active courage is manifested in guiding the family members back from ethical disengagement or stagnation toward attentiveness to multilateral criteria of fairness. Ethical stagnation is assumed here to be the greatest source of failing autonomy and individuation in families.

In fact, relational ethical therapeutic leverages rely on the overcoming of ethical disengagement. Rejunction is the name of the intervention which starts the self-reinforcing process of gaining mutually merited trust. It is self-reinforcing because each member experiences the surge of an inner entitlement to growth and self-actualization earned in return for accountability. Overall, the result for the whole system amounts to restoration of trustworthiness. This outcome is based on a relatively symmetrical investment of trust, an investment that depends upon a regard for "valid" obligations. Yet, it is not for the therapist to determine this validity; it is decided in the process of a multilaterally committed dialogue of mutual claims.

The therapeutic method and attitude of multidirected partiality requires a capacity for deep empathy and for attention given to any member's claims. The required sequential shift of partiality differs from impartiality, the latter an unlikely human stance. Part of the requisite therapeutic skills include sensitive timing and the ability to perceive when a person has reached his limit of accountability. Therapeutic attention is directed at surfacing balances of merit (Dimension IV) rather than at the nature of transactional patterns or of feelings. The multidirected contractual ethics of his work helps the contextual therapist not to base the definition of his task on the overt symptomatic picture alone. For example, addressing the split loyalty predicament which places the child in a referee-confidante role is more significant to consider than any of its symptomatic sequelae.

Indication for contextual therapy does not hinge on any individual diagnosis. Families containing "incurably" sick or damaged members are still good candidates for contextual therapy. Since resource rather than causality is the chief rationale of all psychotherapies, there is no reasonable contraindication to the contextual, ethical enrichment of any therapeutic procedure. Contextual therapy is, however, eminently indicated in cases of vital threat and urgency.

Further goals for the further development of therapy as a whole include an integration of therapeutic knowledge and skills with the ethical dimension. For example, all vicissitudes of the family members' emotional reactions will have to be incorporated into a scheme which acknowledges the unchangeable fact of shared rootedness among relatives. Another important area of investigation lies in the means by which existential (and psychological) guilt develops over symptomatic improvement. Finally, the preventive implications of multidirected partiality and of inclusive concern with all those to be affected are to be explored.

REFERENCE

Boszormenyi-Nagy, I., & Spark, G. M. *Invisible loyalties*. New York: Brunner/Mazel, 1973.

The essential rationale of contextual therapy is based on an ethical dynamic. This position finds validation in both the clinical contribution of family therapy, and in the stressful situation in which contemporary family life finds itself in a society experiencing a multilevel disintegration of trust.

Family therapy evolved from a wish to overcome limitations in traditional psychotherapy. In addition to searching for new techniques, its quest involved an integration of several fields of knowledge. Implicit in the early development of family therapy was the question of whether psychotherapy could become a science that considered simultaneous, multifactored causation of behavioral disorders. Causal factors would include motivations, the vicissitudes of childhood experience, the tragedy of death and limitations, the need and responsibility for others, the ability to develop realistic life plans, an understanding of what the world is about and generativity toward children, to name a few. Furthermore, the young field of family therapy brought to the surface the issue of whether psychotherapy could fulfill its mandate. Moreover, it asked whether psychotherapy should try to be accountable for curing symptoms in one patient (e.g., psychosis, neurosis, depression or school phobia) or should be accountable for the delivery of the curative and preventive benefits of a multidisciplinary consideration of more than one person (e.g., the combined knowledge of psychotherapies based on intrapsychic dynamics, behaviorism and child development).

In a world characterized by rapid technological progress and the exploitative possibilities inherent in computerized efficiency, personal accountability has diminished. Impersonally powerful bureaucracies can flood nutritional sources with carcinogenic substances, poison the atmosphere and wipe out life on earth. A world given to sophisticated and even unintended exploitation of its citizens has little room for trust or integrity among people. Under the circumstances, economic competitiveness becomes life's only "reality." The resulting credibility gap and ethical vacuum become alarming as they apply to matters of parental accountability and parental input into future generations. As the last potential resource for trustworthiness, parent-child relations are the basic fiber of civilization and its survival. The last reserve of trustworthiness lies in the mother's care for the helpless infant born of her body, and influenced by her past. Moreover, the baby is destined to link his parents with the future. The quality of parenting and the quality of life in a new generation are inextricably intertwined, and the connection between the two has been documented by decades of research in developmental psychology.

The fact is that technical progress in time- and labor-saving devices has exacted a huge cost from long-held humanistic assumptions about relationships. For example, nuclear families can no longer anticipate physical and emotional support in child-rearing from extended families and community. The aging are no longer viewed as a potential reservoir of life experience and guidance. Instead, aging is increasingly seen as a process whose singular result is the shrinking of physical powers. The notion of a trustworthy community has all but been abandoned to a generalized skepticism about the integrity of any relationship. A major result of using technology as the primary measure of human progress is evident in a variety of disintegrative phenomena that include the escalating ratio of marital breakdown, the lack of solidarity with the old and the handicapped, large-scale criminality, environmental pollution and a loss of confidence in government and other societal institutions.

DEFINITION OF THE CONTEXTUAL APPROACH

In the late 1950s, a small number of psychiatrists and professionals from other disciplines began to treat families. Faced with encouraging results, they were asked to provide training to thousands of interested helping agents. At the same time, however, a tendency developed to label families and to diagnose their situations in blaming and pathological terms like "malfunctioning," "symbiotic," "schizophrenogenic" and even "obsolescent." These labels added to the burden of family life that was already buffeted by the impact of an ethically stagnant society. In their descriptions of detrimental communication patterns, role distributions, transactional sequences and game rules, most early family therapists seemed to blame family life for the dysfunction of their members. In the main, they failed to support and nurture the family's function as the ultimate resort for sustaining the trustworthiness that alone can provide relational resources for healthy growth and behavior.

Though operating out of a new epistemological context, family therapy became cause-oriented and cognitive in the search for some prescriptive rules that could correct abnormal family functions. However, inadvertently, classical family therapy tended to reinforce a pathological definition of family and thereby undercut the fact that resources for healing continue to exist among family members in the midst of broken and distorted relationships. With emphasis on words like "system," "pattern" and "structure," it became clear that even family therapy ran the danger of turning into a technology for forcibly influencing and changing people. Yet, over the years it became increasingly evident that a humanistic devotion to people in relationships provided the only common denominator of family therapists of differing conceptual persuasions. A decisive gap developed between a cognitive-technological view of family therapy and a therapeutic intervention that concentrated on the ethical sources of stress that impinges on individuals, families and communities alike.

An ethical redefinition of the relational context characterizes contextual therapy[1,2,3,4] whose primary resource is mutually merited trustworthiness. Issues like intermember fairness, integrity, exploitation, entitlement and indebtedness are of primary concern to the contextual therapist whose contract is pluralistic in nature and whose partiality extends beyond one person to include the significant members of his relational world. His aim is to elicit and facilitate the self-reinforcing process of mutually merited trust between closely related people (rejunction). His methodology is to mobilize the latent reserves of trustworthiness through the activation of mutual care, consideration and commitment among family members. The intrinsic multilaterality of the therapist's concern for the survival and welfare interests of each family member constitutes a relational ethic that transcends the scope of traditional individual therapy and classical family therapy.

ASSESSMENT

In forming his intervention strategy, the therapist uses all of his knowledge of the dynamics of human relationships. He recognizes pathology and individual psychological factors, but his main attention is directed to the most powerful relational-ethical leverages. The contextual therapist assesses the deep ethical context of human situations. Having learned to identify manifestations of ethical disengagement, i.e., "stagnation,"[2] he designs his main strategy according to the accessibility of reserves of trustworthiness. The following is an example of a translation from transactional and individual to ethical dynamic dimensions:

> The therapist meets with a suicidally and psychotically depressed young man and his parents. He could focus on the unconscious roots of the young man's irrational ideation or on the overinvolved symbiotic patterns of the two parents' relationship with their grown-up son. Yet on an ethical level, it becomes clear that the young man is trapped in a field of repayable obligations as an alternating confidante between his two desperate parents who will not divorce. Instead they use their son as a captive sounding board for berating each other and their marriage.

An extreme polarization of this split loyalty configuration[5] lies at the bottom of many suicidal or near-suicidal tragedies.

Under the circumstance described above, the contextual therapist will design a rejunctive plan to help form a valid base for trustworthiness between exploitatively parentifying parents and a captively overloyal son. Despite emotional resistance, the parents are helped to learn and acknowledge how they used their child for the substitutive balancing of a displaced relational context. Reworking a captive compliance with the referee-confidante role expectations of his parents, the son is helped to learn more effective and less self-sacrificial ways for repaying his filial loyalty. The outcome aims at increased trust and exoneration, rather than at condemnation and a hateful "severance" of objectionable family relationships. As family members take more accountable stances, each of them in turn acquires inner entitlement for growth and self-actualization.

In contrast with therapy based on power coalitions, entitlement represents an ethical dynamic. Thus a preventive opportunity arises. To be sure, not every child becomes irreversibly caught in the ethical binds of captive split filial loyalty. Still, it is common enough that the recognition of this condition in families could help mental health and other human service professionals avert the development of severely self-destructive conditions (school phobia, psychosis, addiction, anorexia). The following clinical vignette represents a case in point:

Fred, 14, was referred by the court for drug addiction, truancy and repeated shoplifting. An appointment was made to see him with his parents and two older, married sisters. It was easy to understand the mother's bitter disappointment as one listened to the recalcitrant, revengeful and irresponsible statements of the youthful delinquent. As the first stage of his attempt at multi-directed partiality, the therapist was eager to hear the parents' complaints and to lend a sympathetic ear to their embarrassment, shame and disappointment.

As the interviewer extended his interest to the personal aspects of the parents' lives, he learned almost from the beginning that the father was deeply disappointed in his wife. Allegedly in order to avoid his dependently demanding, nagging wife, he drank and spent very little time at home. On the other hand, he was in the habit of siding with his children against his wife, just as his mother used to side with him and his brother against his father. The father's brother committed suicide at 15. Moreover, the therapist learned that Fred's mother was completely unhappy about her marriage and that these marriage partners had long abandoned an intimate relationship. The mother also indicated that she was disappointed in her two daughters for their lack of interest in her difficult problems. However, she attributed their disinterest to their own marital difficulties. The two daughters appeared to be close to each other and sympathetic rather than accusatory toward Fred.

In accordance with the principle of multidirected partiality, the interviewer subsequently sought to reverse the blame and side with Fred on the basis of his intrinsic devotion to the family. This position was made difficult by the destructive nature of Fred's symptoms and by his chronically disrespectful behavior. Yet, based on his conviction about children's fundamental loyalty to their family, the therapist persisted in asking Fred whether, even in the remote past, he remembered occasions when he tried to be helpful to his parents. After a great deal of evasiveness and disconfirming denials, Fred admitted that his mother had no one else to rely upon. It was only he who was available to her whenever she felt abandoned and depressed. Among the family members he alone was willing to spend hours patiently listening to her and offering verbal assurances. The delinquent child was the "parentified" one. That is, he was always reliably available to his mother.

At this juncture, implicit blaming began to point in the mother's direction. Ready to side with her, the therapist expected the mother to acknowledge Fred's responsiveness to her needs. Somewhat reluctant to acknowledge her son's contributions to her life, it was nevertheless impossible for the mother to deny her reliance on Fred in her most difficult, lonely moments. Typically, Fred's behavior started to improve as soon as his filial devotion was recognized. The focus of the contextual therapist could then move on to explore the parents' marriage.

Having sided with both the mother and Fred (and, before the hour was over, with all family members), the therapist assumed a favorable position for demanding accountable attitudes from everyone. This procedure protected him from the blame inherent in being either unilaterally partial or in instigating disloyalty among family members.

The contextual therapist uses the assessment of basic ethical balances for learning the fundamentals of all relationships in a family. The assessment is also used as a stimulus for eliciting responsible attitudes towards each other from each family member. This catalytic function *ipso facto* is a therapeutic component, even when it starts within the first ten minutes of the first interview. As the basic rule of therapy, this multidirected partiality is an actively structuring and guiding principle that leads to an elicitory rather than prescriptive or judgmental intervention. The family members are asked to define their positions vis-à-vis one another's shortcomings and merits. They soon learn that unless they make a strong effort to define their positions, they lose a chance of finally being heard. The cost of the search for trustworthiness decreases as the interviewer guides the family members' attention to the multilaterality of fairness. The family soon learns that once one is heard, it is easier to hear others. They also learn that once the interviewer makes one person accountable, it is easier to let one's self be called to account. In other words, the first steps have been taken toward engagement in a mutuality of trust and trustworthiness.

Of course, the therapist could have proceeded in many other ways to "learn about the material." He could have surfaced evidences of pathology and developmental deprivation as he elicited more and more information about Fred. He could have done the same with any of the other family members. In all of this he could have been guided by separate and discrete curiosities about the psyche of any family member. Naturally, that type of information is valuable but has to be ordered into a contextual understanding of motivational priorities. The fastest way to gain a secure hold over the essential dynamics of a relational system occurs through eliciting every family member's own responsible review of his or her side of mutual entitlements and indebtednesses. This approach addresses the problem of eroding trust that is a fateful impediment to both ongoing relationships and to raising healthy offspring. The lack of trustworthiness in one's relational world is the primary pathogenic condition of human life.

TOOLS FOR INTERVENTION

Rejunction as an Avenue to Entitlement

The goal of contextual therapy is rejunction, that is: 1) an acknowledgment of the principle of equitable multilaterality; 2) an ethically definable process of reengagement in living mutuality; and 3) a commitment to fair balances of give-and-take. In other words, family members explore their capacity for reworking stagnant imbalances in how each of them uses the other and in how they are available to each other. The courage they invest in the review and repair of inadvertent relational corruption and exploitation yields returns in therapeutic resources.

The increase in inner entitlement to autonomy and growth that is gained through renewed commitment to trustworthy mutuality will enable the family members to utilize their ego-strength reserves to better advantage. Consequently, the therapist will be able to use his tactical skills (psychodynamic, transactional, communicational, behavioral) more effectively when he intervenes in a relational context of greater receptivity and in an enlarged capacity for lasting change on the part of overtly and covertly symptomatic family members.

Main Resource: Increased Trustworthiness
Based on Balances of Fairness

Since restoration of trustworthiness in relationships is the goal model of contextual therapy, the therapist has to assess criteria of trust and mistrust. As it is used here, the word trust does not connote a reliable predictability of someone's power-imposed compliance or obedience. Genuine trustworthiness cannot be imposed by either forcible oppression or by manipulative skill. It has to be deserved or merited on the basis of a multilateral input or investment on the part of all partners. The balance of relational fairness depends on a relatively symmetrical investment of trust in caring mutuality. A spontaneous property of people's relational contexts, trustworthiness is the fundamental resource of family relationships.

The conditions of free entitlement are based on a person's fulfilling some of his valid obligations. The question of what constitutes "valid" obligations is a crucial one. The therapist should never pose as a judge of right versus wrong in other people's relationships. His task is to elicit or catalyze a multilaterally committed review of the essential issues of balances of fairness or equity among family members. Valid obligations are based on someone's benefiting (receiver) from someone else's giving (contributor), i.e., on the giver's earned merit.

Multidirected Partiality

Multilaterality is the crucial characteristic of relationships. Relational ethics are created by the fact that every relationship has at least two sides of entitlement, obligation, interest, need, merit and benefit. While traditional individual therapy and even classical family therapy ignore the issue of multilaterality, the key method of contextual therapy consists of a "multidirected partiality" that is based on the therapist's deep regard for the importance of all family members' equitable investment into the trustworthiness of their relationships.[1]

Instead of simply forming a tactical power alliance, the contextual therapist must have the capacity for deep empathy. He also must have the capacity for an "as if" participation in the relational position of each and every family member. From the beginning of the first interview, partiality is shown by listening to everyone's complaints with a readiness to consider any member's justified entitlements. Even more important, perhaps, is the need to hear hidden and unspoken aspects of exploitation and victimization, especially as they affect small, dependent children.

The term "multidirected" connotes a sequential shift to siding with the merit of now one, now another family member. The fact that it also requires sequential, transitory siding "against" someone differentiates multidirected partiality from a traditionally neutral or impartial therapeutic stance or from the generalized notion of empathy.

The "technical" question of timing of sequential shifts in the therapist's partiality is mainly determined by ethical guidelines. Naturally, skill and experience will enable the therapist to accurately perceive the members' needs and capacities for progress. As a rule, then, through listening to one member's side of entitlement, the therapist enables that member to account for his side of the relationship. For example, having listened to Fred's mother's frustrated disappointments about her son's behavior, the therapist can then ask her whether she has acknowledged evidences of Fred's desperate desire to give her devotion, care and loyal concern.

At times a family member signals that he or she is not ready for assuming relational accountability without first receiving more evidence of the therapist's empathic concern. The therapist should see the signal as a request to redirect his concern and to adapt his timing. For example, it is usually unfair and unwise to make a parent concede his or her role as a victimizer without considering the parent's own past victimization as a child.

"Active" Therapeutic Strength: Conviction About Rejunction

Using the illustration of Fred's family, the interviewer could have chosen the path of analyzing the game patterns or the power alignments in any particular period of the interview. He could have challenged the passive father, outsmarted the manipulative mother, fought out the battle of ultimate control with the "all-powerful" delinquent son. He could have given the family prescriptions for changing of behavioral sequences, role distributions, parent-child boundaries and scripts of games. He could have involved the family members in role-playing, sculpting and problem-solving efforts. All of these are useful devices for reaching tactical goals but they do not substitute for the essence of the "active" position of the therapist. From the contextual perspective, an active position requires the therapist to make family members sequentially accountable through multidirected partiality without omitting any member, including the absent ones.

The trust-enhancing impact of the dimension that surfaces ethical balances mobilizes the maximum potential of healing resources. As soon as therapeutic efforts are directed at balances of merit rather than at the nature of feelings or transactions, the self-reinvesting process of mutual trustbuilding has begun.

FOUR CONTEXTUAL DIMENSIONS

In forming his therapeutic strategies and plans, the contextual therapist has to consider four dimensions of relational dynamics:

Facts or Destiny

The factual configuration of one's origins and genetic rootedness in sex, race, nationality, religion and family constitute essential determinants of one's basic nature and the fairness of obligations. The therapist should investigate other factual circumstances surrounding his work. He should know about hereditary conditions, lawsuits between family members, involvements with agencies, divorces, adoptions, financial conflicts, physical illnesses and psychosomatic inclinations. Whereas factual circumstances themselves are often unchangeable, their ethical significance depends on the active measures taken by the members toward balancing their impact.

As Fred's family gradually gets involved in therapy, the factual circumstances of the parents' families of origin attain major significance. For example, therapeutic attempts to give attention to the parents' own problems would automatically tend to diminish their pathogenic impact on Fred. Also required, however, is a more specific search that uncovers areas of the parents' own invisible filial loyalties. Most typically, these hidden devotions tend to be connected with the parents' suppressed filial ambivalence or shame.

One of the most frequent factual sources of deeply felt devotion in combination with ambivalent resentment originates from a legacy of "split loyalty." That is, the child grows up with the unresolvable expectation of being disloyal to one parent as evidence of loyalty to the other parent, and vice versa. For the beginning therapist it is often difficult to see how merely focusing attention on the parents' invisible loyalties can help form a new outlet for channeling hidden familial expectations. Having sided with the parents in their roles as potentially victimized victimizers, the therapist will find it easier to be partial to Fred without the risk that implicit disloyalty becomes the price of the son's therapeutic progress. Knowledge of the facts of the parents' own victimization helps to convert their victimizing acts into valid components of a comprehensive balance of merits.

Needs or Psychology

The contextual therapist has to be sufficiently equipped with detailed knowledge of human psychology. Individuals are mentally confined within their unique brain capacities. Their minds are programmed by a mix of motivational mechanisms (e.g., deeper instinctual needs, guilt, learned patterns, perceptions of reality, avoidance of danger, perceived requirements of relationships) and also by the other three dimensions of the relational context. Psychological and psychodynamic literature generally underemphasize the psychology of concern and caring for others as the self's needs. Instead, considerable attention has been directed at the self-serving needs of persons in artificial isolation from the ethics of their vital interests in relational investments.

Naturally, therapy with Fred's family would inevitably lead into an exploration of the parents' motivations and personal existential vantage points. Behind the parents' frustrated anger at Fred, their own deeper lifelong despairs would begin to take shape. The roots of the mother's depression and the father's psychosomatic inclinations might begin to surface. The mechanisms of displacement, projection and reexternalization would become observable. The therapist's parentification by the family members would become apparent through indications of jealously competitive possessiveness and loyalty conflicts that emerge in transference attitudes toward the therapist.

Transactions and Power Alignments

This is the realm of phenomena first made observable through the emergence of the family therapy approach. As the regularity of transpersonal sequences of behavioral patterns was noticed, it was thought to be analogous to the homeostatic properties of cells and organisms. Feedback characteristics of transactional processes have been categorized as systemically regulated. A new descriptive science of games, scapegoating, triangulation, symptomatic recruitment, transfer of symptom, role complementation, mystification and double-binding then developed. The striking regularity of these phenomena had been overlooked and strategically ignored by practitioners of traditional individual psychotherapy. Conversely, almost without fail, family therapists were able to return school-phobic children to school within days or weeks. This often occurred after years of futile individual child therapy efforts. Characteristically, as soon as the school-phobic or delinquent child was helped to give up the symptom, a sudden shift presented a new family member as the symptomatic one.

The contextual therapist has to obtain as much knowledge of the phenomena of transactional communication sequences and patterns as possible. Provided that the therapist can begin to discern the ethical implications underlying these transactions, their regularities or systemic patterns constitute one window through which the individual-based psychological understanding of each family member can be broadened into a relational context of expertise and competence.

An important aspect of transactional strategic planning pertains to roles played by society's agencies. The school, the court and welfare agencies are vitally important resources that have to be included in a well-orchestrated cooperation that aims at mutual trust rather than at competitiveness. However, the contextual therapist has to remember not to reify and unduly personify transactional-systemic patterns as the ultimate sources of an impersonal "family malfunction" or "pathology." These patterns are epiphenomena of the underlying multiple self-other dynamics, ultimately regulated by the ethics of the quality and symmetry of trust investments and balances of fairness.

Although an important therapeutic tool and the primary "technique" of classical family therapy, a mere prescriptive rearrangement of transaction in itself often risks long-range disloyalty, even if it momentarily succeeds according to the value criteria of the therapist and of society. Furthermore, by defining the terms of other people's family relationships, the transactionally prescriptive family therapist assumes part of the family's responsibility and recruits the family members into a newly found passive dependence on the therapist.

With these cautions in mind, the contextual therapist can find many applications of transactional tactical designs, e.g., for overcoming the parents' resistance to permitting the child to repay filial accountability through means other than self-destructive captive devotion and sacrificed autonomy. A carefully detailed examination of satisfaction patterns will be necessary for discovering the realistic needs of parents which could serve as goals of action plans to be designed by the adolescent in team collaboration with the therapist. The therapist thus becomes a consultant for the catalysis of a living give-and-take of a more equitable kind. Accordingly, Fred would be reassured that the therapeutic design includes an acknowledgment of filial devotion. He would also be liberated for renewed autonomous effort and even for a ventilation of his ambivalent resentment of his parents. Furthermore, his positive regard (transference) for the therapist would be cast into a loyal filial context.

Merit or Relational Ethics

Since merit is an ethical issue, it is not included among the motivational factors traditionally considered in psychology or psychotherapy. Moreover, as a relational balance factor, merit is not contained in one individual's mind. The rapidly changing accounts of the equity of give-and-take determine the fluctuations of merit balances between two people. To the extent that I benefit from your contribution, I become indebted to you and you obtain entitlement on the merit side of your "ledger."[2] Then when I contribute to you or at least acknowledge your credit, I begin to restore the merit balance. The following vignette serves to illustrate how significantly ethical dilemmas contribute to relational imbalances:

A successfully married man displays fear and reluctance over becoming a parent. An only child, he tends to be guilt-ridden over his avoidance of a demanding and aging mother. He views her with ambivalent contempt and resentment.

He is aware that his relationship with his mother carries over to his treatment of his wife, whom he periodically berates and accuses with great passion. To his puzzlement, her ladylike image of womanly gentleness irritates him, though this was a primary motivation in his wanting to marry her.

In reality, his marriage is encumbered with a loyalty conflict. In an ethically invalid substitution, he has moved to exonerate his mother at his wife's expense. If he could be helped to find a way to be realistically available to his mother without jeopardizing his autonomous interests, he may gain new entitlements for marital and parenting commitments.

The contextual therapist must have the conviction that through caring about the partner's justified interests (merits), the self does not merely indulge in noble altruism but obtains the benefits of increased entitlement, i.e., the deepest source of autonomous individuation and growth. Balances of earned merit, i.e., of entitlement versus indebtedness (E-I), constitute the individual's ethical link with his legacy-based obligations as well as with his fellow individuals. By utilizing merit as a stategic leverage, contextual therapy takes a lead in helping the profession of psychotherapy recover from the dehumanization caused by the use of "valueless" pragmatism. This ideology opted to sever the resources of trustworthiness both in contemporary everyday life and in psychotherapy. Viewed from the vantage point of merit as a contextual dimension, Fred should be recruited to become an architect of his family's rebuilt trustworthiness. By investing appropriate new initiatives of trust, he increases his entitlement to acknowledgment of his acts of filial devotion, and to the pursuit of his own autonomous goals, e.g., to forming peer relationships. Consequently, his moves toward autonomy become progressively liberated from encumberment with guilt born of disloyalty. With the help of the therapist, Fred should make efforts to extend reasonable concern rather than self-destructive devotion toward his parents. As a result of these efforts, the parents eventually experience a diminished degree of a sense of loss and pain connected with their son's growth and individuation. Simultaneously, Fred's disappointment and discouragement over the lack of parental approval of his efforts at maturation is buffered through the therapist's skill and expertise.

FURTHER THERAPEUTIC IMPLICATIONS

Significant benefits emerge from the growing recognition of the therapeutic leverage of ethical multilaterality. Chief among them is the fact that it has narrowed the lag that family therapy created between its offer of a systemic understanding of relational mechanisms and its demand for multidirected professional contractual ethics. Underemphasized in classical family therapy literature, it is his multidirected contractual ethics that nonetheless enable the family therapist, or any therapist, to resist accepting the overt symptomatic picture as a sufficient definition of his professional task. As the most blatant example, he should never accept the assertion that destructive marital fighting leaves the couple's small dependent children unaffected and that the children are thus outside of his contractual responsibility and unworthy of his concern.

Under the guiding rationale of its trust-building strategies, contextual therapy includes such particular goals as:

- The internalization of the therapist's empathy and trustworthiness;
- The mobilization of the resources of fair reciprocity via an examination of intermember accountability;
- Including all relating partners into the rejunctive plan;
- The capacity to work with everyone's reistance to change;
- The capacity to differentiate between the unchangeable fact of shared rootedness and the vicissitudes of emotional attitudes like love or hate, friendship or disaffiliation;
- The capacity for a realistic rebalancing of both legacy expectations and stagnant interindividual ledgers;
- The revision and reworking of invisible loyalties;
- Correction of invalid ethical substitutions;
- Work toward deparentification of children;
- Transformation of passively dependent attitudes into actively accountable initiative and planning.

Occasionally, the following more traditional particular goals may also be utilized by the contextual therapist:

- Insight and owning up to one's emotions;
- Prescription, restucturing and the suggestion of behavioral patterns;
- Transference explorations;
- Uncovering secrets;
- Improvement of communication styles and the capacity for listening.

The indication for contextual therapy, family therapy or psychotherapy of any kind does not hinge on individual (medical-psychological) diagnosis of any sort. It depends instead on the severity of the condition, the motivation of the afflicted persons and the availability of a competent therapist. Organic brain damage in a child is "incurable" through psychotherapy. Yet many families of organically handicapped children are prime beneficiaries of contextual therapy. Resource rather than causality is the chief rationale of all psychotherapy.

Contextual therapy includes the techniques and advantages of all reasonable individual psychotherapy approaches. It adds additional leverages of relational resources for helping the symptomatic individual. Moreover, it extends its effects to those whose affliction is hidden but not necessarily secondary. Therefore, there is no reasonable contraindication to the contextual enrichment of therapy in disorders of mind or moderate severity. Furthermore, it is eminently indicated in cases of vital life or death severity. This includes school phobia, anorexia, psychotic disintegration and threatened suicide. Experience indicates that the "language" of fairness versus unfairness is as accessible to people of impoverished urban ghettos as it is to people of high educational or social status. The ethical emphasis of contextual therapy is universally applicable to the human condition.

SUMMARY

Utility

As it now stands, contextual therapy offers a viable approach for treating individuals through mobilizing the resources of family relationships. Additional work will be required for developing a further integration of useful therapeutic knowledge with the ethical dimension of contextual therapy. Such a comprehensive approach will help in situations where other approaches meet severe limitations. Many cases of depression are most receptive to intervention through exploring balances of entitlement and indebtedness. For example, motivations for suicide or self-sacrificial behavior are obviously related to the dimension of merit balances.

Contextual therapy makes use of the resources of trust inherent in hidden relational investments, instead of focusing on an effort to fight pathology or to impose "change" in the service of social conformity. It also helps to produce more reliable, lasting therapeutic change by staving off the development of existential guilt over symptomatic improvement with its implications of disloyalty. Moreover, it recognizes that overdevotion and the covertly overloyal sacrifice of autonomy may contain utilizable therapeutic leverages.

The Therapeutic Contract

The main therapeutic clout of contextual therapy resides in its multipersonal contract, and leads to a need for defining the ethics of relationship. Increased trustworthiness constitutes the aim of this ethic, and is not to be confused with judgmental moralizing or anethical reductionism of the psychological or systemic variety.

Training

Contextual therapy places a great demand on professional education and a new form of training psychotherapists will probably follow from it. Contextual training will benefit supervisory specialists and large numbers of service deliverers. Though contextual therapy continues to gain attention from a variety of directions, the model may encounter "political" resistance on the part of "schools" and "professions."

Prevention

Through its multidirected partiality, the contextual approach is inherently preventive. Its preventive notions are anchored in the present generation's personal investment in the survival interests of future generations of offspring. The preventive leverages are based on a temporal extension of the ethical principles of concern, traditionally defined in medical ethics as *primum nil nocere*.

REFERENCES

1. Boszormenyi-Nagy, I. From family therapy to a psychology of relationships: Fictions of the individual and fictions of the family. *Comprehensive Psychiatry, 7(5):* 408–423, 1966.
2. Boszormenyi-Nagy, I., & Spark, G. *Invisible Loyalties: Reciprocity in Intergenerational Family Therapy.* New York: Harper & Row, 1973.
3. Boszormenyi-Nagy, I., & Krasner, B. R. Trust-based therapy: A contextual approach. *American Journal of Psychiatry,* 137:767–775, 1980.
4. Boszormenyi-Nagy, I., & Ulrich, D. Contextual family therapy. In A. S. Gurman

& D. P. Kniskern (Eds.), *Handbook of Family Therapy*. New York: Brunner/Mazel, 1981.
5. Boszormenyi-Nagy, I. Behavior change through family change. In A. Burton (Ed.), *What Makes Behavior Change Possible?* New York: Brunner/Mazel, 1976, pp. 227–258.

14

Trust-Based Therapy: A Contextual Approach

[This paper was written with Barbara R. Krasner, Ph.D.]

*This chapter connects the crucial relational and therapeutic require-
ments of trust formation with the relational consequences of trustworthiness. Trust and trustworthiness interlock to produce an upward
spiral of balanced relational growth among family members. The
therapist's role is defined as the elicitor of an intermember dialogue
of a trust-enhancing nature.*

*Contextual therapy has emerged from the practice of both classical
individual and family therapies, and its major contribution lies in the
discovery that the key dynamic of relationships is merited trust (Dimension IV). The same is claimed as the foremost therapeutic leverage in
family treatment of any kind. Merited trust applies also to a person's
relatedness to his or her multigenerational roots with their specific
racial, religious or ethnic facets: Having roots and legacies in comn on
is a nonsubstitutive bond among people. And all legacies constitute
an ethical claim on the offspring's consideration.*

*A shift in the concepts of legacy can be discerned in the current
article: "Receiving life, benefits, skills and guidance from their roots,
the offspring are behooved to transmit them in kind to future generations." Today's (Boszormenyi-Nagy & Krasner, 1986) formulations
stress the offspring's duty to sort out and discover what most benefits
subsequent posterity rather than just transmit tradition "in kind."
Hence, real legacy expectations cannot, by their very nature, be "un-*

fair." *By contrast, other transgenerational expectations (e.g., certain parental delegations) can be unfair. The concept of legacy expectations has thus moved from the notion of repayment to the past toward that of reinvestment in the future.*

A distinction between "tactical" siding and merit-guided, multidirectional partiality is suggested by the circumstance that while being temporarily partial to one member, the therapist becomes, simultaneously, partial against another member.

By the fact that his clients turn toward him for help, the therapist is automatically a recipient of trust. How will he use their trust? Will he channel it into his own narcissistic desires for superiority, into his one-to-one relating with a client or into strengthening relationships between his clients?

The contextual therapist's requisite convictions and skills are enumerated in the latter part of the chapter. They all pertain to the elicitation of resources pertaining to Dimension IV of the contextual approach: accountability, fair consideration of posterity's benefits and attention to the fair distribution of burdens and credits.

REFERENCE

Boszormenyi-Nagy, I., & Krasner, B. *Between give and take.* New York: Brunner/Mazel, 1986.

Contextual therapy has emerged from the practice of both individual and classical (transactional-systemic) family therapy. Its basic rationale is that the key dynamic of relationships is the trustworthiness that emerges from mutual consideration of all family members. Its contract maintains a simultaneous, multiple consideration of all the people affected by therapeutic intervention. Contextual therapy is not confined to any one model of practice, although it is founded on specific principles and methods. Its implications are obvious when applied to relationships, yet they are also evident in the aspects of individual approaches that are concerned with the therapist's liability and accountability. Although it encompasses the viable contributions of all schools of psychotherapy, contextual therapy operates out of its specific, ethically founded guidelines and strategies.

Contextual therapy has emerged out of our 45 combined years of psychotherapeutic experience, which includes intensive work with psychotic individuals, extensive experience with children, including the very young, and attempts at healing human suffering across all classes and layers of society (1). The contextual approach incorporates tenets of both individual therapy and classical (conjoint) family therapy, but its major contribution lies in the discovery that the key dynamic of relationships is merited trust. Acknowledging the concept of merited trust leads to a fundamentally new perspective of therapy: simultaneous multilateral consideration of more than one human being. Concern, trustworthiness, adversariness, exploitation, and fair mutuality between family members are heretofore neglected facets of therapy. This radical resource-oriented departure from the traditional (medical or psychological) individual perspective is hard to overemphasize.

For long-range effectiveness, we propose that the foremost therapeutic leverage lies in the processes of trust investments within the family and between family members and the therapist. Because family members are bound to each other by the ethical dimension of mutual trust, or lack of it, we also propose that a sufficiently responsible therapeutic contract is obliged to take account of all persons potentially affected by professional intervention (multidirectedness). Multidirectional accountability is also the key ingredient of therapeutic efficacy. It establishes the therapist's own trustworthiness and provides him or her with a rationale to help avoid the pitfalls of unilateral siding and of manipulation through countertransference. In our view, contextual therapy offers a strategic guideline that holds implications for all forms of psychotherapy.

The term "context" was chosen to indicate the dynamic connectedness of a person with his or her significant relationships. That is, while an individual is a discrete and unique biological entity, dynamically each person's life derives meaning through reference to a social context. Thus the word "context" is used to describe the long-term relational involvement of people, both in its systemic and multi-individual aspects, and includes four key dimensions: the factual, the psychological, the transactional, and the ethical (2). The ethical dimension may be illuminated most simply by the example of a mother who reliably cares for her baby. Her active concern becomes the source of her infant's trust, which, of course, eventually provides the relational and psychological foundations of his or her psychosocial development (3). By being caring, available, and accessible, functionally she helps her infant survive, develop, and function in the world. Her trustworthiness is also an ethical contribution. Whatever its comparative limitations, her mothering is a trustable reality based on personal investment and accumulates merit for her in the unique context of the parent-child relationship. The personal uniqueness of both parent and child is just as much a concern in the contextual view as are their transactional "systemic" roles.

In addition to its key dynamic of merited trust or "merit ledger" (reference 1, pp. 78, 371), context also refers to a person's relatedness to his or her multigenerational roots, with their specific racial, religious, and ethnic facets. The dynamic of merited trust was originally understood as interindividual in nature. In addition, however, having roots in common is transpersonal and can convey a legacy that is the result of expectations handed down from generation to generation. More than a theory, therapy based on trust resources is a pragmatic strategy that helps contextual therapists seize on evident signs of mistrust as potential resources for trust building.

A desired commodity, trust reduces the emotional cost of relational investment. This is illustrated by situations in which people cannot tolerate close relationships despite their desperate hunger for closeness. Trust is required as an initial investment in relationships, after which a person can take further steps toward trust building. It is also a necessity for being able to accept periods of transitory unfairness, a situation that is unavoidable in any relationship. A fluctuation of temporarily unilateral dependence, imposition, or even exploitation characterizes close relationships. Balance in relationships is kept through long-range multilaterality, which bridges and equilibrates short-term periods of unfairness and loss of trustworthiness.

ROOTS AND RELATIONSHIPS

The therapeutic significance of the life-long implications of legacy-bound (parent-child) relationships has been grossly disregarded by the traditions of both classical individual and classical family therapy, not to mention many symptom-oriented therapeutic fads. People stay tied to their families of origin long after it appears that family members have ended their connections with each other either by choice or perforce. Who lived for them, who wanted them, who was available to them, and who made material and relational investments in them are fundamental factors in their attitudes toward the world. Having roots and legacies in common is a nonsubstitutive bond among people that not only outlasts physical and geographical separations from families of origin but influences the degree to which offspring can be free to commit themselves to relationships outside of their original ties, including marriage and parenthood of their own. The long-term legacies of parental accountability and filial loyalty are inescapably weighty. A lack of interaction, negative affect, and even indifferent attitudes and abusive behavior may affect parent-child linkages but per se cannot devalue or terminate their importance. Even strong rebuke or revenge is usually meant to test a parent's or child's willingness to respond rather than to end the relationship. Procreation and roots-in-common invariably supersede the quality of the relation as the stimulus for continuity and mutual concern.

As prior investments in past and future generations, relational legacies are not only a part of a person's factual destiny but are an ethical claim. That is, receiving people are obliged to give. Expecting people are obliged to meet expectations. Over-available or over-performing relatives, for example, are entitled to acknowledgment of their investments and merits. In the first place, common roots, legacies, and linkages to racial, religious, ethnic, and familial contexts are non-substitutable configurations that contribute to an individual's uniqueness. In the second place, common bonds comprise a demand for balance in relationships. Merited trust born of mutual caring is the mainstay of such a balance.

Broader Implications of Intergenerational Legacies

Legacy-based therapeutic strategies are fundamentally different from psychological or transactional designs. As basic contextual determinants of relationships, legacies are created neither by emotional states nor by power alignments. If therapists are unable to base their convictions about the significance of legacies on their own relational experiences, they may well fall into the trap of the typical contemporary observer of human relationships: in this view repayment of obligations emanating from procreation is optional and depends on the participants' feelings and a variety of power manipulations. In subscribing to such a view, therapists surrender the major dimension of their therapeutic leverage.

Without entering into a debate on what constitutes deep versus superficial therapy, it can be said that an overt concern with relational responsibility almost instantaneously leads the therapist into depth dimensions of relationships. The question of relational responsibility is a private aspect of human life and is seldom faced even between partners themselves. Typically, discussion of the issue is either avoided and leads to isolation, to increasing relational (ethical) stagnation, pathogenicity, and untenability of relationships, or to painful and threatening confrontations. The contextual therapist is thus obliged to learn how to guide people through the most heated, direct, and controversial aspects of their relationship, that is, toward responsibility for trustworthiness. Contrary to its surface appearance, the contextual approach is often short-term rather than long-term and direct rather than intellectualized or rationalistic.

TRUSTWORTHINESS AS A PROPERTY OF RELATIONSHIPS

The result of mutual consideration and actual exchange, trustworthiness is always a relational property of at least two people and cannot be reduced to the psychological universe of either one of them. Although it interlocks with the concept of basic trust as a psychological characteristic (3), trustworthiness always results from a multilateral investment of relating partners on behalf of their mutual welfare and life interests. Trustworthiness is a characteristic of mature, nonexploitative (object) relations of any kind and, for example, determines whether an exciting love affair can be converted into an enduring marriage. It connects and channels the vicissitudes of the opposing needs of two or more persons in a relationship. Moreover, trustworthiness enables ego strength to be invested in controlling one's tendencies toward an exploitative misuse of close relationships and ultimately serves self-interest through maintaining the relational resource. Furthermore, caring for another person's needs can enhance personal satisfaction through empathy and love.

Retaining a trustworthy relationship is in the reality interest of all participants. A capacity for consideration and responsibility toward another person is thus to be viewed as neither an outgrowth of traditional guilt-based morality nor as a psychodynamic motive "located" in the superego. In practice, concentration on questions associated with the trustworthiness of close relationships incorporates and uses the therapeutic dimensions of individual-oriented psychotherapy like ego strength, reality testing, projections, and insight into distortions. Yet it also goes beyond them in pursuit of a balanced give and take in relationships. From the perspective of contextual therapy, the balance of give and take in relationships is a more sensitive and more accurate measure of reality distortions than is the insight-oriented self-reflection of one individual.

RESIDUAL TRUST AND FAMILY LEGACIES

In therapy the implications of transgenerational legacies are most readily visible in the "accounts" that exist in the reproductive aspects of parent-child relationships. The legacy of parental accountability originates from the existential fact of reproduction. Having given life to a dependent infant, parents owe it nurturance. Conversely, the legacy of filial loyalty originates from the fact of conception, early human survival, and growth. Children are linked to their parents by the event of birth; they are recipients of biological life, psychological endowment, nurturant care, and techniques for staying alive. Receiving life, benefits, skills, and guidance from their roots, the offspring are behooved to transmit them in kind to future generations. Moreover, it should be noted that in modified form the legacy of filial loyalty exists even when children have been given up or abandoned very early in life. Whatever the degree of parental responsibility or behavior after a child's birth, the child's relationship to the parents who give him or her life is a unique, nonsubstitutable, and unreworkable fact of his or her existence. Even in cases of adoption, paradoxically perhaps, regard for the adoptive child's entitlement to his or her roots tends to improve the relationship with the adoptive parents.

Specifics of a given legacy shape the nature of both parental expectations and filial response to their expectations. For example, the sacrifice of a martyred family member can intensify the heirs' obligation to excel, or, marred by shame, the reputation of a family member can demand exoneration for generations to come. A case in point is the situation of the daughter of an alcoholic father. Bearing the weight of her father's former behavior and apparent failure, she may press her son toward perfection to make up for her filial shame. Overburdened by unfair legacy expectations, her son is faced with the unacceptable choices of abandoning his mother physically or emotionally or of submitting to her impossible demands. More realistically, contextual therapy offers him still another choice: he can help free himself and his mother for a new balance of trust and fairness in their relationship. Overcoming the mistrust, resentment, and stagnation that have accrued from his mother's undue substitutive and compensatory expectations of him, her son can find ways to discover aspects of his grandfather's behavior which serve to exonerate his life. Through active strategic work he can also determine and implement his own terms for accountably fulfilling his legacy rather than becoming entrapped into deferring to his mother's terms or simply learning to evade them.

MULTIDIRECTED PARTIALITY: GUIDELINE TO CONTEXTUAL THERAPY

Multidirected partiality (4), contextual therapy's basic methodology, is used to help the therapist guide clients toward a fresh assessment of legacy expectations and toward more interindividual fairness and trust. It assumes that sooner or later contextual therapists must be prepared to side with all family members, present or absent. It requires a therapist to hear and give courage to each family member as he or she struggles to bring to the surface his or her side. It is a process of consecutive siding with now one and now the other relating partner in order to help family members state their respective terms with some confidence that opposing views can be heard and tolerated. Multidirected partiality is also meant to provide a paradigm that eventually can enable family members to listen and respond to one another's terms.

Multidirected partiality differs from the therapeutic stances of nonpartial neutrality on the one hand and stagnant unilateral partiality on the other. In our view, nonpartial neutrality is probably humanly impossible to attain, and traditional, individual-oriented therapy typically encourages fixed one-sidedness. Conversely, effectively employed, multidirected partiality begins a constructive process of trust building. It also requires that the therapist have the courage to side temporarily against family members as well as with them. It should be noted that consecutive siding with relating partners is a protection against the dangers of countertransference reactions.

Here a distinction should be made between the strategy of multidirected partiality and relational multilaterality, which is an inherently basic aspect of relationships. Multilaterality means that any action or transaction has at least two sides. In ethical terms it means that usually each of the two partners tends to approach the relationship with a self-centered viewpoint. The degree of fairness in a relationship is determined by the relative consideration each partner accords the other. Since neither only one party nor only an outsider can explore the relative merit accounts between them, the partners should be helped to explore and define their own mutual terms for fairness. For example, in case of adoption the adoptive parents should determine the terms of their own vulnerabilities and requirements for consideration but in the long run it should be the adopted child who determines his own terms of needs and entitlements. The therapist's role is to elicit the family members' active search for a definition and then assertion of their respective terms rather than to inject his or her own moral or behavioral value preferences. By offering consecutive multidirected partiality the therapist encourages family members to explore their own multilaterality. However, the therapist is not a contextually rooted participant in the family members' multilateral relationships. He or she is a natural partner only to the multilaterality of his or her own relationships, e.g., with his or her spouse, children, parents, and others of significance.

Identifying Trust in Stagnant Relationships

The following excerpt demonstrates a contextual process examination of trustworthiness among three family members who are stuck in their relationships with each other (stagnation). What begins as an initial diagnosis of an adolescent turns into a relational exploration of multi-individual diagnoses. The clinical material was obtained by way of a multidirected contract through which the therapist became accountable to all family members who in turn were helped to be accountable to each other. The multidirected therapeutic contract would have been in force whether or not all family members were present at the session.

Bob, a 16-year-old adopted, only son of a middle-class couple, was hospitalized after his second suicide attempt. In the evaluation interview Bob's father took a long time enumerating Bob's many doings: school failure, drug involvements, disrespectful behavior, and so forth. As a first attempt at developing trust resources, without disconfirming the validity of the father's concerns, the interviewer asked whether the parents could recall any instance in which Bob offered a helpful, concerned, or caring attitude to them. The mother denied that this had ever happened. The absurd intensity of her response could be taken as evidence of pathological scapegoating on the mother's part. However, the contextual therapist began to wonder about the possible merits on her side. How could he find aspects of her that would justify his contracting with her with genuine partiality? At this moment she was probably close to a point where she could describe the difficulties of her own childhood. The therapist envisaged that she might be manifesting a desperate overreaction to the fact that Bob's growth would soon lead to her loss of his regular companionship. Consequently, the therapist tried to elicit trust through exploring other aspects of Bob's merit, partly to be able to contract with him, partly to give the parents an opportunity to acknowledge his victimization, and ultimately to find new ways for Bob to display filial loyalty.

At another level of concern, the therapist asked Bob about his feelings concerning adoption. Bob responded that he would like to meet his natural mother but could not conceive of doing something that "brutal" to her. By this time the therapist had factual evidence of Bob's capacity for consideration, especially when Bob added that he did not want to hurt his adoptive parents, either. The merit of the victim becomes immediately obvious: he holds responsibility for not hurting the adult world that betrayed him at the beginning of his life.

From here on engagement in issues of trustworthiness became unavoidable and led directly into the therapist's curiosity about the parents' victimization in their own childhood. The movement from stagnation toward trust building had begun.

In this evaluation and assessment, the contextual therapist initially aimed at exploring the relational context of Bob's motivation to commit suicide. In fact, Bob spontaneously responded to the therapist's questioning by linking his self-destructive inclinations to his adoptive mother's habitual and overt disconfirmation of all his accrued merit as a loving son. In response to Bob's disclosures, the therapist pointed out the young man's concerns for both his natural and adoptive parents. Furthermore, he pointed out that it behooved Bob's parents to acknowledge their son's caring and consideration, which reflected favorably on them as well. At this moment Bob was able to say how much he loved his adoptive parents. With this, his mother started to cry and walked out of the room. Subsequently his father was able to reveal that when he was away on business trips, Bob offered his mother comfort in her sadness and anxiety. This acknowledgment gave the therapist an opportunity to be partial to Bob while also endorsing the father's fairness. Obviously, blame was directed at the mother at this point, and even when she returned to the room she still was unable to acknowledge Bob's personal availability. This instance of extreme mistrust presented an opportunity to encourage her to describe the pain of her own childhood experiences. This, in turn, enabled the therapist to be genuinely partial to her as a victim of the past who presently appeared to be a victimizer.

The father's acknowledgment of Bob's active investment in his parents' well-being marked the beginning of strongly directive therapeutic explorations whose goals included 1) beginning to face intermember fairness and legacies, 2) reducing unfair legacy expectations by acknowledging them and redesigning repayment, 3) correcting one-sided, sometimes distorted, always unaddressed views of each other among family members, and 4) rebalancing the give and take among family members. In a brief time all of the family members had taken initial steps toward personal accountability for responsible action. As trust and trustworthiness began their upward spiral, new chances for positive collaboration and balanced relational growth among family members were likely to occur.

By the end of the initial session the famly's concern for each other's well-being began to materialize in the midst of resentment, fears, and accusations. By being prodded to consider the merit as well as the pathology in his or her relationships, in some measure each person could begin to rethink his or her options. The therapist's concern about multidirectionality encouraged each of them to raise his or her side within the hearing of the others, and because they could be heard on their own terms each person was more willing to overcome his or her resistance to listening to the terms of others. After they were helped to voice both satisfactions and disappointments over the quality of their relationships, they could become somewhat freer to dwell on their own parts in contributing to unfair relating. By grasping the notion of joint responsibility for the modes of behavior among them each person was more able to examine interindividual sources of chronic mistrust. All the family members began to comprehend that each of them had made an investment in the welfare of the others and that to be productive these investments needed to be recognized and affirmed rather than discredited or negated. Moreover, no one had been designated as a scapegoat for the situation, and the session had taken place without condemning Bob's parents for the sake of his therapy.

Achieving Autonomy in the Family Context

Given a contractual concern for all family members, the therapist challenged some of the intrinsic unfairness in the family members' ways of treating each other. For example, the parents were charged with the task of learning how to acknowledge Bob's actual commitment and investment in their well-being. They were also asked to rethink on their own the implications of their endless list of demands. Was it actually Bob of whom they had a right to expect so much, or was it unfinished business with their families of origin that had subtly shifted their own filial legacies onto their son (see "the revolving slate," reference 1, pp. 65–67).

Over time Bob has been helped to realign the degree to which he was entitled to live his own life with the degree to which he was required to meet some of his parents' expectations of him. Diminishing the pseudo-adversity between Bob and his parents has established a new sense of security in the family. Fresh confidence about the continuing existence of mutual concern and loyalty among family members has freed Bob to mature in a number of ways. By assuring his parents of his fundamental concern for them, he became likely to win more freedom to commit himself to peer relationships. He was also likely to find more room in which to develop his sexual role and even to explore his biological origins. Eventually he will be helped to achieve this goal through learning how to repay his filial indebtedness in age-appropriate terms. In turn, his parents will be helped to define for themselves specifically what they require of Bob. They will be helped to learn how to state their expectations directly rather than by innuendo and to accept and acknowledge Bob's payments of his loyalty obligations in reasonable "installments." Moreover, they will be helped to learn that he cannot be used indefinitely to compensate his parents for what they may have lost in their own childhoods.

If possible, Bob's parents will be helped to revise their expectations of their son by reconsidering how they themselves have or have not met the terms of their own filial legacies. In clinical descriptions it is customary to ascribe inflexible parental clinging almost exclusively in terms of possessiveness and control through power measures. Conversely, we propose that parents who are overburdened with unmet legacy requirements, whether self-imposed or imposed by their own parents, will inevitably overburden their children. Thus recognizing and reworking long-standing unfairness in their own family legacies will not only free parents from a fruitless expenditure of energy in defensive and retributive behavior but will free their offspring from a similar fate. For example, if his parents were to find sources of trust and appreciation within their original relationships, Bob would become more able to "leave" them and invest his energy in his own welfare and development. Becoming less central to his parents' well-being, because of the investments of other people in their lives, he would feel less helpless. Undefined and boundless obligations invariably lead to destructive parentification of children (1).

In future sessions Bob will continue to be a recipient of therapeutic consideration, but the multidirected contextual approach will incorporate his parents as full partners in the therapeutic effort. As therapy progresses the substitutive function of Bob's symptoms is likely to decrease, and signs of his parents' difficulties are likely to surface with increasing clarity. The parents' childhood struggles will emerge, along with long-standing conflicts over their own invisible filial loyalties.

Their marital problems will also come to the fore. From Bob's side, age-appropriate, peer-related problems will be raised and considered. Suicide will be viewed as an attempt to claim entitlement in the context of his family's unfulfillable, excessive expectations. Children who are locked into the endless spiral of expectation of perfection on the one hand and their parents' withholding of recognition on the other are candidates for self-destructive patterns. We view the threat of suicide as an eminent example of the pathogenicity of mistrust and the value of the preventive use of a family's trust resources, as opposed to pathology within individuals, which is the preoccupation of traditional, individual-oriented therapy.

By extending his efforts beyond the intrapsychic dynamics of one individual, the therapist avoided the trap of psychological reductionism. Instead, he identified the family's resources for helping Bob rather than choosing either to ignore or foreclose them. He drew family members toward responsible individuation instead of simply reinforcing the isolation, emotional distance, and mistrust that already existed among them. He began the multilateral process of identifying and mobilizing the residual trust that resided in the family, even in the midst of long-standing, acrimonious relating.

ELEMENTS OF CONTEXTUAL THERAPY

Contextual Assessment

In a contextual evaluation indications of injured trustworthiness between parents and offspring are regarded as signals for potential trust-building. Fundamental to the evaluation is the therapist's capacity to assess some acknowledgeable merit in every family member. Merit in relationships emerges from prior investments of trustworthiness that are capable of yielding interest and returns in trustworthy relating. Of course, all relational accounts are composed of both assets and debits. Assets are the sum total of past and present investments of care, concern, consideration, and devotion. Debits are the sum total of inconsideration, lack of acknowledgment, neglect, abuse, emotional or physical abandonment, or any combination of acts amounting to a failure of commitment and resulting in accrued mistrust. In any case, acknowledgment of merit is a first step on the way to fair return. In fact, even the process of taking an inventory of assets and debits can serve to readdress ethically stagnant relating. The weight of therapy is thereby redistributed from an emphasis on the removal, interruption, relabelling, or restructuring of pathological behavior to a concentration on resources inherent in the "merit ledgers" or balances of accounts among people involved in a relationship (1).

Therapy

Conducting therapy requires specific training in the contextual approach and skill with a broad spectrum of psychotherapeutic methods. The more comprehensive the therapist's competence, the more he or she is able to assess the facets of a client's context and to integrate the four dimensions of contextual therapy into therapeutic planning. Factual circumstances, communication and transactions, psychology, and merit are elements that combine to determine the outcomes of therapy. In Bob's case, some of his family's factual circumstances include his parents' medical reasons for not having a natural child, the age at which Bob was adopted, and information about his natural parents. The fact of adoption also has a built-in legacy requirement of its own. Despite implicit suggestions of irresponsibility customarily ascribed to people who give their children up for adoption, no adoptive child, or anyone else for that matter, can accept the notion that his natural parent is worthless. Consequently, understanding the reasons why their natural parents gave them up is always a task for adopted children.

In addition to factual circumstances, systemic patterns and role structures associated with a family's communication and transactions are of obvious importance to the therapeutic process. These patterns, sequences, and structures represent the overt, symptomatic level of relational exchanges and are richly characterized in the literature of classical family therapy.

A knowledge of psychology is the third dimension of the contextual approach, which presumes familiarity with intrapsychic development and dynamics. The ego strengths and defenses of each family member, for example, provide the therapist with practical knowledge. In the case illustration Bob's mother may be diagnosed as having a rigidly paranoid type of personality. Her consistent projective inclinations suggest limitations that are to be considered in designing therapeutic strategies. However, initially it is the adolescent's suicidal inclination rather than his mother's psychodynamic configurations that should be the crucial therapeutic and preventive concern. The individually focused question of bypassing the mother's intrapsychic priorities rather than working them through must be subordinated temporarily to the prospect of danger to Bob's life. Once the immediate reality of this priority has been addressed satisfactorily, his mother's entitlement to make claims in her relationships will also be considered. In any case, from a contextual perspective multilateral considerations of entitlement and valid indebtedness should not be guidelines and strategies geared simply to each person's intrapsychic dynamics.

The ethical or trust-building dimension of contextual therapy is its guiding consideration. Given his concern for fairness among relating partners, the contextual therapist presumes that the ethic or filial accountability originates from relational reality rather than from guilt anchored in Bob's superego. Therefore he will be guided by each family member's obligation to recognize the impact of legacy expectations and to acknowledge the merit of each person's contributions to the quality of his or her relationships. This guideline is predicated on the fact that the improved quality of family relationships is a shared interest of all family members.

The multilateral contract marks a transition from diagnosing immediately noticeable intrapsychic symptomatology toward gradually uncovering the facets of relational circumstances. By eliciting trust from all family members the therapist can help each of them turn to him in an atmosphere of growing receptivity to help. Furthermore, the trust elicited by the therapist serves to reveal how Bob's inclinations toward suicide intersect with his mother's relationship with her family of origin.

Trust Building and Therapeutic Conviction

Trust building is both the ideological foundation and the primary tool of contextual therapy. It is the process through which residual trust resources among family members or otherwise significant relationships are identified, elicited, mobilized, and used. It is built on the characteristics that provide balance in life: 1) respect for equitability on every member's own terms, 2) integrated give and take in relationships, 3) mutual consideration and "use" of one another, and 4) redistribution of returns from the joint accounts of trust investments.

Clearly there are other powerful forces at play in determining the visible behavior of relating partners. People are also motivated by needs for affection, dependence, and sexuality. People are inclined to use each other unilaterally as objects for transference, displacement, and substitutive retribution. Contextual therapists integrate these factors and others like them but nevertheless proceed from the central conviction that evolving interindividual trustworthiness is the basic fiber of durable relationships and the shortest route to eradicating skewed and distorted behavior.

Knowledge, skill, and personal conviction are all elements in a therapist's capacity to channel and use trust. As a qualified helping professional, the therapist presents himself as worthy of his clients' trust. Over time he will become privy to private aspects of his clients' lives and help them investigate the loyalties in their families of origin, their marriages, and their capacity to parent. As various family members turn to him for help he himself becomes a major if interim recipient of their trust investments, in part because they sense his conviction about multilateral equitability. Trust between therapist and client can flow in a variety of ways:

1. From the outset the therapist receives trust through the client's act of contracting for help. This initial and usually tentative line of trust may be strengthened through the client's response to the therapist's elicitory measures aimed at encouraging people to take initiative on their own behalf.

2. Once clients have returned trust offered to them by a therapeutic investment in their situation the therapist has his own choice to make in terms of how he will use their trust. The therapist can accept the clients' trust, channel it into his own personal relationships, grow and mature from it, and use it to secure his commitment to a responsible

performance of his difficult work, or he can convert his clients' trust into a reservoir that supplies his narcissistic desires of superiority and offers him a power-based notion of therapy. He may even use it as unilateral leverage for refueling his own personal relationships.

3. In the tradition of individually oriented therapy, trust can be channelled into a one-to-one relationship between therapist and client. This mode of using trust can create escalating demands in managing an intensification of transference and countertransference attitudes and needs.

4. Rechannelling trust into the process of strengthening relationships between family members is an alternative to the exclusivity of trust development between client and therapist. Using this option the therapist can inject his own regard for accountability and integrity in relationships. He can help family members reveal one another's unacknowledged consideration and contributions. Through his multidirected trustbuilding efforts, the therapist can elicit responsible attitudes that may lead to a more genuine dialogue (5) among family members.

Using multidirected trust building as a therapeutic methodology requires a knowledge of legacy expectations, a degree of personal maturity, and a set of convictions that can be brought into dialectic exchange.

The skilled contextual therapist operates with a set of convictions that emerge from both his personal and professional experience:

1. Trustworthiness is a decisive relational factor that cannot be reduced to the individual psychologies of the family members.

2. Trustworthiness follows the regulatory forces of earned merit rather than of power. For example, when a person is "successful" in unilaterally exploiting his partner's trust, he inevitably loses ground in maintaining trustworthiness (balance of accounts).

3. Multilateral investments of trust and consideration among family members enhance each person's entitlement to more satisfactory living (multi-laterality). At least in part this conviction must emerge through the initiative, personal, and familial experience of the therapist.

4. The therapist's task is to elicit multilateral investments in rela-

tionships and to identify healing resources for all relating parties (multi-directed partiality). This task is to be differentiated from any tendencies on the part of a therapist to impose his own value judgments.

5. A person's inherited legacy expectations cannot be ignored without an increase in the emotional costliness of living (legacies as present here-and-now relational contexts).

6. Children should not be forced to guarantee age-inappropriate nurturance to their parents or be used as unilateral, captive investors in their parents' depleted accounts of trustworthiness. This conviction is based on the further understanding that both parents and children benefit from balanced parent-child accounts (equitability of interests between parents and children).

The capacity to apply contextual concepts and convictions lies in a variety of skills:

1. Using multidirectionality to elicit and catalyze the active participation of all family members in discovering and mobilizing pockets of residual trust resources (1, chapter 5).

2. Helping people develop appropriate terms for repaying realistic legacy expectations within their specific contexts.

3. Helping unreceptive parents accept their children's attempts to repay them in "installments."

4. Eliciting multilateral investments from participating members of long-term significant relationships without the therapist becoming depleted through the effort. That is, the contextual therapist cannot function indefinitely as a primary source of trustworthiness for his clients or he becomes a captive to expectations that he supply hope, trust, dependent support, limitless empathy, and one-sided partiality to family members.

Many signs indicate that our era has reached a dangerous extreme of relational disintegration. Belief in linear progress toward individuation has resulted in a cost to relational responsibility. It has led to a frightening fragmentation of even nuclear families and to widespread grossly inadequate, often dehumanized child-rearing patterns. Moreover, the disintegration of both small and large communities raises the frightening possibility of a generalized downward spiral of trustworthiness, a condition that leads to pathogenic social patterns.

SUMMARY

The contextual approach stresses relational factors as resources for individual health and strength. Its focus on interindividual trust in family life and legacies introduces a fundamentally new perspective to therapy: the simultaneous consideration of more than one human being as the valid subject of therapeutic intervention. The approach retains an interest in both the singularity of individuals and the transactional-communicational systemic discoveries of classical family therapy.

Therapeutic focus on actively facing and planning for balanced relational accounts leads to a resource-based orientation to therapy. Contextual therapy takes care not to negate signals that indicate pathology but interprets them as evolving from a condition of stagnation between two or more people. Stagnation is usually the result of a lack of trustworthiness in relationships.

Work with families evokes the importance of trust and trustworthiness more sharply than individual-oriented therapy. Close and continuous observation of many families leads the therapist to rediscover the significance of trust over and beyond its worth for early childhood development. If basic trust is essential to emotional development in early childhood, merited trust is a fundamental need of adults. Born of multilateral investments of care and consideration among family members, merited trust is the primary principle of contextual therapy, and trust building is its primary strategy. Initially, merited trust is governed mainly by basic legacies. Parental accountability and filial responsibility are basic legacies that leave an impact, whether or not the participants' behavior seems to justify an investment in each other's welfare. Real or prospective legacy sharing is a residual trust resource that can compensate for transitory unfairness.

Contextual therapy is a complex scheme of interlocking concepts and methodological strategies. Its implications and skillful application require extensive study, training, and experience. While trust building is its guiding principle and its primary goal, at base the contextual approach is eclectic and noncompetitive. It underlies and incorporates all viable therapeutic orientations and strategies. The contractual implications of multidirected consideration of all persons affected by the intervention is a guiding principle for psychotherapy as a whole, and in our view this contract is bound to affect all forms of future professional practice, including individual therapy or counseling. In addition, contextual therapy's approach to relationships may have far-reaching implications for a fresh and creative reconsideration of disintegrative social patterns.

Finally, it should be noted that the multilateral perspective of contextual therapy should lead to an ethic of relationships that requires family members to define or redefine the balance of their relationships. In no way should this process be confused with judging or moralizing. Instead, it is a caring responsibility for the future, i.e., prevention in a genuine sense. The study of early development provides evidence for the relevance of present family behavior to the life options of the dependent offspring. At a more advanced state of evaluation, the value of any psychotherapy will have to be assessed in terms of both curative and preventive impacts. Its multidirected accountability does not only render contextual therapy ethically sound and legally secure, it also provides it with a built-in preventive relevance.

REFERENCES

1. Boszormenyi-Nagy, I., & Spark, G. *Invisible Loyalties: Reciprocity in Intergenerational Family Therapy*. Hagerstown, Md: Harper & Row, 1973.
2. Boszormenyi-Nagy, I., & Ulrich, D. Contextual family therapy. In *Handbook of Family Therapy*. Edited by Gurman A. S. & Kniskern D. P. New York: Brunner/Mazel, 1980.
3. Erikson, E. H. Problems of ego identity. In *Psychological Issues*, vol 1, number 1. Edited by Klein, G. S. New York: International Universities Press, 1959.
4. Boszormenyi-Nagy, I. From family therapy to a psychology of relationships: fictions of the individual and fictions of the family. *Compr. Psychiatry*, 7, 408–423, 1966.
5. Buber, M. *I and Thou*. (Translated by Kaufmann, W.) New York: Charles Scribners' Sons, 1970.

EDITORIAL: BEYOND THE SUPEREGO

What small child has not said to his parents, "It's not fair"? Parents themselves can be heard to remonstrate with their young children, "Now, be fair!" or, on the other hand, "Life isn't fair!" Both children and parents seem to know what each other means by "fair"—each tacitly agreeing to the concept of equitable treatment. Boszormenyi-Nagy and Spark have described in *Invisible Loyalties* (1) how parents act on the basis of their notions of fairness, which derive from their own experiences of just and unjust treatment. These legacies of trans-generational justice are passed on wittingly or unwittingly—perhaps leading to unfair or unrealizable claims on their offspring.

In "Trust-Based Therapy: A Contextual Approach," which appears in this issue of the *Journal*, Boszormenyi-Nagy and Krasner assert that intrafamilial trust is the basis of mental health and the foundation of psychotherapy, a radical shift in our current thinking. Their implied assertion that an important aspect of human relating is an intuitive sense of justice is akin to John Rawl's definition of "justice as fairness" as a basis of the social contract. This article—a summation of work with families over many years—integrates the insights of psychoanalysis and the concepts of systems theory as applied to families but proposes a more inclusive scheme based on intrafamilial ethics.

The ethical dimension that Boszormenyi-Nagy and Krasner empha-size is neither the superego of the Freudian model nor the traditional morality of religion. The authors refer to this dimension as "merited trust"; it refers to the long-term balance of fairness between the gen-erations and within couples and derives from the existential fact that human beings are born into some form of the family and, inevitably, must come to terms with what they deserve, can expect to receive, and what is expected of them within that institution.

People act in ways they expect will gain them reciprocal behavior in return, and when they are treated in ways that they feel their past behavior has not merited, they feel treated unjustly. The bond of trust has been broken and the consequences are often mental "ill health." Parents expect to be and feel accountable to both their children and society for their treatment of them and in turn expect a certain loyalty from their children. Children do feel and act "loyal" to their parents—

whatever forms this loyalty assumes. Uniquely among psychiatrists, Boszormenyi-Nagy and his collaborators have observed, investigated, and "treated" the twisted and fractured bonds of trust within families. We agree that a sense of justice is a dimension of human affairs which transcends individual psychology and is the relational matrix within which people seek and find value in their lives.

Researchers such as Bowlby have given us ample documentation that "attachment" is a fact of human existence. Students of object relations have provided clinical data and explanatory theories to this effect, perhaps best expressed by an abused child patient of Fairbairn's who said, when asked if she wanted a "new, kind mummy," "No, I want my own mummy" (2). It is a human characteristic that we do have and need relationships and that each of us judges the ethical quality of these relationships.

The work of therapy is a "pragmatic strategy." It consists of identifying the remaining resources of trustworthiness in troubled families and disentangling the "invisible loyalties" that have perhaps come to be expressed in distorted ways. *However, that parents are "accountable" to their children and that children are "loyal" to their parents is accepted as a basic premise, whatever way these loyalties are expressed.*

Just as parents are accountable to their children, therapists are accountable to their patients and to the significant others who will be affected by changes in one individual. Therapists cannot be neutral but must rather be partial in a "multidirectional way"—hearing each family member's claims on his or her own terms. Primary relationships and loyalties continue even if actual relationships with parents and grandparents have been severed. They are based on "roots in common." These are not substitutable by any other relationship and "contribute to an individual's uniqueness." Second, common bonds constitute an "ethical claim" requiring that relationships remain in fair balance and that trust be merited and maintained. Therapists have the opportunity to help a family to restore its uniqueness and integrity.

What is important about this article is that it makes us sit up straight and reexamine certain assumptions as we go about our work. It asserts that human beings *are* "entitled" to and do deserve a modicum of fairness, that "mutual trust" based on consideration and caring accumulates "merits," and that "merits" accumulated deserve to be recognized and repaid over the long term. This does not imply that life will always be "fair" in the short run or that people are "entitled" to all that they might wish. It does, however, maintain that long-term bonds of familial trustworthiness help people through periods of unfairness. It denies "the trap of the contemporary observer of human relationships: in this view repayment of obligations emanating from procreation is optional and depends on the participants' feelings and a variety of power manipulations."

Some questions come to mind: How does love enter the picture? What of giving that is motivated by the wish to give pleasure to someone one loves? Perhaps the authors are implicitly suggesting that the unconditional love between parent and child or in marriage exists as an aspect of roots in common while "merited" trust is a broadened conception of the semiconditional love of adult life. The complexities of how these dimensions of trust and love are worked out in human families need further elaboration.

In conclusion, however, we feel that this approach to helping people should enrich the work of all therapists, whether they choose to see individuals or families, and, we hope, further the already visible movement toward integration and an end to sectarian squabbles. It behooves all therapists to consider seriously their patients' "loyalties": it suggests that even in work with individuals the enduring value of the individual's family and social context must be appreciated or therapy may be merely temporarily palliative or even destructive. The overriding implication is that civilization and decency in human conduct need not be a repressive force but can be, and often is, a liberating source of mental health and creativity.

REFERENCES

1. Boszormenyi-Nagy, I. & Spark, G. *Invisible Loyalties*. New York: Harper & Row, 1973.
2. Guntrip, H. My experience of analysis with Fairbairn and Winnicott. *International Review of Psychoanalysis*, 2, 145–156, 1975.

Judith Grunebaum, M.S.W.
Henry Grunebaum, M.D.

15

Contextual Therapy: The Realm of the Individual (Interview with Margaret Markham)

Contemporary therapists cannot ignore the balance required between the needs of each individual on the one hand and relational networks on the other. The contextual therapist acknowledges his accountable concern for all consequences of his interventions for the entire relational context. In this he will utilize his knowledge of overt and covert psychological determinants; however, he will not yield to a systemic-transactional reductionism any more than to a psychological reductionism.

The contextual therapist is interested in both the self-directed (centripetal) and other-directed (centrifugal) aspects of relational consequences. Centrifugal consequences are to be understood first and foremost as facts of reality, just as much as the forward-thrusting performance of genes is a fact of reality, and only secondarily as "ought" or value.

The resolution of the antithesis between two partners' self-dictated, centripetal claims lies in the phenomenon of entitlement. Entitlement depends on merited worth rather than on psychological phenomena such as affect, cognition or drive. Constructive, that is, duly merited, entitlement leads to real freedom of true autonomy and individuation. Its dialectic basis is receiving through giving. Entitlement is a source of freedom to enjoy life, creativity and courage of commitment; it allows one to claim one's own rights and to live free of psychosomatic illness. It is an ethic which benefits both actor and recipient.

By contrast, destructive over-entitlement (first defined in this paper), though actually earned through one's role as a helpless victim, leads to a derailment of the use of accrued merit. It can result in a striking lack of remorse over destructive behavior in other relationships.

In the accountability for relational consequences, the earning of entitlement becomes a major contextual therapeutic guideline and concern about posterity becomes its highest priority consideration. Whereas the adult's responsible concern for posterity represents a major resource, the child is himself a reservoir of relational resources. For example, a twelve-year-old terminal cancer patient may have still greater emotional resources than the depleted, grief-stricken parent of the dying child.

In conclusion, relational thinking has to be revised according to a joint consideration of consequences for both the acting individual and for others. A sharp separation between centripetal and centrifugal consequences has proven to be costly to Western societies. Recent interest in the Japanese model of more concerned industrial management is one sign of an emerging awareness of the costliness of callous self-serving managerial patterns.

E arly in his writings Freud began to distinguish between two vital forces—psychic reality and external reality. As he delved into and expanded the concept of ego, he relegated to this level of the psychic spectrum the managerial function for an individual's dealing with external reality. Nonetheless, no matter how wide Freud's spotlight swept, ultimately his psychoanalytic approach focused on the understanding of a single psychic universe—the realm of the individual. Despite this emphasis on the individual, reality demands recognition of two seminal facts: that a child does not develop in total isolation but in constant contact with others, and that an adult continues to live out his span in a network of interrelationships.

In the past few decades a multitude of therapeutic approaches—group therapy, family therapy, dialectical intergenerational therapy—have paid tribute to the key role of such intersocial factors. At times, however, the transactional aspects were given far more weight than their due at the cost of relegating the importance of the individual to virtual limbo. At the Houston meeting of the American Academy of Psychoanalysis, contextual therapy was proposed by a Philadelphia psychiatrist as a means of striking an equitable balance between the needs of the individual and the demands of a relational framework. The following interview touches on many of the main points in that presentation by Ivan Boszormenyi-Nagy, M.D., chief of the family therapy section at Hahnemann Medical College and Hospital.

Psychiatric News: What are the chief hallmarks of contextual therapy?

Boszormenyi-Nagy: In contextual therapy responsibility for all consequences of relationships is transformed into a therapeutic guideline and methodology. It is neither psychoanalysis per se nor antipsychoanalysis. The components of the context are persons in relationship with one another. Thus, even while seeing one individual, the therapist should utilize the leverages of the entire relational context for the benefit of all persons in relationship with one another. By the same token, no family therapy should exclude a regard for the individual even though it has to depart from the stance of classical individual therapy. His psychological nature comprises just one aspect of man's relational reality.

PN: Does this accentuation of relational values clash with traditional Freudian concepts?

Boszormenyi-Nagy: Actually, many of Freud's basic concepts originated from assumptions about relationships, e.g., dependence, primary identification, Oedipus complex, projection, displacement, transference, etc. He explored the consequences of motivational forces and their vicissitudes as they affect the prospects of the individual's health or illness. Freudian psychology made enormous discoveries of people's hidden unconscious motives. Today, manifest conscious intentions and goals of relating can no longer be regarded as simple linear cause and effect reactions. As a matter of fact, it has become everyday wisdom to explain and understand the meaning and goals of relating entirely from the standpoint of an alleged Freudian sophistication about hidden motivation.

PN: How does contextual therapy differ from other modalities, for instance, family therapy?

Boszormenyi-Nagy: In the beginning of classical family therapy great discoveries were made about the transactional regulation of behavior and of pathology. Predictable sequences were described, that is, homeostatic feedback-like patterns of communication and visible interaction. Moreover, this "systemic" view yielded valuable structural or configurational understanding of *covert* relational determinants of the behavioral orchestration in families. However, the evolving systemic-transactional reductionism started to parallel its counterpart which it claimed to obviate: psychological reductionism.

Interesting to note, the key to the door of depth relational phenomena and to the contextual extension of system-based thinking in classical family therapy came from Martin Buber, and only to a lesser extent from relationally based ego theory. Buber's concept of the dialogue came closest to a requisite framework which can describe two or more individuals in a personally engaged relationship. Actually there is no psychological theory capable of considering the dynamics of two selves simultaneously from the multiple subjective vantage points. Where the contextual approach transcends the symmetrical notions of the dialogue and the feedback characteristics of systemic-transactional classical family therapy is in its concern about posterity as the highest priority of all consequences to be considered.

PN: Isn't such overriding concern with posterity somewhat of a departure from basic psychoanalytic concerns?

Boszormenyi-Nagy: Whereas psychological theories characteristically disregarded balance *between* persons, systemic theories disregard persons. Although systemic theories have been able to explain the nature of business or ordinary social relationships, they could never fully grasp the uniquely committed and asymmetrical nature of parent-child relationships. The balance of give-and-take in life is irreversibly asymmetrical between parent and child. The essence of what we receive from our parents can only be repaid through posterity. Just as we have been unilaterally fed by input from preceding generations, we have the duty and privilege of aiding posterity in the face of increasingly complex and frightening odds.

Feedback-related homeostasis, is, of course, a major part of physiological regulations. However, much more of the characteristics of the essence of biology lies in the nonfeedback-like, forward-thrusting performance of the genes which program both growth and obsolescence of one generation after the other.

PN: What were the considerations that gave initial impetus to the development of contextual therapy?

Boszormenyi-Nagy: It has evolved from a search for defining the mechanism of effective psychotherapy for some of the most challenging "pathologies." The early formulations that led to contextual therapy relied first on justice as a social dynamic: later on fairness and trustworthiness became motivating factors, to be succeeded more recently by *entitlement.* All these concepts have certain characteristics of an ethical nature. Yet, the term "ethics" is likely to evoke severe distortions and misunderstanding since it seems to be connected with moralizing, adjudicating, value preferences, and idealism. Moreover, an attempt to characterize the pertinent dimension of responsibility for consequences to the partner as "relational ethics" has not succeeded in overcoming these difficulties.

Even the term "value" is frequently misleading. Inevitably values have a judgmental or prescriptive, normative character. Yet the fact that relationships have consequences for the partner is primarily not in the realm of value or "ought." Consequence is first *a fact of reality*; something that *is*. Yet, inherently it implies the initiator's responsibility for centrifugal consequence, especially if the partner is in no position to reciprocate or retaliate on a symmetrical basis.

ENTITLEMENT

PN: What inference does this hold for contextual therapy?

Boszormenyi-Nagy: I believe that first of all the contextual therapist deals with the factual nature of the centrifugal impact or consequences of relational reality, and only secondarily with the ethics of that responsibility which may effectively be assumed for those consequences. Specifically, the contextual approach adds this centrifugal aspect of relational reality to *a new, extended, motivational understanding.* The resolution of the antithesis between the self-dictated, centripetal needs of two partners lies in the concept of *entitlement.*

PN: You've referred to entitlement a number of times, but isn't this an individualized concept? Just how does it fit into the schema of contextual therapy?

Boszormenyi-Nagy: Entitlement is a fundamental phenomenon of the relational context and as such does belong to the individual. It emerges in each partner through the capacity for striving to care about the other's needs and interests. Reality dictates an oscillation between centripetal and centrifugal concerns on everyone's part. In one sense, the therapeutic goal can be described as the therapist's mobilizing — through a catalytic action — the family member's motivations for earning entitlement.

The word "earn" suggests that the essence of entitlement consists in the nature of merited worth, rather than in a psychological phenomenon such as affect, cognition, or drive.

PN: I think the word entitlement is often misapplied. Could you define it more precisely?

Boszormenyi-Nagy: I agree; the term is, at best, imperfect and often leads to misunderstanding. To put it more precisely, entitlement is not simply an arrogant claim or a narcissistic attitude held in one mind. Entitlement accrues on one side of the merit balance of a relationship. Therefore, it can be earned by a person *only* at the cost of caring about the partner. Entitlement is valid only in the context of the relationship in which it is earned. Entitlement on one side quickly yields to indebtedness as the partner also earns merit to a sufficient extent. Thus, it is a *justified or earned claim* — a consequence of caring and of responsible consideration of the partner's merit.

The goal of enabling family members to earn entitlement has implications for the main contextual therapeutic guideline. Multidirected partiality is the crucial method. In brief, as each person is serially being asked to state his justified relational position, each gets motivated also to hear the other and to respond. A search for the learning of consequences for everyone concerned is a long and tedious one for both family members and therapist. Yet it is probably the most effective and least wasteful method for supporting the viability of relationships, a desirable consequence for both the living and for future generations.

In actuality, relationally earned constructive entitlement, in contrast to destructive over-entitlement, leads to freedom and security for each individual's living. The person capable of earning entitlement through relationships is more able to claim his due in relationships, to enjoy life, including sexuality, to undertake the risks of new relationships, and to be free of either psychosomatic illness or self-destructive patterns of behavior.

PN: Exactly what do you mean by destructive over-entitlement?

Boszormenyi-Nagy: For one thing, having earned entitlement does not necessarily lead to a sense of entitlement. On the one hand it is possible to feel entitled without having earned actual entitlement. On the other, parents can deprive their child and thereby increase his intrinsic entitlement. At the same time, by failing to acknowledge the child's stake in the relationship and making him boundlessly accountable, they can indoctrinate or delegate the child with a low sense of entitlement, engendering a persistent sense of indebtedness. Destructive entitlement can later lead to a striking lack of remorse over destructive marital, social, or even parental behavior. This freedom from remorse is not a psychological distortion. Tragically it was actually earned through having been exploited. It is a consequence of a destructive reality. Moreover, through sparing their own parents from blame and instead taking it out on innocent others, children earn further destructive entitlement through remaining invisibly loyal, captive victims of the past.

In its purest form entitlement requires, therefore, the dialectic of receiving through giving, in sharp contrast to the linear concept of having more through withholding. It integrates and eliminates the antithesis between self-gain and the merit of fair consideration of others.

PN: Isn't that quite quixotic and somewhat at odds with Freudian perceptions of motivations?

Boszormenyi-Nagy: Unquestionably, the scope of psychology is encompassed within the existential realm of one person's brain. Psychodevelopmental history begins with late embryonic life and terminates with the individual's death. Freud described variations within the confines of the centripetal concern of his relational psychology—the narcissistically relating person is obviously characterized by a self-serving world view. Psychodynamically, however, even the "object" of the maturely relating person is essentially regarded from the vantage point of the self's interest. The object satisfies the particular needs of the self and, therefore, the relationship should be retained primarily in the self's interest. The maturely relating person shows concern for the interests of the partner but, ultimately, he is seen as being motivated by relational consequences exclusively for himself.

A few years ago J. Sandler and W. G. Joffe expressed the view that there is no room for altruism in psychodynamic theory. They maintained it is both theoretically and clinically important from the point of view of psychic adaptation to realize that there is no such thing as unselfish or altruistic love or concern for another person. Rather, the ultimate criterion in deciding whether or not to strive for or maintain a particular relationship is the effect that relationship has on the central feeling state of the individual making that determination.

PN: What do you visualize as the special contribution that contextual therapy can make to individual and family psychotherapy?

Boszormenyi-Nagy: The knowledge of relational reality, that is awareness of the consequences of one's relationship for the partner as well, is an added resource for the planning of therapeutic strategy. It is crucial to understand that contextual strategies are not aimed at erasing the consequences of past relational impact, but at *repairing and enriching* the prospects for the future. In this context we have to elicit one of the key resources of trustworthy relationships: that is, the confidence that the giving of consideration to another individual does not have to lead to self-depriving sacrifice.

The consideration of consequences of relational reality does require a new perspective on therapeutic contract. No matter if we call it individual, marital, or family therapy, ethically the therapist is engaged in an invisible contract with *all* persons who can possibly be affected by the outcome of that therapy. Therefore, contextual therapy is characterized by a broad contractual accountability rather than by insistence on conjoint sessions. Moreover, responsibility for the consequences for the self and others is a more relevant contextual therapeutic goal than mere production of "change." Contextual therapy explicitly explores and elicits responsibility for relational consequences for the partner's side. It aims at enabling all relating partners to gain through the earning of constructive entitlement. Since family therapists usually work with both parents and children, they are likely to witness the transactions that tend to have lasting consequences for children. Nat-

urally, for any parent to assume liability for such longterm consequences is frightening and often made ambiguous by a genuine lack
of knowledge. The integrity of the psychotherapist requires that he pay
vigilant attention to the implications of both research and clinical
observations on the consequences of parenting behavior on children.
Specifically, contextual therapy does not stop with an analytic contemplation of pathology or developmental damage in the offspring.
Full attention to the impact of the behavior of *all* participants should
result in maximum impetus for improvement.

PN: You characterized contextual therapy as differing from classical
family therapy in that the former places concern about posterity as the
highest priority of all consequences to be weighed. How does this apply
clinically?

Boszormenyi-Nagy: I can best answer that by relating a specific instance
that illustrates the application of both the earning of entitlement and
the regard for generational mandates: A terminally ill 12-year-old cancer
patient faced a not uncommon situation. Her parents became depressed
and the pediatric hospital staff became concerned about the effect of the
parental attitude on the young patient. The nurses raised the question
whether the mother's visits should be terminated to spare the daughter
from her emotional demands and suggested that the visits be replaced
with some specially selected toys or discussions about school matters.

From a contextual point of view, the relational resources had to be
assessed first. In the fact of inevitable loss, the options for receiving
through giving were reviewed. It seemed conceivable that the dying
child still had more resources for giving than her parent. This assumption, of course, contradicts the standard, centripetal assumption of the
child — especially a sick one — as being a primarily dependent and needy
recipient, a pure "taker." A corresponding and basically sound assumption is that it is the parent who should *always* be the giving resource
for the child, especially a sick one.

PN: But isn't that invariably true?

Boszormenyi-Nagy: Not necessarily. In this particular case, from a contextual standpoint, through the daughter's terminal illness the parent gets progressively deprived from earning entitlement. The parent can no more increase efforts at giving the best for the child's future. In addition to their own protracted mourning over the loss, the parents are running out of options for fulfilling the mandates of their parental accountability. By contrast, the daughter is still able to make major contributions to the depleted, bereft parents by expressing her caring and loving. As a result she can also earn entitlement through repayment of filial gratitude. To be cut off from her mother's visits would have amounted to accelerating her departure from life lived as a relationship. With this in mind, strategies had to be drawn up to help this terminally ill daughter to take care of the mother. This *she* accomplished by encouraging her mother to knit a sweater according to a mutually agreed upon design and color choice. This plan worked with success and as a result, since then a similar review of resources has been applied to other cases of terminally ill children.

PN: What do you see as obstacles to wider use of such contextual dynamics?

Boszormenyi-Nagy: One of the most significant difficulties in trying to bridge the depth aspects of psychodynamic and relational approaches lies in a tendency for psychological reductionism — characteristic of our era. Psychodynamic and other psychological motivational theories can rely on elaborate and articulate conceptual schemes. The language of relational phenomena is relatively undeveloped, often lacking precision as well as subjective and personal depth. One of the greatest difficulties in describing the intuitively sensed key leverages of any psychotherapy has been a relative lack of language for relational phenomena. This is especially true with processes that involve responsibility of the self for his relational impact on the partner. Consequently, the temptation to define relational phenomena in terms of their secondary, psychological impact on individuals has been enormous. It is no wonder that, at first sight, relational phenomena appear to be less deep and less precisely definable than psychological ones.

Intrinsically, the sum total of psychotherapeutic observations on causal connections of human behavior amounts to a giant research project on the descriptive criteria of relational consequences. Here lies the ultimate preventive mandate of the psychotherapy profession. Contextual therapy regards the individual to be virtually committed to transgenerational benefits received and to personal gains tied to his caring for posterity. Related to Erik Erikson's notions about "generativity," the sorting out and fulfillment of mandates for posterity is to be viewed as a complex motivational source. As his highest priority, the contextual therapist is unwilling to ignore options for eliminating unnecessary, often inadvertent damage to be inflicted on small children.

PN: As admirable as these aims are, don't you think they call for some drastic revisions in social attitudes before they can succeed?

Boszormenyi-Nagy: The centrifugal aspect of relational reality has immense, unexplored implications for research, therapeutic method, and the requisites for effective, preventive family planning. It is probably identical with that glue which makes communities or work settings worthy of people's trust and commitments. This "ethical" dynamic of viable relationships is based primarily on the factual reality of our impact on others, rather than on adherence to value traditions or taboos.

It is probably true that Western society has shown a progressive decline of responsibility for the consequences of relationship. Many factors have contributed to this, including industrialization, mass mobility, mass communication, and the disintegration of family ties. Large scale societal moves seem to amount to irresponsible borrowing from the funds of the future rather than readiness to plan to provide resources for the future. Government and big business collude to cut funds from public education and from support for the family. The posterity is, of course, a captive investor to face the risks for the consequences. It raises the possibility that it may lead to future generations being justly entitled, in addition to feeling entitled for being destructive.

Implicit in psychotherapy are the roles of both a quasi-scientific student of the enduring consequences of human relationships, and of a catalyst eliciting the safeguards for the human worth of a future inseparable from the present. Through a responsible learning of the phenomena of consequences, and effectively conveying their factual nature to society, the psychotherapy profession could contribute to a practical value-renaissance in the West. Our inherent sharp distinction between the individual's rights or self-contained interests, and his regard for the total impact of his relationship will have to be revised. The price of their disjunction has already proved too costly.

16

The Contextual Approach to Psychotherapy: Premises and Implications

[This paper was written with Barbara R. Krasner, Ph.D.]

This chapter further outlines the nature of the relational context as the foundation of therapeutic method. It elaborates on the four relational dimensions as the clustering of the total spectrum of therapeutic principles and methods. Special attention is given to the contextual therapist's commitment to the multilateral therapeutic contract.

Certain contextual guidelines apply to any modality of therapeutic technical approaches. For instance, the therapist will inevitably collude with the damaging impact of a destructively fighting parental couple if he accepts their premise that their small children will not need therapeutic attention. One parent's subtle protectiveness of a child against the mistrusted other parent can be a more detrimental relational context (split loyalty) than violent parental fighting or even divorce.

For the treatment of ethical stagnation we mention three methodological guidelines: ethical reengagement, the bridging of manifest adverseness, and the reassessment of legacy expectations and payments. General operational characteristics include the translation of individual or symptom-based problem definitions into relational configurations and the courage to examine structural exploitation even at the cost of siding against the beneficiary.

In emergencies such as risk of suicide, child battering, incest, psy-

251

chosis, serious delinquency, and so forth, contextual therapy is not adverse to actively structuring interventions.

Legacy expectations can be fulfilled following the offspring's terms or they can be postponed, but they cannot be denied or indefinitely ignored without paying a heavy price. If it is accompanied by guilt feelings, a failure to recognize legacy obligations may lead to self-impairing behavior or even to psychosomatic reactions.

The more recent investigations of distributive justice and injustice (Boszormenyi-Nagy & Krasner, 1986) are foreshadowed in the current article's statements: The contents of each person's legacy are received as objective components of given circumstances. This destiny of inherited facts and their ethical implications are more than a mere construct. "Some people grew up with luck, i.e. health and environment, that is better than average, others with luck that is far worse than average." The task for the contextual therapist lies in learning how certain facts in a person's relational world are transmitted into ethical obligations.

Concerning the relationship between Dimensions II and IV, it can be stated that the availability of trustable relationships lowers the threshold for the participants' ego strength requirements. A major distinction between needs and merit lies in the fact that the psychological dimension can tolerate substitution without a loss of symbolic meaning. In contrast, imbalance of fairness cannot validly be transferred out of the original relationship; for instance, lack of merit transferred from a filial to a marital account results in new unfairness. Even certain unilateral therapeutic models (child therapy, classical behavior therapy) may serve implicitly to reinforce intrinsic scapegoating of the "patient."

There is further stress on the dynamic priority of vertical accounts of rootedness. The parent-child relationship is interminable even by large geographic distance, lack of interaction, negative affect, indifferent attitudes, or abusive behavior. Parents and their children represent to each other resources of tremendous potential. The combination of the legacy of filial devotion and the child's existential need to repay incurred debts to his parents comprises one of the greatest avail-

able human resources for therapy, prevention of illness, and a more fulfilling life.

REFERENCE

Boszormenyi-Nagy, I., & Krasner, B. *Between give and take.* New York: Brunner/Mazel, 1986.

INTRODUCTION

The purpose of this chapter is twofold: to describe the therapeutic utilization of the ethical or merited trust dimension of relationships, and to use this dimension as a strategic guideline capable of functioning as the integrative factor in all useful psychotherapeutic approaches. In brief, the ethical dimension focuses on responsible, trustworthy action in relationship. It is not to be confused with a "moralizing" or judgmental position that compares one value with another. In our experience personal accountability for trust and trustworthiness in relationship constitutes a depth dimension of human life, attainable in the short-run, provided the therapist is ready to encourage necessary facing. However, the task of facing and sometimes confronting often offends the relational ideal of well-mannered tact.

To the contrary. Generally, the appeal of psychotherapy is founded on people's desire to diminish suffering and to increase satisfaction in living. Popular therapeutic methods are most readily embraced as a result of their claims of direct curative power. The simple, all-encompassing premises of such methods meet with people's longings for a flight from life's complexity and from the burden of responsibilities. A promise of quick relief from suffering and an immediate increase in self-assertive gratification fits into the cultural orientation and myths of our era. On the other hand, at the turn of the century Freud discovered fundamental aspects of motivation. He also converted a sophisticated and dynamic scheme into what we now know as psychotherapy. In psychoanalytic therapy the client is required to be able to develop new capacities for satisfaction, partially through curbing unrealizable wishes and partially through accepting the limitations of reality. The minority who qualify as good analytic or "uncovering" patients indeed achieve an improved integration of motivations and feelings; that is, through the expenditure of hard effort, they arrive at a less costly formula for living. However, all individually focused therapeutic strategies lack a guaranteed return in terms of the trustworthiness of the client's relationships with others.

Self-serving progress toward "doing one's own thing" may bring disservice to the self through fragmenting a person's vitally needed relational world. Fair consideration of the interests of others is therefore in the best reality (ego) interest of the individual. The capacity to acquire and retain at least a few trustworthy relationships in the face of increasing dehumanization and alienation in the public world cannot be equated with either altruism or with guilt-laden compliance fueled by superego demands. The apparent contradiction between self-interest and consideration of others can be bridged dialectically through the relating partners' shared need for trust. Chronic mistrust is self-defeating in the realm of close relationships and even in society at large. It is also self-defeating in the context of the individual.

Many readers will welcome an effort at defining the nature of deep, often invisible fibers that hold relationships together. Others will be more interested in "here-and-now" results. These readers may view a concern with "root" relationships as superfluous, time consuming, or troublesome, and stress the singular importance of manifest peer contacts. It would be unrealistic to deny that the realm of peer relationships is the most important arena for decision-making and is the forum for deeply-involved emotional experiences. Yet a person's satisfactory peer relationships are enabled by strength developed from directly experienced trustworthiness in intergenerational relationships. In the authors' view, the ethical dimension of trust between relating partners is the invisible thread of both individual freedom and interindividual balance. A concern with this ethical dimension requires time and life experience. And while it poses fresh demands on the evolving therapist, the dimension of merited trust will also benefit him.

THE NATURE OF THE CONTEXT

The contextual approach under discussion in this chapter introduces a comprehensive relational view of psychotherapy. It is a major reformulation of what earlier was described as "dialectical intergenerational family therapy" (Boszormenyi-Nagy & Spark, 1973). Resource rather than pathology oriented, the contextual approach offers a promising design for preventing individual and relational imbalance and breakdown. In essence, its strategies are guided by multilateral balances of entitlement and indebtedness between relating partners, and are built upon a balanced integration of the significant relational premises (overt and covert) of existing therapies. More than an additional psycho-therapeutic technique, the contextual approach acknowledges the basic dynamic and developmental contributions of the Freudian approach, for example, but questions and expands its individual based limitations as well. In its attempt at an integrative relational conceptualization, contextual psychotherapy takes exception to psychologically or "sys-temically" reductionistic assumptions about the determination of hu-man behavior. A variety of factors currently lend impetus to the de-velopment of such a challenge and make the establishment of a more comprehensive therapeutic orientation necessary:

> The fact that recent developments in the field have extended and diluted the concept of psychotherapy and made it so diversified that its common denominator has been stretched almost beyond recognition.
>
> The fact that there is now reason to doubt whether therapists of differing ideological and technical orientations share identical premises or can even communicate meaningfully about their work.
>
> The fact that pressure is building for the development of strin-gent requirements for professional accountability and economy of service delivery.
>
> The fact that the family approach has emerged with both a claim of effectiveness and a growing following, yet without an appropriate integration into the larger body of psychotherapy. In fact, some authors define their approach to family therapy as if it were mutually exclusive of psychological understanding.

Clearly, widespread confusion over the nature of psychotherapy is proliferating, and presents a hazard for consumers as well as for pro-fessionals. At a time when it is fashionable to question the creditability of psychotherapy as a whole, it seems necessary to marshal all of its reliable evidence into a convincing, mutually supportive, cohesive, and logical argument.

There is increasing recognition that psychotherapy's medical origins, tending to stress the ideal of quick and effective symptomatic relief for one patient, has served to eclipse factual information about its reliance on basic psychosocial resources, specifically, trust-building relationships. The medical origins of psychotherapy have frequently stressed a causal, rather than an empirical method of cure. These expectations often lose sight of the fact that psychotherapy has to depend on a resource rather than on a pathology orientation. The medical goal of treatment aimed at a causal elimination of pathogenicity has not yet become applicable to psychotherapy. There is a tendency to overlook the fact that individual breakdown and imbalance are relationally reinforced. Here constructive bridgebuilding seems desirable for the further development of the relational implications of Freud's doctrines. Viewed historically, the implicitly "relational" components in Freud's theory of the object directedness of human instinctual drives have become more explicit through the teachings of Harry Stack Sullivan and Ronald Fairbairn. More recently, another type of humanistic elaboration has been offered in Kohut's (1977) psychology of the self. From the side of philosophical anthropology, the relational premises of human life have been posited and developed in the teachings of Martin Buber. Moreover, on the practical side, the field of family therapy has compiled a substantial body of clinical experience with relationships. Nonetheless, the key dynamics of a multilaterally perceived human context remain largely undefined even though their usefulness as therapeutic resources has been documented by the clinical effectiveness of the family approach.

THE MULTILATERAL THERAPEUTIC CONTRACT

Primarily, the paradigm of a multilateral therapeutic contract implies an ethical reorientation for the whole of psychotherapy, including traditional contractual arrangements geared to only one "patient." Implicit in the modality of conjoint, nuclear family therapy introduced during the 1950s, the ethical reference was avoided and thinking was diverted into general systems theory. In the late 1960s, intergenerational family therapy introduced the paradigms of transgenerational linkages and ethical therapeutic leverages (Boszormenyi-Nagy & Spark, 1973). It also expanded the temporal dimension of contractual goals and responsibilities to several generations connected via reproductive destiny and legacies rather than through simultaneous transaction.

A multicentered consideration of the welfare interests of each of the participants in a given context is a major depth characteristic of the contextual approach. In the first instance, "multilaterality" is a basic ethical rather than psychological dynamic that evolves from the fundamental fact that all relationships are built on two or more sides. Each side is comprised of differing legacies and interindividual balances of needs and entitlements, and is anchored in each person's welfare and survival interests.* Ethically, a person is neither an isolated entity nor a singular center of his and his partner's universe. Nor can two or more individuals consistently merge their joint interests without consideration of their separate commitments to and investments in relationships. Any assumption of a persistent, total merger of two or more people's interests is deceptive, illusory, and doomed to failure. For the fact is that the entitlements of closely related individuals are dynamically polarized. They may be either competitive or mutually supportive, but their relational outcome is never a matter of indifference for either person. No relationship can be understood and managed without some capacity for multilaterality. In the second instance, "multidirected partiality" (Boszormenyi-Nagy, 1966, 1973) describes a therapeutic approach whose contract and processes are governed by the multicentered nature of interrelatedness. It recognizes, addresses, and utilizes the ethical dynamics of equity and trustworthiness that are always key issues in human relationships.

Multidirected partiality is an approach rooted in a therapist's decision to accept contractual accountability, in view of the inevitable multilateral outcome of his work. It also depends on a therapist's

---

*The term "interest," by itself, may connote psychological, need-based experiential or even power-transactional dynamic properties. By contrast, survival or vital welfare interests have to be defined in the context of their own fatefully factual, existential givenness. The inherited legacy of an individual originates from the factual destiny of his or her being, e.g., gender, member of a race, ethnic, or religious group.

capacity to actualize courage, risk-taking, and the exposure of both personal claims and legacy obligations between and among family members. Contrasting with both directionless therapeutic impartiality and unidirectional advocacy, multidirected partiality is an attitude of a serious search for and expectation of periodic rebalancing of significant instances of unfairness. As an ethically integrative principle, multilaterality and its corollary, multidirected partiality, constitute the "basic rule" of relational dynamics and of the strategic rationale for contextual therapy. This rule and its pragmatic implications provide the foundation of contextual interventions and, in our view, should serve to eclipse evasive reliance on the therapist's "intuition" or personal "value" orientation. For example,

> A therapist's collusive acceptance of a childishly fighting couple's premise that their small children are free of "problems" may represent a fundamental violation of the children's interests and entitlements to a full and productive life. The consideration of captively exploited children has to be regulated by the basic rule of multilaterality because the welfare interests of all family members are in fact at stake, and the therapist is at liberty to ignore one side at the cost of others.

Contextual therapy is not only characterized by its emphasis on multidirected partiality but also by its focus on the patient's originally relevant relational context. Contrasted with the psychodynamic tradition, the contextual approach differentiates between therapeutic methodologies that aim at assistance through essential reliance on the trust resources of a person's family, and approaches that offer help through utilizing strategies within a substitutive, e.g., transference context. In our view, the familial context holds greater therapeutic leverage and is the decisive factor in designing ethically relevant intervention strategies. In fact, the term "context" may be defined as a relational entity comprised of both transactional systems and unique elements that can have no valid substitute without altering the meaning of the whole. Per se, transactional, "pattern," "structure," and "system" can remain unaffected if appropriate substitutes take the place of the principal characters of an individual's original context.

Conversely, their essential symbolic nature makes many psychodynamic or emotional configurations substitutable. The essence of displacement, transference, fixation, repetition, compulsion, and many other phenomena is that they can be reenacted vis-à-vis new relational partners without consecutive psychological change or maturation. Moreover, in a psychological sense, a capacity for substituting partners is even a desirable attribute.

To be sure, in the course of growth the original context of family relations must yield to substitutive relationships. In the maturation process parents are inevitably replaced by peers, teachers, elders, and superiors in a variety of ways. Yet there are no ethically valid surrogates for the original context of family relations. Despite its capacity to evoke familiar patterns of emotional reactions and transactions from the subject, in its ethical sense the substitutive context lacks the intrinsic trust implications of the familial context. The fact remains that my friend is not my mother nor does my therapist "replace" my father. Moreover, attempts to resolve intrapsychic conflict through psychologically substitutive relationships run the danger of ethical disengagement, can invite disloyalty, and can cause stagnation or relational corruption. From a contextual perspective, relational corruption is an existential condition promoted by unilateral exploitation and by unbalanced intergenerational accounts that reinforce flight and evasion of mutual responsibility as a family's accepted mode of relating. Relational corruption, in its subtle, misleading, and collusive manipulativeness, is usually a more damaging contextual characteristic than overt, brutal destructiveness. One parent's subtle protectiveness of a child against the other parent, for example, can be a more detrimental relational context (split loyalty) than violent parental fighting that leads to divorce.

If multilaterality and an emphasis on the subject's originally relevant context are major characteristics of the contextual approach, "rejunction" is its basic strategy. The therapeutic strategy of rejunction, fundamental for the mobilization of the resources of trustworthiness, is essentially based on two criteria: (1) the intrinsically regenerative nature and nonsubstitutability of the relationships of people with roots-in-common (especially of parent-child relationships) and (2) a multilateral consideration of welfare interests from a dialectical perspective of mutual fairness and accountability. Rejunction should not be confused with a thrust toward clinging togetherness. On the contrary, anything that undermines the trustworthy credibility of individual integrity drives people away from each other. Exploitative clinging to one's children, for example, has to be examined in the light of multilateral interests. Reasonable steps have to be made toward the autonomous development of the child. The "permission" for individuation represents an important trust-generating or rejunctive measure. Recognition of the regenerative resources of parent-child relationships serves to liberate people from the culturally imprinted prejudice that defines family ties as predominantly restrictive and despotic. Moreover, the mutual welfare interests of parent and child are timeless and ineradicable.

In practical terms, rejunctive strategies are usually effected in the face of bitter disappointment, denial of concern, exploitation, and even vindictive destructiveness. For example, divorcing parents carry an enormous burden of emotional turmoil, love turned into rejection and hatred, and are often enmeshed in bitter disagreements. Nonetheless, from a rejunctive perspective, a couple's apparent adversative interests should not be equated with a disregard for the long-term welfare interests of dependent children. It is axiomatically certain that the life prospects of young children will be more profoundly and lastingly impacted by the outcome of effective therapeutic intervention than those of their parents. Furthermore, aside from benefitting from increased entitlement from their investment, parents will always share an interest in providing optimal trustworthy input in their children's survival and welfare. For ultimately, parental and filial self-interests coincide through the mutually needed trust-building implicit in continuing in a responsible parenting team that functions despite divorce. There are at least 3 stages in the process of rejunction. They include,

Ethical re-engagement of family members through reassessing the balances of fairness and of accountability, and through a renewed capacity for acknowledging positive contributions from all sources

Efforts to bridge manifest adverseness between parental and filial welfare interests through the planning of more realistic and

appropriate strategies for attaining new balances of fairness
    Efforts to effect new supports for multilaterally trustworthy
relationships through an ongoing reassessment of legacy expectations and payments.

Given their basic goals, neither rejunctive strategies nor their underlying theories depend on conjoint sessions or on any particular methodological modality. The skillful use of the rejunctive rationale enables contextual therapists to be consistent and personally supportive while pointedly confrontative on relevant issues. Effective intervention is unthinkable without a therapist's conviction about the value of trustworthiness as a needed resource for reworking legacy assessments; and about the necessity for rebalancing criteria for relational involvement. The successful outcomes of rejunctive intervention include a diminished need for pathological symptoms; increased autonomy or ego strength, and increased freedom for and entitlement to more satisfying relational engagements.

    Practiced in therapeutic modalities that are oriented to individuals, couples, families, groups, and relational networks alike, contextual therapy is characterized by the following operational capabilities. *From the side of the therapist* contextual therapy requires:

The therapeutic ability to translate individual and symptomatic problem definitions into multilateral, relational configurations that encompass the fairness and welfare interests of more than one contractually agreed-upon client
The therapeutic courage and ability to apply the principles of multilaterality to personal relationships. This includes:
(1) A willingness to consider the entitlements and merits of all parties concerned
(2) Courage to examine structural corruption even if it temporarily means siding against the beneficiary of corruption
Therapeutic conviction about the intrinsic value of the joint effort between therapist and client that rests on an offer of professional accountability and fairness *and* on every client's accountable commitment to multilateral fairness in relating
The therapeutic intention to overcome the universal human tendency

to scapegoat one person in vindication of the self or of another. Occurring in therapist as well as in their clients, this one-sided tendency is often directed at an individual's parents

The therapeutic capacity to help lead family members into active pursuit of emotional maturity and integrity, despite self-deceptive resistances. That is, toward confronting their fears of aggression and inappropriate hostility and shame over desperate longings for dependence, among other factors

The therapeutic ability to side empathically with each family member in turn. Family members are consecutively included in the therapist's considerations whether or not they are present at sessions (multidirected partiality)

The therapeutic ability to acquire the skill, experience, and courage to provide leadership in desperate relational emergencies like suicide, child battering, incest, psychosis, serious delinquency, and destructive scapegoating among other conditions often considered as indications for institutional management of the individual involved.

From the side of family members contextual psychotherapy requires:

The capacity of each family member to define their claim of subjective fairness, and to develop courage to assert their respective sides of entitlement

The capacity of each family member to hear each other and to care about each other's subjective vantage points on entitlements and interests

The capacity of each family member to strive toward a trustworthy balance of positions in the family as well as to move toward their own idiosyncratic goals

The capacity of each family member to acknowledge their personal accountability for the outcome of changed attitudes and behaviors and their impact on more vulnerable members of the family, such as young children

The capacity of each family member to support and gain from a mutual regard for everyone's attempts at fulfilling legacy obligations

The willingness and ability of each member to discriminate between expediency and integrity in personal relationships

The capacity of each family member to claim and grant tolerance and privacy for needed moratoria; that is, the time required for change to occur. The time required for equitable reworking and correcting displacements, projections, and denials is an example of the need for moratoria in interrelationships.

In our view, the therapist's multidirected concern for the vital interests of all affected family members can hardly be contraindicated.

A comprehensive approach to the premises of psychotherapy is bound to help practitioners within their subspecialties or technical preferences. Whether he works with adults, children, couples, families, or groups, the therapist's concern with the discharge of parental accountability toward small children, for example, is incorporating a leverage of decisive ethical consequence and extending his range of effective therapeutic options at one and the same time. Furthermore, the therapist working with individuals will gain important clues from a contextual examination of the background of traditional individual-based limiting factors, e.g., ego weakness, resistance to insight, and severely distortive transference tendencies. The following clinical anecdote serves to demonstrate the implications of an integrative view:

> For Anne, age 5, her dad is strong, handsome and generally great. What's more, he always seems to be right when he argues with mom. On one occasion, Anne's one-sided devotion toward her father made her mother cry. The incident left Anne with bad feelings.
>
> Anne finds herself in a family situation marked by two characteristics: One Freud called oedipal. The other can be termed "multilaterality." The oedipal condition is created by Anne's psychic development and her initial responses to the sexual difference between her and her father. Given this undeniable fact, Anne and her mother are involved in unavoidable hurtful and competitive conflicts. Anne's partly inevitable oedipal victories over her mother and feelings of oedipal guilt lead to a variety of intrapsychic conflicts for the girl. Anne would feel the same way with any set of parents. In technical terms her parents represent components of an "average expectable human environment" (Hartman, 1964) or external reality.
>
> On the other hand, Anne and her relational input also compose her parents' external reality. On the day of one argument, the girl

was unaware that mother had been the target of an insensitive attack from her own mother. Furthermore, on the same day, father had told mother about his young secretary in glowing terms. And earlier in the week, mother had been made anxious by wrinkles. These factors and her recent conflict with Anne made mother feel like she was carrying a heavy burden.

She would probably have felt the same way with any female child. Anne represents a component of her mother's average expectable human environment or external reality.

In relationships, one partner's external reality, traditionally viewed as average or nondynamic, constitutes the psychodynamic fulcrum of the partner and vice versa. Contextual multilaterality recognizes the simultaneous dialogue between at least two ego, id, and superego universes.

From a contextual perspective, the competent psychotherapist is able to discern the dialectical interplay between a person's intrapsychic dynamics and ever fluctuating balances evolving from the external realities of interindividual relatedness. He is therefore advised to be familiar with the manifestations of developmental phases, basic drives, superego formation, defensive avoidance of conflicts, projection, displacement, resistance to treatment, transference tendencies, and grief mechanisms among other individually-based sources of knowledge. He should also be able to assess and intervene in imbalances of entitlements that are rooted in subjectively experienced "ethical" expectations and disappointments. A flexible use of all effective "technical" therapeutic leverages is the hallmark of the contextual approach. Yet the development of a guiding focus is required for a therapist to make adequate use of a dialectical, multipersonal model of ethically balanced trustbuilding that recognizes pathogenicity in human relationships but is not delimited by it. In the case of Anne and her mother, both suffer from the pain of their conflict and their resulting mistrust and guilt. Under these circumstances, the contextual therapist should aim at creating new trust between them through a search for the terms that appear fair from both sides.

The contextual approach is rooted in the fact that despair over a lack of trustworthy intergenerational relationships, and its accompanying retreat from ethical (fair) engagment with significant family members, often lies behind conditions normatively defined in terms of individual psychopathology. In large measure, the therapeutic capacity to address this reality emerges from a solid grasp of the complexly interweaving manifestations of multilateral, multidimensional, and legacy-based ethical dynamics. Multilateral consideration as the generic core of a therapeutic approach is relatively new, of course. In distinction to traditional psychodynamics, it defines human motivations, liberation, fulfillment, entitlement, and situations of health and sickness in dialectically dynamic relational terms. Additional knowledge will be required for the full utilization of contextual therapy as a pragmatic methodology.

LEGACIES

The enabling guidelines of contextual therapy are closely associated with a recognition of the potentially liberating elements in the legacy that in all its variable forms is the heritage of every human being. Transpersonal in function, the relational configuration of the legacy constitutes an ethical imperative that transcends the issue of the concrete behavior of a given set of parents or children. It also transcends filial disappointment and regret over the specifics of one's upbringing. Legacy expectations evolve from the fact and implications of generative rootedness rather than from the quality of parenting or the nature of filial response. It should be noted that legacy expectations are not fixed chains of destiny that inevitably define a person's existence. People need not live with the burden of having failed to meet unilaterally determined legacy expectations, but can participate in defining their own terms and options for fulfilling these inherited demands. On the other hand, though the fulfillment of legacy-bound obligations may be avoided or postponed, it cannot ultimately be denied nor indefinitely be ignored. A flat refusal to act on one's account, or at least to acknowledge it, results in existential indebtedness which may or may not be accompanied by guilt feelings. A failure to recognize legacy obligations and a sense of remorse often results in self-impairing behavior or even in psychosomatic response. Conversely, the very attempt to fulfill legacy expectations augments the possibility of individual entitlement, freedom, and autonomy regardless of outcome. Efforts to fulfill legacy expectations can occur in a variety of ways, some of which are taught or "delegated" by the parent generation (Stierlin, 1974), and some of which are decided by the offspring's terms. The nature of optional responses depends on the degree of a person's flexibility and creative initiative. In any case, a person's capacity to address and act on legacy requirements can be greatly assisted by the therapist's ability to advise practical solutions that are both realistic from the offspring's side and more acceptable from the parents' side.

FOUR DIMENSIONS OF THE CONTEXT

Grounded in relational dynamics as well as in psychodynamics, the contextual therapist identifies relational trustworthiness as the crucial resource for individual health and maturity. His efforts to reinforce the fiber of trustworthiness in significant relationships provide the unifying understructure and the common denominator of tactical measures. His successful investment in assessing and actualizing relational resources among family members tends to take priority over incomplete, nondialectical symptom modification and the elimination of pathology as goal definitions. Consideration of the unique entitlements of all family members as discrete individuals *ipso facto* limits the utility of partial or transactionally reductionistic models and terms like system, structure, network, communications, transaction, homeostasis, feedback, and behavior. From a contextual perspective, the hypothesis underlying the use of behavioral prescriptions, psychodynamic interpretations, power tactics, tasks, and transactional-communicational restructuring are unidimensional in orientation. Their ability to address interlocking balances that affect all dimensions of relatedness is therefore unnecessarily limited. In contrast, comprehensive and multilateral guidelines and strategies proceed from the perception of four crucial relational dimensions that are interlocking in nature. These include:

Facts (Destiny)
Needs (Psychology)
Transactions (Power Alignments)
Merited Trust (Balance of Fairness).

The four dimensions of contextual therapy constitute the relational essence of the human condition. Intersecting and intertwining in nature, each of them represents a relational determinant that informs psychotherapeutic intervention of all kinds. Each of the four crucial dimensions of contextual therapy retains its own technical implications for intervention. A brief review of them and their specific characteristics underscores the necessity for an integrative therapeutic approach. Fact and merit should be considered from within their original primary contexts. Need and power can be considered from within original and substitutive contexts alike. The therapeutic leverages of all psychotherapeutic approaches are translatable into one of the four dimensions.

Facts as Destiny

In the first instance, the factual contents of a person's destiny include sexual, racial, ethnic, religious, and familial identities. Other factors may include:

Beauty or ugliness, hereditary illness or severe brain damage, or greater or lesser brain endowment
Early loss of parent(s), adoption, or questionable paternity
Prominent predecessors and a consecutive legacy of excellence, shameful parentage and a legacy of failure, martyred ancestors and the accompanying indebtedness over survivorship
The benefit of the successful marriage of one's parents, or the burden of a legacy of split loyalties resulting from damaging relationships between immature, manipulatively hostile parents.

To some degree, each of us is obliged to find ways to rebalance and exonerate the shortcomings of our families of origin. No one is intrinsically free of the implications of the filial loyalty and the parental accountability that constitutes life's two fundamental intergenerational legacies. Intergenerational legacies, like physical characteristics and genetic endowment, are nonnegotiable components of individual survival and welfare. They are based on the configuration of facts but become ethical claims in their own right and involve the dimension of merit as well.

The factual basis of intergenerational legacies impacts individual vested interests and the welfare interests of all family members. Consequently, each person's rootedness and family constellation provide a dynamic clue to his or her entitlement and indebtedness. For example, by its very nature, the birth of a brain-damaged child weights a family's obligation to consider the welfare interests of each family member in its own peculiar way. The child's very existence predetermines a relative deprivation of the dependency needs of healthy siblings. It also escalates the siblings' obligation to consider the special indebtedness and entitlement of their depleted parents. In the same vein, the fact of birth into an historically suppressed group imposes its own particular indebtedness. Here, each person inherits the obligation to care about the specific survival interests and causes of his or her own loyalty group. In an analogous way, the adopted child who is kept in secrecy about his origins may risk entrapment in an unactualized ethical concern for unknown, natural parents. In any case, the welfare interests of individual family members are always factual givens and the obligation to consider each family member's interests is an ethical dynamic. The expression "it behooves us" connects existential facts with the necessity of assuming mutual, if consecutive responsibility for family members.

The inherited configuration of facts that precedes and surrounds human existence constitutes a dynamically formative part of human destiny. The contents of each person's legacy are received as objective components of given circumstances of a highly specific nature. The task for the contextual therapist lies in learning how certain facts in a person's relational world are transmuted into ethical obligations, expectations, and demands. The destiny of inherited facts and their ethical implications are more than a mere construct. Some people grow up with luck that is better than average. Other people grow up with luck that is far worse than average. But no person's background constitutes a destiny of completely unfulfillable obligations.

Needs or Psychology

Like the factual contents of a person's destiny, psychological factors constitute a nonreduceable entity. Psychological factors contribute to the strength and meaning of relationship which in turn benefits from the degree of complementation between the needs of partners. Essentially, however, psychological realities belong to the individual level of systemic organization. Each person's psychological universe is contained in his or her brain functions. The distinction between fact and need as determinants of a person's relational context can be illustrated by the actuality of a child's physical handicap and social deprivations on the one hand, and his consequent attitudes, thoughts, and feelings about having been thus deprived on the other. Hereditary illness, for example, affects a person's destiny even if the fact never penetrates his personal awareness. On the other hand, a person's absorption of the fact of hereditary illness may give rise to fear, resentment, depression, and dependent character traits among other psychological elaborations. It is obvious that some children grow up in a more unjust world than other children. It is equally obvious that some children face a greater burden of frustration of their basic needs and rights than other children. Moreover, they vary according to the extent and nature of the psychic consequences of their existential destiny.

To be sure, the dimension of individual psychology includes the component of trust. Erickson introduced the notion of basic trust as the foundation of the individual's psychosocial development. Moreover, trust and trustworthiness serve a life-long resource for need-satisfaction, stability, and hope. The stronger the individual, the more he or she will be capable of postponing immediate gratification and of taking a realistic inventory of options. Beyond basic trust, however, lies the issue of the adult need for trustworthiness. Without the resources of at least a few trustworthy relationships, people appear much further removed from hope and satisfaction. Conversely, the availability of trustable relationships lowers the threshold for ego strength requirements on the part of participating individuals.

The individual and his psychic motivational system constitute the need level of relational dynamics while merited trust or a balance of fairness represents the ethical level. Fairness as a crucial relational determinant never displaces the reality of human need but includes and transcends it. The significance of an individual's instinctive motivations, thought organization, and emotional-affective experiences remain intact and valid. Interlocking in function, the relational dimensions of psychology and merit are distinctive in nature. The major distinction between psychology and merit, however, lies in the fact that the psychological dimension can tolerate substitution without a loss of symbolic meaning. For example, a client may transfer his dependent need-configuration from the parent to his relationship with the therapist or employer. The role-appropriate need-configuration can then be elaborated and resolved in a transferred, reality approximate, "inappropriate," substitutive context. Freudian psychoanalysis clearly chooses to reply on a substitutive parent-child context (therapeutic transference) as the main relational avenue for accomplishing change. In contrast with psychologically meaningful displacements, entitlement or indebtedness based on an imbalance of fairness cannot validly be transferred out of the original relationship in which injuries and distortion actually took place. In this view, displaced accusations, e.g., with the spouse as object instead of one's parent, are ethically invalid and trust destroying.

The internal object relations theory of psychic function (Fairbairn, 1952; Guntrip, 1961) provides an important link between the psychological and ethical components of distorted behavior. According to this view, the deepest functional level of the mind is intrinsically relational. The tendency to ascribe "badness" to a relational partner hinges on the universal human reliance on good and bad "internal objects." It also hinges on the everpresent human inclination to perceive closely related people through the looking glass of internal configurations. An emotional need to "externalize" internal badness may inappropriately converge with the ethical demands of filial loyalty and even be reinforced by them. For example, through scapegoating someone else, a person can retain invisible loyalties to parents whom he apparently, if ambivalently, resents or despises. Retributive behavior meant for a parent but aimed at a mate may momentarily decrease the actor's guilt-laden tension. Under the circumstances, however, the dynamic linkage of unsettled ethical accounts between parent and child is likely to stay outside of an individual's awareness. Unfaced and unresolved, unbalanced intergenerational unfairness functions as an intrusive, mystifying element in later relationships. This process of displacement has been termed "the revolving slate" (Boszormenyi-Nagy & Spark, 1973). Characteristically, the person who unjustly lays blame on another person in order to protect his parents tends to be immune to guilt toward the innocent victim of the revolving slate. A lack of merit transferred from an invisible filial account to a third party results in a person's false capacity to claim entitlement, at the tragic cost of new unfairness done to another aspect of the human context.

No therapist can benefit from disclaiming the significance of early development, learning, psychopathology, and other facets of individual psychology. Nor is there any real benefit of parsimony for the therapist in ignoring either historically imbalanced accounts between people with roots-in-common, or the directly inflicted if subjectively experienced injuries that are living issues among family members. The task for the contextual therapist lies in assessing the place of each of these relational dimensions within the context of each client's life. Successful intervention depends on the therapeutic capacity to discern the manner in which individual psychological determinants interlock with the dimensions of factual destiny and merited trust as well as with transactions or power alignments.

Transactions or Power Alignments

Many aspects of day-to-day existence are manifestly competitive and power-oriented. Traditional socio-anthropological interpretations of human behavior and activities have long been conceptualized according to role and power conflicts between competing entities or between authority and opposition to authority. In political science as well as in the social sciences, theories tend to be reductionistic in their exclusively power-based analyses of the nature of decision-making, male and female role conflicts, class struggle and war, among other factors. These analyses usually overlook the fact that the greatest social influence is often connected to an ethically-based leverage that involves self-sacrificial defeat and death on the part of a loyal member of a family or ethnic group. In a literal sense, sacrifice of all power rather than direct power gain is the essence of the social martyr. Be that as it may, a concern with the dynamic structures and processes that determine power alignments and interindividual and intergroup struggles for control has continued to impact the thinking of most authors in the field of family therapy and social dynamics. For example, sequences of transactional patterns and structures are frequently interpreted as sufficient determinants of relational behavior (Haley, 1976). It is evident, of course, that styles of communication can lend themselves to identifiably exploitative games. Consider, for instance, the difficulty of escaping "double-binds" (Bateson, et al., 1956). Even the psychodynamic context of an individual's needs that requires another individual as a need-object intrinsically represents a power arena for unilateral exploitation, possession, and contest. Moreover, psychotherapeutic contracts between patient and therapist also imply a power alliance. Individual therapy is aimed at enhancing the effectiveness of one person's life. Its traditional contract and goals tend to fall short of a contextual consideration for the health, pleasure, success, competitive competence, and freedom from incapacitating symptoms for significant people in the patient's life. Child therapy and family therapy are usually contracted by an adult authority who defines pathology, and thus run the danger of working toward one-sided, potentially exploitative goals. The unilateral structure and goals of therapeutic modalities like child guidance and classical behavior therapy may also implicitly serve to justify covert scapegoating as a legitimate mode of relating.

At a minimum, traditional individual or symptomatic-based pathology orientations disclaim the component of loyal devotion in the "patient" member's stance. The resulting therapeutic compliance not only protects a potentially exploitative family "establishment" but also burdens the symptomatic member by implying that he alone is responsible for change. Consequently, the client is locked into an insoluble double-bind: on the one hand, the symptomatic role can function to confirm a person's implicit devotion to his family. On the other hand, he is regarded as the apparent source of the family's difficulties. Under the circumstances, the substrate of the family's implicit if covert pathogenic context remains intact. The family's subtle exploitation of the "designated patient" and the family members' own personal and relational imbalances stay basically untouched. Given the relational ethical stagnation of his family and his own therapeutically sponsored disengagement from them, the symptomatic family member usually invests himself in substitutive relational efforts and fails to initiate efforts to bring his family to account for their responsibility for injury and exploitation. Even if psychological gains are made, a major resource for relational trust-building is collusively abandoned by both the family and therapist.

Unless all relational dimensions are faced and considered, transactionally "active" therapists paradoxically may reinforce a stagnant, dependent continuation of ethical inactivity and disengagement among family members. Conversely, through strategies based upon the therapeutic implications of a mutually accountable reinvestment in fair relationship, the contextual therapist elicits a penetratingly active process of trust-building among all family members. As he sees it, the task is to guide symptomatic and nonsymptomatic family members to a subjective redefinition of their own accountability for relational entitlement and indebtedness. The successful accomplishment of this task is highly dependent on the therapist's use of multidirected partiality. In the case of a family with a delinquent adolescent, for example, the contextual therapist accepts the socially desirable, transactionally prescriptive goals of improved behavior. However, he considers the ethical issue of a subtle, exploitative parentification of the delinquent adolescent as the most dynamically significant factor in the situation and soon finds ways to surface the youngster's covert loyalty to his parents and family. At the exact moment when all credit is denied to the delinquent, the therapist may show his curiosity about any sign of the youngster's devotion, concern, or availability.

Merited Trust or Balance of Fairness

Merited trust or a balance of fairness (also known as relational ethics) is founded on the observation that each family member is entitled to fair consideration of his survival and welfare interests simply by virtue of his birth and existence. It also assumes that any malfunction may represent a desperate effort on the part of one member to signal an imbalance of trustworthy give-and-take within the family unit. That is, like other designated patients, the delinquent has merit on his side. In fact, his overt behavior may be a function of invisible loyalties and, as such, can amount to a contribution rather than a deficit in the family system. In many instances, an unrelieved focus on symptomatology is myopically unilateral in nature and may be equated with chronic indifference to a person's deeply-held if deviously expressed loyal family devotion. Short-sightedness of this kind can result in factual exploitation of the designated patient, and in ethical disengagement and stagnation among all family members. In turn, ethical stagnation leads to the essential pathogenicity of relationships and, if fixated, is a poor prognostic sign in the long run. On the other hand, the multilateral recognition of merited trust even in the midst of striking pathology serves to establish concern and trustworthiness as bases for reciprocity between people with roots-in-common.

A fundamental dynamic force, actualizing residual trustworthiness in parent-child relationships is society's ultimate resource for re-establishing the cohesion that currently seems threatened. The intrinsic merit inherent in avoided or denied close family relationships is a therapeutic and preventive dynamic that is used and abused for recharging the batteries of badly buffeted adult hope, purpose, and meaning. The dynamic interactions and outcomes of fair consideration between relating people are existentially observable and not to be confused with the world of "ought" and the prejudicial moralizing associated with it. Balances of fairness are not interchangeable with abstract moral values, assumptions about moral, psychological development, or code-like, reified religious and cultural doctrines. Nor is merit to be confused with superego configurations or the psychological experience of relating partners.

Using merited trust as the core determinant of relationships, the contextual therapist can guide family members to a fresh appraisal of the requirements of a fair balance between their mutual welfare interests. He can help families' dormant resources of trust, and teach them how to design ways of give-and-take that can intervene in chronic mistrust and seemingly desperate "cut-offs" among family members. In the process of reversing mistrust and unfairness, the contextual therapist can also help family members divest themselves of causal factors that underlie distorted exressions of invisible loyalties. To be sure, the actual task of discovering satisfactory patterns of dialogue and exchange remains the responsibility of relating persons who have to learn to overcome tendencies to scapegoat "bad relatives."

MERITED TRUST AS A MOTIVATIONAL DYNAMIC

Integrative in intent, contextual therapy is anchored in factual and ethical relational determinants, and incorporates the dimensions of power and need. Its generic rationale, however, is specific in nature and in the first instance has to do with multilateral balances of entitlement and indebtedness between relating partners. In particular, merit that belongs to parent-child interactions is intrinsically trust regenerating and has motivational as well as developmental implications for human growth and stability. The inescapable weightiness of the long-term legacies of parental accountability and filial loyalty create an inherent and nonsubstitutable interdependence between the survival and welfare interests of parent and child alike. Inevitably, vertical accounts of rootedness stand as the most influential of all relational balances. Geographic distance, lack of interaction, negative affect, and even indifferent attitudes and abusive behavior may affect the linkages between parent and child but per se are unable to end them. Even revenge or passionate rebuke is usually meant to test a parent's or child's willingness to respond rather than to terminate the relationship between them. Parents and children can seem to hate each other but their anger is secondary to longed-for trust. The fact of procreation invariably supersedes the quality of the relation as the stimulus for continuity and mutual concern. The roots of the individual's existence itself are thus a source of basic contextual trustworthiness (Boszormenyi-Nagy, 1976).

If parent-child relationships are decisively influenced by legacy expectations, they are also affected by an asymmetry of power, i.e., the unequal power differential that exists between parents and their dependent children. The facts of asymmetrical power and its potential misuse underscore the dynamic significance of merited trust as a relational dimension whose importance grows in direct proportion to the degree of asymmetry. Initially one-sided, accountability between parents and children is built on a prior contract of two legacies: parental accountability and filial indebtedness. The child's survival and existence as a helpless infant are predicated on some adult's actualized commitment to be a caring parent.* Abrogation of an *a priori* agreement to provide parenting automatically victimizes a child and is one example of the misuse of asymmetrical power. The child's developmental vulnerability provides an additional framework and time span in which parents can victimize their offspring through the misuse of unequal power.

Exploitative parental behavior will affect a youngster's life at two levels: (1) behaviorally and emotionally, an immediate here-and-now response will take place in the form of a child's tears, anger, and self-destructiveness, and (2) a delayed "developmental" and motivational response will result in the guise of defective character formation, social alienation, an incapacity to learn, and paranoid suspicion, among other manifestations. A delayed response to parental exploitation invariably takes place, and serves to telescope past transactions into the present and future. Delayed filial responses to past occasions of exploitation by parents represent an unbalanced ethical account that eventually must be assessed and reworked lest the cost of the imbalance be conveyed to future generations.

The misuse of asymmetrical power is only one source of exploitation by parents. A second source lies in the native readiness of children to meet the existential debts that they owe their parents. To that end, children make themselves available to parents beyond the call of reasonable duty, even when such availability exacts considerable personal cost and sacrifice. Consequently, a source of usually inadvertent parental exploitation lies in the adult tendency to "parentify" young children. By definition, parentification implies the subjective distortion of a relationship in which one's children or mate are treated as one's parent (Boszormenyi-Nagy & Spark, 1973, chapter 6). The tendency to parentify is not only a sign of relational dysfunction but also exists in reasonably balanced relationships to a lesser degree. Carried to ex-

---

*"Children's Inherent Rights" (Boszormenyi-Nagy & Spark, 1973).

tremes, however, parentification becomes a vital ethical issue if it exhausts a child's relational resources and results in a deficit financing of filial devotion at the cost of personality development. The dangers of parentification are easily missed by overburdened parents who are depleted by the demands of today's complex, impersonal world. Ensconced in nuclear families and isolated from trustworthy relationships with extended kin and community members, depleted parents inevitably turn to their own children for nurturing. Despite its potential misuse, the fact remains that children provide huge resources for their parents in the form of wished-for and actual trustworthiness despite filial limitations of knowledge, authority, and functional competence. The combination of the legacy of filial devotion and a child's existential need to put himself in a position to repay incurred debts to his parents comprises the greatest available human resource for day-to-day life, for effective therapy, and for the development of preventive planning in individual and relational breakdown and imbalance.

If filial devotion gives rise to a child's investment in repaying existential debts, parental investment gives rise to an accumulation of entitlement based on merit. Moreover, parental ability to accept filial efforts to rebalance early accounts is parallel in importance to the child's willingness to "pay back." The same paradigm of investment and devotion, with its fair and unfair balances of entitlement and indebtedness, exists as well in long-term relationships outside the parent-child tie. In relationship, entitlement and indebtedness co-vary in direct proportion to two people's give-and-take. See Figure 16-1.

The quantitative fluctuations of the balance of fairness between two power-equal partners can be described by the formula $(E_1 - I_1) = -(E_2 - I_2)$. Entitlement and indebtedness constitute the two end poles on the continuum of relational ethics. The formula describes the ongoing ethical context of the relationships between partners 1 and 2.

In an ongoing interindividual exchange, any act of giving or receiving automatically shifts the status of an account toward a new balance or imbalance. For example, a man's reluctant but positive co-operation in his wife's pursuit of education and career eventually increased the degree to which he was entitled to actualize his own interests beyond his profession. That is, his entitlement grew in direct proportion to her indebtedness for his consideration of her welfare interests. On the

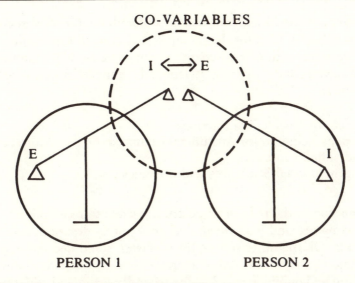

Figure 16-1. *Intrinsic Balances of the Ethical Context*

other hand, her indebtedness lessened as her husband claimed his entitlement. As I do something for my partner, my entitlement increases. Conversely, my partner's attentive consideration of my interests indebts me and compels me to find ways to enable his entitlement. Entitlement founded on multilateral concern depends on my capacity to consider your interests. Interlocking in function, your welfare becomes my welfare insofar as the fulfillment of your interests entitles me to your consideration of my interests. From a multilateral perspective, one person's fair consideration of the other can be sustained because each of them has a self-serving investment in maintaining an accountable, trustworthy partnership.

TEMPORAL MULTILATERALITY

Time is an important factor in relational investments. Considerations of timing pertain to a flow of energy and to a demand for patient consideration in relationships as well as in the therapeutic process. In the therapeutic process, time and its use are major factors in therapeutic strategies concerned with fair balances of multilateral entitlement and indebtedness. In fact, for the therapist, the issue of time required for effective intervention is inseparable from questions of multilateral priority setting and weighting. Relationally time can be subdivided into four units:

Sequences of Visible Transactions
Timespans Required for Attitudinal Change in One or More Persons
An Individual's Lifespan
Transgenerational Sequences and Linkages

On one side of the temporal spectrum, visible transactions are "factual" in nature and lend themselves to a purely descriptive study of behavior. On the other side of the spectrum stand decision-making, motivations, and satisfactions that are subjectively timed realities whose initiation and outcome may last for seconds, years, and a lifetime, or for several generations.

Sequences of *short-term, visible transactions and interactions* are exemplified by events like a new educational or occupational achievement, or the conclusion of a court-supported visiting arrangement between divorcing parents. Purposive (goal-oriented) in direction, such events occur within a clearly measurable timespan. Sequences of visible transactions are usually interspersed with moratoria that provide the time frame for attitudinal change. Without intervening periods of apparent inactivity, relating partners are neither able to integrate discrete transactional steps nor to absorb the implications of observable interactions in terms that affect long-term changes in attitude.

Attitudinal change connotes a realignment of motivations that may or may not be accompanied by visible behavioral change. For the contextual therapist, the most significant attitudinal changes in relationship evolve from progress toward trust-building that is time-determined. Re-engagement in an avoided parent-child relationship, for example, can effect a profound change in long-held attitudes of resentment and indifference (see case illustration, chapter 12, Boszormenyi-Nagy & Spark, 1973). An aging mother's terminal illness may motivate her daughter to seek and show warmth and intimacy after a 35-year period of cold and distant attitudes. Moreover, for the first time since her child was very young, mother may now be in a position to assume a receptive attitude toward her daughter's approaches. Suddenly, a final chance for both parties to rework the past, rediscover trust, and influence the future frequently proves to be a stronger determinant in relationship than the need to maintain retributive attitudes that function as reinforcing factors of a prior, long-term engagement.

Birth itself establishes each individual as a living link between past and future generations. Born into legacy expectations on the one hand and cast into potential responsibility for parenting children on the other, between conception and death each of us is also faced with the task of living life in optimally self-fulfilling ways. At a minimum, individual survival and a relatively satisfying existence within one's personal context constitute life's purposive design. By nature, however, the purposes and goals of one life span intersect and overlap with the purposes and goals of past and future life spans, and thus intertwine with a multigenerational chain of legacies. Marriage and the foundation of new family units continue the forward movement of these legacies, and, in our view, are paragons of creative challenge for every human being.

Paradoxically, perhaps, the process of individuation exists in dialectical relation to a person's capacity to act on the demands of inherited legacies. That is, the biological space in an individual life span that is creatively assigned to fulfilling legacy expectations provides options and opportunities for redefining the parameters of personal autonomy. Needless to say, some people are more fortunate than others in the degree to which their legacies are enabling or binding, and freeing or confining.

An individual's freedom to address legacy expectations in his lifetime is directly connected to his ability to engage in peer relationships, to marry, and to commit himself to a new generation. Ostensibly, marriage is a vehicle for long-range relational commitment that potentially can span two lifetimes. In fact, the promise of continuity of commitment through shared parenting is a major factor in weighting marriage with a higher degree of ethical accountability than that ordinarily associated with friendships. As a rule, adult-to-adult commitments of most kinds are essentially symmetrical and, if they survive, do so within enough of a balance of give-and-take to satisfy each partner's interests. When a relatively fair consideration of each other's welfare is no longer possible in friendship or in marriage, separation or divorce takes place. On the other hand, a "divorce" between parent and dependent child is neither feasible nor ethically symmetrical because the welfare interests of successive generations irreversibly "telescope" into each other.

Figure 16-2 illustrates the analogy between a telescope and the *transgenerational sequences and linkages* of delayed injuries that are incurred through imbalanced accounts in intergenerational legacies. As the segments emerge in sequence, holes become visible in each of them in turn. In contrast to individually-oriented therapists whose interest lies in only one segment of an extended system, the contextual therapist sees the telescope in its expanded state. In the case of child placement, for example, he is not only concerned with the visible effects of adoption or of foster care arrangements on a child's current life, but also with their implications for the child as he grows up to be a parent and grandparent, and for other members of the extended family, born and unborn. Moreover, knowledge that telescopes transgenerationally provides the source of specific methodological leverages in therapy.

The therapeutic capacity to choose appropriate time perspectives is not only a determinant in goal setting, but also provides a basis for

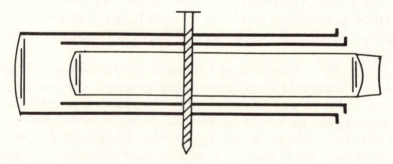

Figure 16-2. Transgenerational Telescoping

evaluatory criteria of psychotherapeutic change.* The fact that long-range time sequences in general and transgenerational linkages in particular are difficult to visualize should make them no less a consideration than visible, short-term criteria for change. Its concern with long-range time sequences makes contextual therapy a preventive approach *par excellence*, as the young child becomes an investor in future relational assets and debits, and credits and liabilities.

THERAPEUTIC IMPLICATIONS

The contextual approach offers a variety of challenges to the future of psychotherapy. These include:

A reconsideration of trust as a therapeutic factor in lowering the cost of developing ego strength, as well as a concrete aid in strengthening the ego of a person in a given context

Open attention to legacies as past resources of trust that have been transmitted to the present and future of each human being and can (1) serve to foster an appreciation of legacy as a principle of liberating potential, and (2) extend the storehouse of measures through which people can fulfill legacy expectations on their own terms of entitlement

Opportunities for combining therapeutic goals concerned with one individual's success and personal expediency with an explicit contractual concern for the integrity of everyday transactions, parent-child solidarity and trustworthy relations in extended kinship systems and the community

Fresh options for overcoming traditional splits between symptomatic, short-term, crisis-oriented therapeutic change and multilateral, long-term, fundamental therapeutic change

The refinement of a catalytic elicitory methodology that can be in-

---

*In contrast with everyday observers of life events, the contextual therapist has to learn to differentiate between time frames of visible events and interactions and those associated with long-term dynamic linkages that function as invisible connections between current events and their future implications.

corporated into the practice of all modalities of therapy, without
the therapist having to abandon his preferred subspecialization or
technical competence
A redefinition of prevention that is more accountable and more effective
by virtue of its move beyond unilateral and "categorical" symptom-
based planning to a grasp of intervention that is multilaterally feasible and resource oriented rather than delimited by pathology
Recognition that while historic severances from roots through voluntary
or forced migrations (Haley, A., 1976) can never be undone, in fact,
the relations between people with roots-in-common function as
potential sources of trustworthiness and provide a basis for reworking the disintegrative phenomena of society-at-large.

From its inception the family approach has raised questions of an
integrative nature. Initially, it seemed to offer additional technical
leverages that could readily be incorporated into already existing psychotherapeutic modalities. As it discovered its own ground and strengths,
family therapy gradually began to evolve as a discrete profession. In
the authors' view, however, eventually the family approach may make
its sturdiest contribution to psychotherapy by continuing to uncover
a relational dimension of human behavior that has long been implied
by theoreticians, but never pursued to its creative endpoint. If in fact
the ethical dimension of trust between relating partners is the invisible
thread of both individual freedom and interindividual balance, family
therapy's most fundamental contribution to psychotherapy need neither
be limited to new strategies nor elevated into a clearly unnecessary
competitive profession. Ultimately, family therapy's lasting contribution may lie in its emphasis on the multilateral implications of each
client's own context, and the contractual therapeutically responsible
implications of a contextual approach.

REFERENCES

Bateson, G., Jackson, D. D., Haley, J., & Weakland, J. Toward a theory of schizo-
    phrenia. *Behavorial Science, 1*, 251–264, 1956.
Boszormenyi-Nagy, I. From family therapy to a psychology of relationships: Fictions

of the individual and fictions of the family. *Comparative Psychiatry, 7*, 408–423, 1966.

Boszormenyi-Nagy, I. Behavior change through family change. In A. Burton (Ed.), *What makes behavior change possible?* New York: Brunner/Mazel, 1976.

Boszormenyi-Nagy, I., & Spark, G. *Invisible loyalties: Reciprocity in intergenerational family therapy.* Hagerstown, MD: Medical Dept., Harper and Row, 1973.

Fairbairn, W. R. D. *An object-relatedness theory of the personality.* New York: Basic Books, 1952.

Guntrip, H. J. *Personality structure and human interaction: The developing synthesis of psychodynamic theory.* New York: International Universities Press, 1961.

Haley, A. *Roots.* Garden City, New York: Doubleday and Co., 1976.

Haley, J. *Problem-solving therapy: New strategies for effective family therapy.* San Francisco: Jossey-Bass, 1976.

Hartman, H. *Essays on ego psychology, selected problems in psychoanalytic theory.* New York: International Universities Press, 1964.

Kohut, H. *The restoration of the self.* New York: International Universities Press, 1977.

Stierlin, H. *Separating parents and adolescents: A perspective on running away, schizophrenia and waywardness.* New York: Quadrangle, 1974.

17

Commentary: Transgenerational Solidarity — Therapy's Mandate and Ethics

The ethics and mandate of therapy are seldom fully recognized. The apparent disintegration of lasting human relationships may impinge on posterity with heavy consequences. As high mobility, loss of relational continuity, and fast rates of change diminish security in adults, parents will increasingly turn to their children for the fulfillment of their adult emotional dependency needs. In remarried families, children are often expected to fit in with enthusiasm equal to that of their remarrying parent joining a new mate.

Moreover, in mistrustful marriages, children are easily overlooked in their roles of referee or guarantor of solidarity. In doing so, the destructively entitled, exploited child is expected to carry the burden of responsibility that was formerly provided by the extended family. At this juncture therapy and prevention converge. Therapy's mandate includes the task to inform society at large about the implications of preventable transgenerational consequences.

The ethics of therapy are inseparable from the ethics of relating and the ethics of science. In order to reach its goals, scientific inquiry has to be free of bias. Therapy is not a scientific endeavor. It aims to serve the client's interests—the therapist has to be benevolently biased toward the client's welfare. The therapeutic contract defines the sides. Ever since Hippocrates formulated it, the therapist is known to be ethically obligated to give priority to the client's side, to his or her health interests. I consider health synonymous with unimpeded survival and pathology as an interference with the quality of survival. But the context of relating raises the question: whose survival?

In contrast with physical medicine, in psychotherapy the consequences of therapeutic intervention can never be confined to one client's interests. Even in classical, individual therapy, the patient's spouse, children, and parents too will be subject to consequences of the outcome, whether the consequences are favorable or unfavorable, whether or not the therapist intends and knows so. In other words, at least implicitly, therapeutic design and contractual ethics include the health interests of all potential beneficiaries and victims of the interventions.

The emergence of family therapy did not create the conflict among the interests of the various family members, but it has made it difficult to ignore such conflicts. Since family members are often opposed to one another's sides, it is unlikely to help all of them by a single intervention design. Among family therapists, reference to a systemic understanding appears at times as a ground for professional hubris or even as a shibboleth. Yet the systemic view does not by itself resolve the controversy of interests and the contradiction between personal consequences affecting closely relating persons. A systemic view of recursive feedback processes has some explanatory value for the motives of the persons involved and for therapy, but it does not eliminate the ethics of responsibility for consequences. I propose that *interpersonal consequence* is the most important aspect of close relating and that it is the basis of both relational and therapeutic ethics.

In terms of general systems theory, accountability for consequences has to rely on the level that is the ultimate source of human actions and decision: the person. In this sense, a family includes at least two major systemic levels; (a) the family as one whole unit, composed of interacting individuals, and (b) a congeries of various individuals, each being a whole system of respective responsibilities for his or her actions.

Physically, psychologically, and legally, the nuclear family is dissolvable, but the individual is indissoluble. The fact that there are "circular" conflicts between family members does not by itself dissolve the family. Only if one or both of the spouses qua individuals decide to pursue their lives divorced from each other, will dissolution follow as a consequence. Ethically or legally, it is the individuals who can be made accountable for decisions and for the consequences of those decisions.

Responsibility for consequences is heaviest with respect to the interests of future generations. And there is no pattern of essential reciprocal influence or feedback between remote generations. Generation I will affect generations II, III, and IV, but not the other way around. The sequential chain of time is irreversible but not untouchable.

Any assumption of pathogenesis treats the pathogen as a preexisting set of conditions and pathology as the resulting consequence. If incestuous sexuality with a small child is the pathogenic condition, the resulting factual psychological, transactional, and ethical consequences constitute the pathology to be treated. The pathogenic fact has already occurred before the client was referred. It cannot be removed post facto. Yet life goes on and presents its manifold options nonetheless. There are resources in every participant's options. I suggest that, instead of acting through the removal of pathogens, all therapy is *resource-based*.

Consider the case of the incestuous father's family. Besides being a part of a system of recursive current transactions, the incestuous parent's act reflects consequences resulting from his *formative past*. In contrast, the abused child lives in a *formative present* that may have lasting consequences for her future survival. Moreover, if she is lastingly affected, she may have a corresponding impact on her children. The chain of consequences points toward the interests of posterity.

In most cases the chain of consequences is not as easy to see. Perhaps the most widespread "pathogenic" conditions of our era are the fragmentation and deterioration of the quality of close relationships. The main result of these two factors is a destructive "parentification" (2) of young children by their parents.

Fragmentation of extended family ties has been continuous as a result of increased mobility and geographical dispersion of working men and women and as a result of women's more active pursuit of careers.

A deterioration of long-term commitment to man-woman relationships has come about through increasing frequency of divorce and, for certain segments of society, the welfare support of mothers with dependent children. Inevitably, as support through lastingly committed adult relationships diminishes, parents will turn to their children for the fulfillment of their own adult emotional dependency needs.

The overwhelming adult reliance on young children can take overt or covert forms. In its overt form this exploitation of young children can be expressed through sexual or aggressive abuse of the child as the object of adult needs.

In its covert form, exploitation of children follows from their captive role as providers of trust and their lasting investment in relationships compared with the shaky commitments of adults. Children are easily overlooked in their role as referee between mistrustful married or divorced parents and as captive "fiduciary" guarantors of solidarity and happiness within remarried families. In their search for a satisfying adult solution, parents tend to assume that their adult freedom for lasting commitments is beneficial or at least understandable to their young children. Unfortunately, these myths tend to interfere with responsible adult concern and exploration.*

In cases of both overt and covert exploitation of children by their parents, the destructively parentified child is made to absorb a significant part of responsibility that used to belong to the extended family. The child's affection, devotion, trust, and trustworthiness are implicitly expected to keep the family together. Through their regressive acts and failings, many parents recruit their young children to try to keep them "in line." Although the parentified child performs an indispensable function for both family and society, he does so at the expense of his emotional maturation and trust in the world.

As it is widely assumed, the child's exploitation may have consequences not only for the child himself but also for potential new victims,

---

*One aspect of covert exploitation of children takes place through parental abandonment and neglect.

people on whom the victimized person will tend unfairly to "take-it-out." Essentially, the victimized child will suffer two kinds of damaging consequences: (a) a distorted, mistrustful or even antisocial personality development, and (b) a *destructive entitlement* (1). Entitlement to be destructive usually includes a blocked sense of remorse over harming others. This ominous inclination is a major factor in the multigenerational escalation of exploitive parenting and antisocial behavior.

Looking at the enormity of the consequences of destructive parenting, the therapist is faced with the ethics of responsibility for both healing and prevention. In fact, the preventive outcome of his work will cover a much wider ground than the healing aspect. The therapist, of course, cannot reverse the disintegrative developments in postindustrial society. On the other hand, the therapist should not be an accomplice in disregarding the child's fate in what could be designated as "pure marital therapy." If the couple have small children, the therapist cannot be excused for an indifference to prospective consequences to the next generation.

To claim that no one can predict future consequences is not enough. The therapist can still insist that the parents work on exploring and defining not just their own respective sides but the children's sides as well. It is through such *self-delineation* that responsibility for the interests of the offspring can be naturally elicited. Exploring and defining the children's burdens will liberate the parents as persons and as spouses. Whether they will stay together or decide on divorce, the spouses will lastingly benefit through *self-validation*, i.e., through establishing their respective ethical worth.

This contextual model of therapy as a self-delineating and self-validating dialogue builds safeguards against a multigenerational escalation of destructive entitlement. As the parents earn constructive entitlement through the consideration of future consequences for their young children of the parents' mistrustful, exploitive battle, therapy and prevention converge under the umbrella of *transgenerational solidarity*: the context of both therapeutic mandate and ethics. This is where the legacy of family therapy points as a guideline for the growth of therapy as a whole. Also it is at this juncture that therapists have an ethical contribution to society's future. Therapy's mandate includes learning about intergenerational consequences and informing society about this field of knowledge.

REFERENCES

1. Boszormenyi-Nagy, I., Interview with Markham, M. "Contextual Therapy: The Realm of the Individual." *Psychiatric News, 16*, 16–26, 1981.
2. Boszormenyi-Nagy, I. & Spark, G. M., *Invisible Loyalties: Reciprocity in Intergenerational Family Therapy.* New York: Brunner/Mazel, 1973.

18

Transgenerational Solidarity: The Expanding Context of Therapy and Prevention

This paper explores the mandate of therapy in the context of the quality of human survival. Transgenerational solidarity is, of course, a biological "mechanism" of the survival of each higher species of animals. Each parent-child relationship constitutes a link in the chain of transgenerational survival. In most animals, the quality of parenting is usually sufficient or else the offspring dies. Humans can produce parentally deprived, yet surviving, offspring.

The maintenance of the quality of survival in all living things is embedded in a capacity for evolutionary progress. Thus, in Schroedinger's words, living things circumvent the typical subordination of matter to progressive disintegration and simplification (entropy). Living things possess "negentropic" features. In this paper it is suggested that the negentropic progress of technical sophistication may lead humanity toward a progressive disintegration of the quality of lasting relationships.

Naturally, the destructive consequences of technical advancement cannot be reversed. However, therapists of families owe it to posterity to provide society with a preventive formula for constructive parenting. In contextual therapy the chance for earning entitlement is being offered as a built-in guardian of quality parenting. It is based on a relational ethic which is bound to benefit both the giver and the receiver of due concern. In so doing, this ethic advocates neither pure altruism nor pure "rugged" individualism. The contextual explanation for why this ethic is so often disregarded lies in the phenomenon of destructive entitlement. Hence, constructive and destructive entitlement are rooted both in an individual's inner world and in his relational context.

The context of this ethical realm between persons is explored here with the help of the concept of the intrinsic relational (e.g., transgenerational) tribunal. In a sense, this tribunal is the extension of the earlier notions of interpersonal merit ledger, or more accurately, the equilibrium among several coexisting merit ledgers.

This article searches for a common denominator for the requirements of that which therapy and prevention address in their broadest terms: 1) genuine criteria of autonomous individuation in the context of real relationships that have to be sorted out vis-à-vis random internal relations that inform the private epistemologies of each partner's idiosyncratic goals; 2) the dialogue of mutual self-definition anchored in the balance of inherent commitments to mutual self-validation through fair give and take—the basis of relational ethics, i.e., responsibility for consequences to others; 3) the systemic regulation of behavioral patterns of marriages, parent-child relationships, nuclear and extended families, and larger community metworks; 4) an intrinsic tribunal of transgenerational solidarity as the basis of prevention and as the manifestation of human species survival, e.g., concern about environmental health; 5) negentropy as the "locomotive" of biological evolution and, via ethics of receiving through giving to posterity, the guardian of both parent-child and peer relationships in a progressively automated world.

A confusion of basic notions characterizes the current understanding of the mandate of therapy. There are signs of declining public support and questions are being raised by government, the insurance industry, and the medical profession. All of this occurs at a point of an unprecedented "market acceptance" of a multitude of individual and family based therapy approaches. Yet the various techniques seem to have contributed to fragmentation rather than to a broadened common basis of understanding.

The term *therapy* is used here in its broad generic connotation. As a starting position, it includes all interventions that aim at bringing out the healthiest possible performance of human beings. In this sense it includes: psychoanalysis, psychotherapy, group therapy, family therapy, couples therapy, child therapy, geriatric therapy, etc., with all their schools and branches. It should not, however, include manipulation of one human being in the selfish interests of another person, a political party, an army, a business enterprise, etc.

In this article the suggestion is made to include the dynamic of transgenerational or species solidarity under the mandate of therapy. However, the quality of the individual's life remains a major touchstone for therapeutic goal, and the point of reference for the focus remains each person him- or herself. This multiple individual view in no way compromises another, the "systemic," view of relationships, a major tenet of classical family therapy. These two views can be subsumed under the perspective of relational reality and of intergenerational accountability. Inevitably, the quality of individual satisfaction depends on responsibility for relational consequences, ultimately for the offspring. Denial of consequences weakens prospects for coping with relational reality.

The reasoning behind this article originates from contextual therapy but its propositions address the unity of therapy and prevention. The term *contextual therapy* will be applied to the author's approach as it has evolved over a quarter of a century (Boszormenyi-Nagy, 1962, 1965a, 1965b, 1966, 1972, 1976, 1979; Boszormenyi-Nagy & Spark, 1973; Boszormenyi-Nagy & Krasner, 1980, 1981, 1986; Boszormenyi-Nagy & Ulrich, 1981).

Contextual therapy is not simply a school of family therapy. It represents a search for the common denominator of therapy as a whole. Currently, the integration of biological therapy, individual psychotherapy, and systemic family (relational) therapy can only be empirical and fortuitous, rather than rational. The three methodologies may coexist with one another in a treatment plan but they are mutually nontranslatable. Yet, considering the inevitable interlocking between individual and relational realities, selective reliance on any of the three approaches would be oversimplifying and reductionistic. I propose that through transcending the realms of biological, psychological, and systemic transactional regulation, we arrive at the sphere of the ethics of responsibility for long-term consequences of relating. Without consideration of this indispensable foundation, relational reality cannot be understood.

As an umbrella of therapeutic synthesis, *responsibility for relational consequences* has to comprise biological, psychological, and systemic-transactional criteria. The ethics of relational responsibility cannot be contradictory to any of these three descriptive and explanatory ideologies. Appropriate concern establishes one's integrity and ethical worth. This prospect of mutual self-validation is a major option of both donor and receiver for benefiting from relational resources. (Boszormenyi-Nagy & Krasner, 1986). Our responsible caring feeds into the substrate of posterity's fate. The fiber of responsibility for consequences connects the health of the present with the preventive interests of the future. However, in order to become a therapeutic guideline, the ethics of relational responsibility has to be translated into intervention methods and strategies.

Whereas no form of individual psychotherapy or family therapy is based on a scientific causality that equals, for example, bacteriology, there seem to be core assumptions about consequences that could serve as a common denominator among the essentially complementary rather than integratable congeries of therapeutic methods and philosophies.

THERAPY IN THE CONTEXT OF HUMAN SURVIVAL

Humanity faces a new historic reality of possible self-imposed extinction, and no informed human being can ignore its threat without committing a serious, almost pathological denial. The prospects of this reality threaten our own lives and, even more likely, our children's lives. Progress in transportation, computers, electronics, lasers, nuclear devices, etc. has speeded up the processes of even peacetime destruction to such an extent that they have far outpaced the growth of proven human responsibility. These accelerated processes contribute also to a progressive disintegration of reliable human relationships. Consequently, the nuclear family—fragmented by unabsorbable burdens— may follow the decline of the extended family. Divorce, single parenthood, teen motherhood, sperm banks, carrier pregnancy, genetic engineering, etc. are new social forms and realities which challenge our ingenuity. Whether one chooses to ignore the parenting implications of these phenomena or not, everybody's quality of life is affected either by their direct impact or by existential guilt over inaction.

One of our central theses is the key learning of decades of efforts directed at effective therapy: the healing resource of reliable and trustable human relationships. If reliable relating is vitally necessary for health, what are its functional criteria both among adults and children? In the long run, the consequences of the quality of each parent-child relationship add up to the quality of transgenerational survival. I propose that the reliability of relating can best be defined in ethical, rather than psychological terms. In contrast with value ethics, i.e., a concern with right and wrong, relational ethics emphasizes responsibility for consequences for others.

Exactly because the quality of our relationships has consequences for the survival of the future, relational ethics is not some collection of abstract moral values but the realistic criterion and the main "mechanism" of survival. Both constructive and destructive inputs can have lasting transgenerational consequences. They affect the offspring's capacity for trust. Once the trust of a child has been badly damaged, chances are that his or her children will grow even more mistrustful.

Having received from the past and owing to give it back to the successors, each person is cast into an unspoken ethical contract with the justice of transgenerational solidarity. If one generation returns less than it has received, this justice is bound to be violated. Thus, I propose that the most crucial generational consequences do not constitute a feedback. Even if they are part of circular transactions, they essentially feed forward.

The ledger of giving and receiving between generations impinges on the offspring's chances, his good or bad luck. Yet, not every injustice originates from personal malice or neglect. Destiny itself brings with it the prospect of the offspring's unfair victimization. For example, extreme degrees of bereavement combined with rejection are not only incapacitating circumstances, they represent a "distributive" injustice too. Certain children are exposed to more than the average human's share of bad luck. Yet will anybody ever own up to the responsibility or compensate, for example, for someone's: losing a parent at an early age and being rejected by the other parent; being affected by hereditary illness; having become parent of a brain damaged child; having been born uncommonly unattractive; having found out that the man he believes to be his father actually is not; discovering at a young age that he has an incurable disease?

If loss of reassuring, concerned relationships engenders serious misfortune for the offspring, recent history pictures an ominous course of each successive offspring's progressive bereavement of hope for security. The loss of stabilizing, supportive, if burdensome, ongoing family relationships places each subsequent generation into a more exposed, vulnerable condition.

However, the greatest burden of transgenerational deterioration of trustability may not originate from bereavement itself but from the adult generation's attitudes. If, for example, adult effectiveness is used for the deceitful exploitation of the weak offspring rather than for caring concern and support, the child's reasons for trusting the world are rightly jeopardized. Moreover, placing the burden of responsibility for his helpless predicament on the young child himself is always a sign of adult relational corruption. Perhaps the divorcing or unattached parent cannot help his or her child obtain a network of reassuring relationships. Yet, accepting adult responsibility for this condition still remains a constructive adult option. Conversely, to assume that the young child alone will find his or her supportive adult relationships represents a dangerous gambling with adult credibility. So does an expedient reference to the "resilience" of children betrayed and abandoned by the adult world. Even more destructive can be the burdening of the young child with responsibility for settling the parent-parent mistrust, i.e., placing the child into the predicament of split loyalty (Boszormenyi-Nagy, 1976; Boszormenyi-Nagy & Krasner, 1986).

This leads us into one of the most burning questions that has to be posed to helping professionals: How can we instruct the public about adult behavior's consequences for posterity? Decades of claims to healing competence and to scientific understanding of the effects of therapy obliges us to formulate at least a basic guideline for do's and don'ts.

Certain detriments inherent in the factual contemporary disintegration of family relationships are:

a decreasing store of relational stability and continuity, e.g., of community and extended family;
a decreasing life span of marital commitments;

an increasing divorce rate;
an increasing percentage of single parent homes;
an increasing percentage of early teen pregnancy;
an increasing rate of transitory, non-marital cohabitation;
an increasing reliance on nonrelational stimulation, e.g., violent television scenes, chemicals;
an increasing percentage of families with absent parents;
a decreasing prevalence of personal commitment to occupational choices;
a decreasing quality of life due to overpopulation (in certain areas of the world);
a high rate of unemployment.

It is my suggestion that many of these large scale social shifts are consequences of diminishing trust reserves.

Other detriments for posterity originate from ignorant, irresponsible, deceptive, or corrupt adult attitudes and assumptions:

that children can and should take care of themselves as adults do;
that small children never take responsible postures in families, but if they do, it proves that they don't need adult caring;
that society itself will take care of "its" children;
that relational difficulties can be solved by "cut off";
that an increasing adult freedom of partner choices automatically serves the children's interests as well, etc.

Concurrently, the violent and sexual abuse of children seems to be escalating and children are increasingly more frequently abandoned, neglected, or simply not claimed by parents. Children of welfare families are often deemed precious because of the welfare check their existence will bring to the household. More importantly, children in any family are likely targets of inadvertently displaced adult retaliation.

Responsibly caring about posterity is an extension of the contextual principle of the therapist's factual accountability for therapeutic impact on the lives of all persons related to his or her patient(s). In contrast with physical medicine, the effects and consequences of any psychotherapeutic intervention cannot be confined to the person of the patient.

Even if the treatment is considered classical individual therapy or psychoanalysis, we know that each of the patient's significant therapeutic changes may affect the lives of those related to him or her. It is even more expectable, both in a positive and in a negative sense, that the patient's children will be subject to a profound impact from changes in their parent's attitudes. Thus, an intrinsic inclusiveness of therapeutic contractual responsibility has wide-ranging ethical and legal implications for any kind of therapy. Our hypothesis requires, then, the extension of all therapeutic responsibility mainly to the interests of posterity. Conversely, as a corollary, the extension of fair consideration to posterity's interests is bound to impart therapeutic benefits to the present generation.

THERAPY IN THE CONTEXT OF
THE SURVIVAL OF LIVING THINGS

Immersed in an inorganic world bent on entropic disorderliness, the gradual disintegration of all higher forms of energy and matter, paradoxically, living things not only have managed to sustain themselves but tend to evolve into forms of higher complexity and order. The gradual evolution of increasingly complex forms of plant and animal species appears to support Schroedinger's (1962) classical thesis that living things are capable of utilizing "negentropic" mechanisms that seemingly contradict the inorganic world's obligatory entropic trend toward disintegration. Instead of elaborating on his theoretical assumptions, we shall borrow Schroedinger's words: living things can "suck orderliness" out of an essentially disorderly world. Gregory Bateson (1979) called this capacity the "central mystery of evolution."

How does the human species as a whole, and family relationships in particular, fit into this natural order?

Based on the threatening implications of technical progress, mankind faces a new ethical task. Technical progress is unreliable and cruelly indifferent to human survival needs. It has effectively increased the rate of destructive possibilities without correspondingly safeguarding our security and our quality of life. Moreover, its ominous threat for the future forces the current generation willy-nilly into the role of the wrongdoer vis-à-vis posterity. In order to survive, humanity needs a new, appropriately effective ethics of responsibility to thwart its likely destructive consequences to posterity (see Jonas, 1979).

What can the average parent do about the industrial pollution of the atmosphere or the threat of nuclear destruction? Virtually very little. Yet how many parents tend to blame themselves: Why did I bring my child into this kind of world? How fair is it to expect the parents to shield the offspring from an unpredictable destiny? Nonetheless, the offspring are entitled to search for someone to whom to attribute responsibility for the "mess" they inherit. Often they regard the parents as irresponsible, selfish beneficiaries of undeserved advantages. In revenge, the helpless, scapegoated parent, too, becomes entitled to hit back in callous unconcern. Yet who is to be blamed? As technology "progresses," each generation is held to owe more than it has received. The unfairness of this circumstance tends to enhance each generation's entitlement to be vindictive. How can therapy account for a realistic cause for grudge in future generations?

Concepts of across-the-board species solidarity were seldom formulated aside from earliest Christianity and, partially, the League of Nations and the United Nations. "Partially" also in the sense that the latter two have remained partial to "recognized" governments in opposition to all non-self-governing loyalty groups. As a whole, humanity seems unable even to form a responsibly constructive game plan for the prevention of intergroup "terrorism." Invariably, on the other group's side this terrorism amounts to justifiable heroism. Loyalty to one's subjugated or disfranchised group, historically, has been the source of the noblest forms of devotion and self-sacrifice. I believe that without a workable formulation of multilateral consideration between loyalty bound groups, references to generic human solidarity remain futile. Yet our international "order" has not even developed a forum for the genuinely multilateral consideration of the claims of various religious, racial, or ethnic groups. This lack of any rational forum can drive any desperate group into "terrorism." Intergroup violence replicates intrafamilial violence.

Human progress has consequences for posterity. Without responsible thought given to the good of posterity, by omission or by commission, these consequences may turn out to be randomly or predictably detrimental. Inertia toward responsibility for the ominous consequences of technical progress to posterity amounts to an entropic feature in human life. The random accomplishments of scientific progress are never going to do the job of responsibly responding to the survival needs of posterity.

Paradoxically, therefore, technical advancements, the fruits of intelligence themselves, pose a threat to the negentropic prospects of any form of life on Earth, even though all biological evolution culminates in the achievements of the human brain. With its boundless hunger for stimulation and curiosity for new things, human intelligence has also prostituted itself for the good of destructive intraspecies competition. Since posterity has no vote and cannot voice its own survival interests, the traditional ethics of self-denial and renouncement of pleasure will not suffice to give the future its due. I suggest that transgenerational solidarity and quality of survival depend on a contextual and consequential definition of ethics. According to this Janus-faced ethics the party who "multilaterally" invests due caring also earns entitlement. The investor's personal gain thus hinges on the terms of the good posterity. The doer's gain manifests itself in an enhanced quality of his or her own life as well. One goal of contextual therapy, "rejunction" (Boszormenyi-Nagy & Ulrich, 1981), aims at the renewed unity between the self-serving and the altruistic motives of closely related persons.

THE EARNING OF ENTITLEMENT:
A FORMULA FOR INDIVIDUATION.
THE SELF'S ETHICAL VALIDATION

Next I propose to connect negentropy with Martin Buber's (1958) notion of the "dialogue" as the *sine qua non* of the individual's existence as person. Buber writes that there is no complete I without a Thou (you). Only through responsibly addressing Thee (you) do I become an I. According to this dialogic principle, mutual regard for each other is in the best existential interests of both relating partners.

This is true not only via each party's extractively self-serving benefits but, more fundamentally, through the partners' mutual definition of each other's autonomous, differentiated personhood. In this ethically self-delineating and self-validating sense, giving become inseparable from receiving.

A core concept of contextual therapy (Boszormenyi-Nagy and associates, 1972, 1973, 1976, 1979, 1980, 1981, 1986), the earning of entitlement links the individual with transgenerational solidarity. Through considering the offspring's inborn, inherently deserved entitlement to nurturant care, the parent earns entitlement. Through responsibly facing the ethical imperative of the claim of species solidarity, the donor simultaneously enhances the quality of both his or her own and the receptor's life. Concern about relational consequences improves the quality of relating on the one hand and the prospective quality of each partner's physical and emotional health on the other. Concern about the environmental effects of progress is, thus, one of the key tests of social-relational maturity and health. In other words, due to its asymmetrical vulnerability to consequences, posterity commands an unconditional, inherent entitlement to consideration. In turn, through its offer of consideration, the present itself can become an entitled beneficiary.

A major relational resource of our times, however, frequently goes unrecognized: the young child's offering of loyal devotion and trust to the adult world. The recognition of this resource would not only require the reversal of the stereotype: adults are caretakers and little children are hungry, empty receptacles of adult offerings. It would also throw new light on the adult's needs for an uncontested acceptance by the family, i.e., on a deeper level, our implicit parentification of young children through their trusting acceptance and availability. Is the adult going to reciprocate, acknowledge, or exploit the child's offerings? Naturally, here lies one of the main options of parents for ethical self-validation, namely, through responsible recognition and due concern.

The discovery of specific ways in which each member can validate his ethical worth through due concern vis-à-vis the other not only diminishes the cost of their reciprocal consideration but it becomes a forceful motivational factor for their personal maturation (Boszormenyi-

Nagy & Spark, 1973). It frees up the donor to live a fuller, more enjoyable and creative life. Then, since he receives and experiences the resulting inner freedom and health, he becomes spontaneously motivated to earn entitlement again. In this way earning of entitlement through fair give-and-take becomes a determinative, self-sustaining dynamic of relating. It is a major option for every partner's ethical *self-validation*. Consistent with the good of posterity, reciprocal trustability becomes the "golden rule" of "relational negentropy." Moving from the family to the larger scenario of human species survival, the prospect of anyone's earning of a right to better health through considering the necessities of others will represent a store of orderliness and hope in our world of seemingly increasing relational chaos and random aggression. The prospect of recognizing the gain for the self because of contributing to others becomes a valuable glue that helps trustable relating prevail. This makes relating persons coinvestors, even if, by necessity, some of their specific interests conflict.

In the contextual sense, this balanced mutuality of coinvestment of partners is an important safeguard for relational fairness and responsibility. The ledger of fair give-and-take, however, has to extend also into the future. Responsibility for posterity is a fair expectation, even if the investor generation cannot reap the benefits of the offspring's returns. In a domino-like fashion each generation can "repay," essentially through giving to its successors. Thus caring about posterity's fair chances represents transgenerational solidarity or, expanding Buber's (1948) term, it safeguards the "justice of the human order." Just as negentropy in nature points toward increasing orderliness, responsibility for the defenselessly exposed offspring addresses a relational component of negentropy. Conversely, a random, raw prevalence of self-serving "rugged" individualism represents an entropic aspect of social process. Destructive overentitlement is one of its major driving forces and its sad consequences.

DESTRUCTIVE OVERENTITLEMENT

One of the main obstacles to a person's ability to offer due responsibility and caring to others lies in his or her having earned *destructive overentitlement* (Boszormenyi-Nagy, 1981). Earned destructive entitlement is one of the consequences of an overwhelming victimization of a child by his or her parenting environment. The child is usually defenseless against adult "intrigues," especially if they utilize the child's spontaneous loyal devotion, concern, generosity, and caring availability. Whether the child is exploited through exposure to sexual or violent abuse or through being entrapped between two mutually mistrustful and blaming parents' contradictory expectations of his or her filial loyalty, the child not only gets deprived but destructively entitled, too.

An important preventive consideration pertains to the reversibility of pathological personality formation. Certain stubborn character traits are due to inborn characteristics, others to lasting or irreversible early conditioning. We know that early influences are critical in all higher animals. The effects of imprinting are characteristically permanent and typically manifested with considerable delay (Lorenz, 1981). If detrimental early learning leads to both pathology and one of therapy's greatest stumbling blocks, every effort should be made to prevent the formation of long-term detrimental effects. In other words, can therapists do more than trying to repair serious damage already done? If so, which principles of therapy provide the guidelines for preventive societal "engineering?"

Destructive entitlement is, however, not reducible to the psychology of pathological character formation. It is quite difficult to distinguish between the psychology of a pathological character development on the one hand and the ethics of an ongoing unbalanced, injured ledger of fairness that exists between the child and the exploitative parents on the other. As an ominous moral surplusage, destructive entitlement always leads its owner to a tragic relational ethical dilemma. As far as his formative relationships are concerned, the victim's overentitlement was actually earned and deserved. Yet destiny, i.e., his human context, will never own up to accountability for past vicissitudes which, in addition, may not even have been consciously perpetrated by anyone. No doubt, the victim's attempt to take it out on a third person is always unfair. Even though he is entitled to compensation according to the unsettled ledger of past relationships, he is never so entitled in the current instance. Substitutive retribution is ethically always invalid, even if psychologically understandable. Unfortunately, through seeking the remedy to his overentitlement via wronging other relationships, often without knowing, the victim becomes himself an unfair victim-izer. His accumulated destructive over entitlement usually prevents him from facing proper remorse over his current existential guilt, accruing as a result of his exploiting others.

Destructive entitlement itself becomes a major entropic input into the chain of successive generations. Each parent generation may be decreasingly inclined (and in part less obliged) to offer security to the offspring. They may be, however, less aware of destructively parenti-fying their children. By their irresponsibly vindictive, neglectful or blaming attitude, parents may force their children to carry depleting amounts of adult responsibility.

In doing so, parents violate the justice of the human order and the violation tends to escalate over generations. The more their own parents were insensitive to their vulnerability, the more will parents themselves be insensitive to their vulnerability, the more will parents themselves be insensitive to their children's helpless predicament. Thus, inadvertently and tragically, each parent generation becomes its off-spring's captive opponent. The contemporary scene of increasing rates of violent and sexual child abuse seems to illustrate this blind antagonism even on an overt level. I suggest that rather than ignorance, faulty learning, or negative attention seeking, the parent's destructive overentitlement is the main cause of the escalation of today's neglectful or destructive parental behavior.

EXTENSION OF THE CONCEPT OF INTERPERSONAL LEDGER: AN INTRINSIC TRIBUNAL

Faced with the difficult question: Who determines the extent of concern due in a given relationship? Contextual therapists had to rely on a concept borrowed from Buber (1948), "the justice of the human order," as a quasi-objective criterion of interpersonal fairness. As formulated earlier (Boszormenyi-Nagy & Spark, 1973), the objectivity of relational justice is not an independent entity. It really is a dialectical criterion derived from the simultaneous consideration of the balance between two (or more) relating persons' subjective, self-serving rights and entitlements. Just how much concern is *due*, for instance, between my mother and myself depends on a dialectical consideration of the subjective terms of the rights and interests of both of us.

While I was a helpless infant, I had a claim to my mother's total consideration. As two grownups, the due expectations in our ledger have become essentially symmetrical. Now, however, that she is an old, ailing lady, she has a new claim on my sympathetic concern and attention. The bilaterality of give-and-take necessitated the development of the notion of relational "ledger" (Boszormenyi-Nagy & Spark, 1973), composed of the fluid balances of reciprocal fairness of both observable transactions and resultant interpersonal (even intergenerational) consequences between relating persons.

Despite its relative objectivity, the notion of an interpersonal ledger has retained a comparatively transactional or perhaps to some readers a feedback-like flavor. This is even more true of the concepts of interpersonal "contract" and "quid pro quo," both widely used in the literature on classical, transactionally based family therapy or marriage counseling. The latter concepts can easily explain here-and-now, behavioral, transactional, feedback-like events. Yet, while transactions capture the barter-like aspect of the interhuman dialogue, by its nature, responsibility for consequences transcends the scope of the transactional patterns themselves. Consequences flow into the future.

In contrast with "contract," the term "ledger" includes an implication of a unilateral, non-feedback-like consequential process, applicable to parent-child relationships. Because of its generative nature, the parent-child relationship has to contain forward thrusting consequences. Inadvertently, the parent has to deal out fateful cards to the young child whose mind is malleable, gullible, and open to early conditioning, and whose developmental timetable is uniquely rapid and consequential. The child and his or her existence, of course, do exert vital influences upon the parent, but under no conditions are the consequences equally fundamental, formative and irreversible. The most significant intergenerational consequences flow from parent to child and rarely vice versa.

The requirements of species survival constitute the reality of *transgenerational solidarity*. As an invisible third party, this solidarity participates in family relationships, especially in intergenerational ones. The rules of its intrinsic covenant provide the ethical guidelines for close relationships.

Although individuals can rightly be hypothesized to be essentially motivated by needs for food, power and stimulation, social systems are inevitably regulated also by balances of justifiability. Newborns are justified to nurturant care, parents to their children's filial loyalty, adolescents to an emerging autonomy. Yet justifications among humans inevitably conflict among themselves. Some of those conflicts are brought to actual courts, others are lived out between relating partners with a more or less shared awareness of an assumed justice of the human order. It is as if the totality of human relationships would represent an *intrinsic relational tribunal* whose decrees are meted out through the relational behaviors themselves.

The quest for an objective human justice has long preoccupied people's minds. Through their religious systems, human civilizations have created their idiosyncratic notions of cosmic justice. In tangible reality, people incarnate chaotic random congeries of destructive entitlement, revolving slate (Boszormenyi-Nagy & Spark, 1973), and substitutive vindication. This may become obvious in case of "pathology." In ordinary instances, the private sphere of close relating absorbs much of the ricocheting impact of life's injustices. Small children and often pets are captive shock absorbers of these forces. They become scapegoats and silent hostages to the frustrations of the adult world. Yet severe exploitation of children leads to their learning of destructive entitlement and to serious consequences for posterity. Ultimately, the balance of alleged and real justifications will be subordinated to the intrinsic tribunal of transgenerational solidarity, the guarantor of our species survival.

I propose the term *intrinsic transgenerational tribunal* as an extension of the dyadic parent-child ledger into an inclusive consequential criterion that spans countless generations in the survival of the human species. The fact that the irresponsible, ultimately exploitative behavior of a certain divorcing couple may affect the future parenting capacity of their 3–5-year-old children, invokes the fate of a third generation, at the very least. The tribunal stands for the outcome of consequences for posterity and it reminds the present of its responsibility for the future. It represents the evaluation of the sum total of all vertical and horizontal relational ledgers from the vantage point of both posterity's sheer viability and the prospective quality of its life.

THE BASIS OF THE INTRINSIC TRANSGENERATIONAL TRIBUNAL

The criteria of the basis of the intrinsic intergenerational tribunal depend on transgenerational solidarity. This solidarity requires both:

(a) priority of consideration of the welfare of posterity, and
(b) multilateral fairness in the relationships of contemporaries.

The reader could ask here: Are these requirements dependent on the value attitudes of therapists and on specific cultural taboos? Yet, responsibility for existential consequences transcends the injunctions of any idiosyncratic value system. Existential guilt depends on the factuality of consequences of the injury we do to the justice of the order of being. In other words, the extent of injury suffered by the victim rather than the extent of the perpetrator's capacity for guilt feelings constitutes the criteria of existential guilt, therefore of the intrinsic transgenerational tribunal, too. Internalized injunctions or taboos, on the other hand, are specific to the superego configurations or to the stage of moral psychological development of a given person. The tribunal's criteria for judgment could never be predicted from religious, cultural, or superego morality of any particular type. Only an ongoing monitoring of factual consequences for the other can determine the impact on the, always multilateral, balance of interpersonal fairness.

As the basis of the judgments of the tribunal, consequences for another relating partner imply a factual reality rather than a psychological process. Relational ethics stresses the factual reality of both inflicting of injury and earning of merit. The balance of these consequences determines a great deal of relational burdens and benefits as they fall upon each and every relating member.

In order for any therapy of the future to encompass the mandate of concern about transgenerational consequences, therapy cannot be governed by either psychological or behavioral-transactional-feedback criteria alone. The ethical resources of close relationships can no longer be taken for granted without paying a heavy penalty.

The psychological, including psychodynamic, understanding of human beings will, however, always remain a useful therapeutic tool. The knowledge of psychic motives is always one key to the understanding of human relational reality. Yet the laws of psychology characteristically refer to the functions of one mind, i.e., the property of one human being. There is no psychology that simultaneously accounts for the motivational rationales, e.g., internal object relations, of several persons. Especially, it is impossible to describe the psychology of as yet unborn persons. By contrast, the ethical criteria of relational consequences heavily focus on the interests of all persons to become affected, including the unborn offspring.

Systemic or transactional feedback theories have well served the purposes of classical family therapy. Patterns of interactional behavior have described certain lawful characteristics of the behavior of simultaneously coexisting relational partners. Feedback theory is not suitable, however, for the explanation of long-term transgenerational consequences. The impact of the present on yet unborn generations is largely unilateral, nonfeedback-like. Consequently, posterity cannot help but be affected by its past, but it cannot influence the already buried ancestors.

Without the resource of ethical self-validation, the person is not free to unfold his or her psychological potential. No authentic self-validation can occur in an existential void, in a life which lacks social purpose and worth. Neither psychological guidelines nor transactional-systemic rules can by themselves guarantee that vital component of self-validation which derives from worth obtained through interpersonal benefits and social relevance.

PROCESS

The implied tribunal is not a forum or "system" that is separate from the aggregate relational intentions and actions of the participants *qua* discrete and separate individuals. As all relating partners take turns in claiming their respective justifications, each enacts his or her share of the forum that ultimately validates the criteria of the fairness of the balance. From here on the tribunal can be considered as one of the major relational determinants. As one person's claim bounces off, so to speak, from the claims of others and claims mutually rearranged themselves, a new "geometry" of justifications sets in. Naturally, young or yet unborn offspring cannot voice their claims and justifications, and it is our task to care.

Through addressing the fairness of consequences, the tribunal becomes a causative source of further consequences. Along with facts, psychological factors and transactional, i.e., recursive feedback, homeostatic and other systemic patterns, the tribunal constitutes a major dimension of relational determinants. By their mutual acts and by the collusion of their justifications people may redeem each other or sentence one another to living in Hell, to developing psychosomatic illness, etc. In a sense, the tribunal thus executes its decrees: The party who fails to earn merit vis-à-vis his relational partners or lastingly ignores his factual accountability for damaging consequences to posterity may become depressed, insomniac, anorectic, addicted, ruined by success, sexually malfunctional, relationally stagnant, accident-prone, or psychosomatically ill. As a psychological consequence, conscious or unconscious feelings of guilt may or may not accompany the person's disentitlement, i.e., the accumulation of existential guilt on his or her side.

The husband who, based on substitutive justification, and, additionally, on invisible loyalty to his parents, takes out his retaliation on his wife, both acts out and invokes the intrinsic transgenerational tribunal. At the same time as he metes out vindication justifiable in the context of his filial ledger, he inflicts new injustice in the context of his marriage. Viewed from the vantage point of his children, he also injures the justice of a new parent-child order of being. By imposing on his children the heritage of split loyalty, he is bound to offer them less trustability yet extract from them more trust than it is his due. As the children earn destructive entitlement, they will act it out in ways that may not punish the parents but will impose new injustice on further relational contexts.

MULTIPLE LEDGERS WITHIN ONE TRIBUNAL

The consideration of the phenomenon of the "revolving slate"* (Boszormenyi-Nagy & Spark, 1973) requires an extension of the jurisdiction of the intrinsic relational tribunal from one interpersonal ledger to the totality of the members' relationships. The total "hearing" procedure has to cover the consequences as they affect the concurrent ledgers of claims to fairness within and between the competing partnerships that compose the whole. The phenomena of destructive overentitlement (Boszormenyi-Nagy, 1981) and "revolving slate" illustrate how two relational ledgers can be linked to each other through one person's accountability to the tribunal as a whole.

Each of these relationships has its discrete jurisdictional domain or ledger, and the overall relational tribunal has to monitor conflicts, the validity of shifts, and substitutions between the jurisdictions of the various relationships of each person. It seems that the principle of distributive justice, too, has to be invoked here: It is unfair not to give all relationships their due. Preferring the basic rights of one relationship over the other would violate this principle. It is unfair to lastingly ignore one relationship in order to benefit another. The relational tribunal thus contains criteria of fairness *both* within and between ledgers or domains of relational jurisdictions.

The concept of the intrinsic relational tribunal is difficult to accept for a number of reasons. To many people, the term "tribunal" sounds harsh even though they can conceive of an implicitly conflictual nature of relationships. To many people the notion that it is more than a

---

*In the revolving slate, a fixed account between two people gets turned by one partner against a substitute, innocent target who is made accountable for the debts of the original debtor.

psychological or systemic metaphor, that it is a monitoring, recording and executive process, could make the tribunal sound anthropomorphic. Some people may react to this notion as if the tribunal were a rigid authority, a doom or dark destiny. Others may feel that contextual therapy expects people to stay in a gloomy, overresponsible contemplation forever. To many people the very idea of stressing any accountability sounds, of course, unpalatable and "counterculture." In this sense there exists a social taboo operating against the very ideas of responsibility and ethics.

Yet appropriate attention paid to this facet of relational dynamics is one of the most liberating aspects of therapy. Naturally, people cannot be continuously concerned about balances of fairness in their relationships. All that can be expected of humans is a periodic monitoring of consequences from both the self's and the other's vantage points. The horizontal requirement of the fairness of give-and-take between peers has to be balanced with the vertical aspects of *intraspecies solidarity*. One form of caring about posterity consists of caring to review and revise the legacy expectations of the past for the benefit of the future. This is an extremely important task, for example, in cases of religiously, ethnically, or racially mixed marriages. The task of the present is to sort out the precious pearls that posterity should inherit from the heritage of its past.

IMPLICATIONS AND CONCLUSIONS

Today's social and technical pace has accelerated the processes of "relational entropy" or disintegration. The traditional structures of society: religion, community, family, marriage, etc. are unable to generate sufficient impetus for responsible caring to halt disintegration of relational continuity and stability. Because of lack of structures for their channeling, much potential relational resource and good faith fails to materialize. As a result, both prospective donor and prospective recipient are shortchanged. With the progressive disintegration of trust-ability and trust, millions of young people get lost in such symptomatic phenomena and desperate indirect reaching out for help and for negative attention as violence, vandalism, drug addiction, child abuse, early teen pregnancy, suicide attempts, etc. Yet, in a seeming passive aggressive attitude, society-at-large may increase entropy through its permissive indifference and decline of caring leadership. Genuine responding to desperate indirect reaching out would require a consistent strength and responsibility that is decreasingly available in society. The "symptom" which tends to represent a request for a trustworthy, if firm, response, remains unanswered. The ignored, abandoned offspring generation becomes both emotionally frustrated and destructively over-entitled, even if some of its legal rights are formally being codified. It is imperative to sustain the caring quality of formative intergenerational relationships.

I propose that the relational predicament of our age results primarily from a relational fragmentation and disintegration of earned trustability rather than, as it may superficially appear, from a rigidity of family patterns and rules. Disintegrative forces bombard children's brains through television and the "values" of desperate peer groups. More importantly, many bitterly disillusioned adults are unable to infuse their children with trust. Instead, they drain the trust offerings of their children. Yet blaming the family's "pathology" without attempting to resupply it with trustability would only further increase relational entropy and disintegration. The microcosm of the family can seldom countervail the massive messages from an increasingly exploitative and extractive, computerized business and political world. Through our own inaction we contribute to the implicit exploitation of posterity. As therapists, it behooves us to stand for transgenerational solidarity.

Therapy itself can, inadvertently, collude with the entropic side of societal trends if it subscribes to any of a number of self-defeating goal notions:

(a) that the goal of individuation is a self-serving (rugged) individualism, and that evidence for the powerful relational resources of good faith, trust, solidarity and options for ethical self-validation via earning of entitlement can be dismissed, as is characteristically done in the practice of classical individual therapy;
(b) that a manipulative inducement of superficially problem-free, here-and-now behavior patterns suffices as the goal of therapy,

thus overlooking the goals and spontaneity of conscious or unconscious motivation as the crucial determinants of each individual's behavior, as is typically assumed or alleged in classical
marriage or family therapy;
(c) that the removal of the presenting symptom in the identified
patient is the goal of therapy, as is frequently claimed in classical
behavior therapies and in certain "strategic" family therapies.

Many therapists believe that they should be value-free and above
partiality to their clients' "moralistic" claims to justification. Yet I am
convinced that close relating cannot be maintained without a capacity
for a tolerant "let live" in exchange for the self's claims to a right to
"live." Furthermore, each person's rights to here-and-now fulfillments
of needs are deeply interwoven with his or her willingness to fair
consideration of the other's needs and interests. The quality of people's
present relating does depend on their sense of long-term consequences
of care about fairness. This is the foundation of their relational trustworthiness; the main criterion of relational viability. Thus, even short-
term therapy requires concern about the fair balancing of long-term
ledgers.

The contextual therapeutic attitude of "multidirected partiality"
(Boszormenyi-Nagy, 1966; Boszormenyi-Nagy & Krasner, 1986;
Boszormenyi-Nagy & Spark, 1973) extends to all family members the
expectation that they delineate their claims to justification.

The emerging picture of conflicting justifications helps to understand
conflicting motivations. By extending partiality to the destructive entitlement of the currently victimizing parent, the therapist helps ex-
tinguish the motivating strength of the heretofore unrecognized consequence of past damages. Having acknowledged the parent's past
victimization, the therapist can then expect a more accountable behavior toward the next generation. In the meantime the parent's entire
defensive apparatus may get mobilized. Nonetheless, the therapist who
aims at inducing the self-reinforcing motivational spiral of earning
entitlement, will help his or her clients to arrive at a new self-per-
petuating spontaneity of motivation. Although this therapy demands
commitment and courage on the part of the therapist, it is not based
on the therapist's own value priorities.

The driving force of the therapeutic process is the conflict between the justifications of the relating partners and each member's need for the self-reinforcing spiral of earning entitlement, without which neither trustable relating nor responsible parenting is possible. The therapy of the future will have to learn to translate between a long-range trust-building agenda and a helpful methodology of short-term relief from suffering.

The notion of the intrinsic relational tribunal encompasses the reality of conflicting justifications among closely relating people. Thus, ethical consequences are interwoven with the psychological consequences of the conflicts between needs and wills of closely relating people. To put it in another way, people are motivated both by their needs and by their justifications. The helpless, the wounded, the blind and the handicapped are, by the reality of their hardship, justified to extra concern. Typically, the helpless infant is accepted to be justified to caring attention. Once grown, the adult is expected to absorb the blows of his or her fate. Therapy and prevention remain incomplete, however, without accounting for both people's justifications (entitlements) and for their "sense" of personal justification.

The extension of therapeutic concern to human species survival offers important messages to society-at-large. Ultimately, it parallels a more concerned attitude toward environmental protection. The requirements of a genuine species solidarity would not stop at prohibiting genocide initiated by any self-appointed master race or nation on the one hand or violent protest staged by a suppressed ethnic group on the other. Instead, species solidarity will require the formulation and documentation of each human loyalty group's claims to justification. Only if humanity will be able to listen to justifiable thought conflicting demands will it become fair to expect people to devote their energies to mutually sorting out their claims and alleged justifications. As long as indignant ethnic, religious, racial, etc. groups find no ears to talk to, their energies are bound to be channelled into destruction.

The intrinsic tribunal of transgenerational solidarity underlies the larger societal process as its crucial dynamic for survival. For example, the worker's solidarity with the nation and the company's solidarity with the laborer makes the "Japanese model" of industrial management successful in a keenly competitive era. Conversely, our essential disregard for "mankind's conscience" leads to exploitative oppression of ethnic or racial groups until wars, terrorism or revolutions emerge as tribunal through havoc. Even the fear of a nuclear holocaust seems to play the role of an intrinsic tribunal through its implied threat to species survival. Similarly, the admonitions of the emerging environmental activism of our times represent one of the tribunal's criteria for transgenerational solidarity.

Returning to the realm of close relationships, a regard for the quality of any and every individual human life requires that future accumulation of destructive entitlement be kept at the lowest possible level. The induction of destructive entitlement undermines transgenerational solidarity. It engenders justifications to revengeful actions, ultimately murder, child abuse, terrorism, prejudice, war or even genocide. It also creates insensitivity to the survival interests of humanity as a whole.

Through its relational concerns, contemporary therapy is in a position to live up to its broader mandate instead of merely manipulating the behavior of the victims of relational or biological calamities. Therapy ought to be able to translate its insights into practical formulae for societal prevention on the one hand and for remedial goals and methods on the other. Therapy's literature tends to underrate its mandate. Therapy anchored in the relational-ethical context should take its place among other efforts explicitly aimed at the prevention of irreversible damages to the quality of human survival.

REFERENCES

Bateson, G. (1979). *Mind and nature*. New York: E. P. Dutton.

Boszormenyi-Nagy, I. (1962). The concept of schizophrenia from the perspective of family treatment. *Family Process, 1*, 103–113.

Boszormenyi-Nagy, I. (1965a). Intensive family therapy as process. In I. Boszormenyi-Nagy & J. L. Framo (Eds.), *Intensive family therapy* (pp. 87–142). New York: Harper & Row.

Boszormenyi-Nagy, I. (1965b). The concept of change in conjoint family therapy. In A. S. Friedman et al. (Eds.), *Psychotherapy for the whole family: Case histories, techniques and concepts of family therapy of schizophrenia in the home and clinic* (pp. 305–319). New York: Springer.

Boszormenyi-Nagy, I. (1966). From family therapy to a psychology of relationships: Fictions of the individual and fictions of the family. *Comprehensive Psychiatry, 7*, 408–423.
Boszormenyi-Nagy, I. (1972). Loyalty implications of the transference model in psychotherapy. *Archives of General Psychiatry, 374–380*.
Boszormenyi-Nagy, I. (1976). Behavior change through family change. In A. Burton (Ed.), *What makes behavior change possible?* New York: Brunner/Mazel.
Boszormenyi-Nagy, I. (1979). Contextual therapy: Therapeutic leverages in mobilizing trust, Report 2, Unit LV. *The American family*. Philadelphia: The Continuing Education Service of Smith, Kline and French Laboratories.
Boszormenyi-Nagy, I. (1981). Contextual therapy: The realm of the individual (Interview with Margaret Markham). *Psychiatric News, 16* (20 & 21).
Boszormenyi-Nagy, I. & Krasner, B. (1980). Trust-based therapy: A contextual approach. *American Journal of Psychiatry, 137*, 767–775.
Boszormenyi-Nagy, I., & Krasner, B. R. (1981). The contextual approach to psychotherapy. In G. Berenson & H. White (Eds.), *Annual review of family therapy* (pp. 92–128). New York: Human Sciences Press.
Boszormenyi-Nagy, I., & Krasner, B. R. (1986). *Between give and take: A clinical guide to contextual therapy*. New York: Brunner/Mazel.
Boszormenyi-Nagy, I., & Spark, G. M. (1973). *Invisible loyalties: Reciprocity in intergenerational family therapy*. New York: Brunner/Mazel (reprinted 1985).
Boszormenyi-Nagy, I., & Ulrich, D. (1981). Contextual therapy. In A. Gurman & D. P. Kniskern (Eds.), *Handbook of family therapy*. New York: Brunner/Mazel.
Buber, M. (1958). *I and thou* (2nd rev. ed. with postscript by author added.) Smith, R. C. Trans. New York: Charles Scribner's Sons.
Buber, M. (1948). Guilt and guilt feelings. *Psychiatry, 20*, 114–129, 1957.
Jonas, H. (1979). *Das Prinzip Verantwortung [The Principle of Responsibility]*. Frankfurt: Insel.
Lorenz, K. Z. (1981). *The foundations of ethology*. New York: Springer.
Schroedinger, E. (1962). *What is life? The physical aspect of the living cell*. New York: Macmillan.

19

Contextual Therapy and the Unity of Therapies

This article reviews some of the integrative premises of the contextual approach. This integrative intent had been implicit in the origins of the approach: intensive individual and systemic family therapies. The all-encompassing respect of the approach for other therapeutic modes and rationales became explicit in 1979 with the formulation of the four dimensions of relational reality (facts, psychology, transactional patterns and context of fairness).

Obviously the unity of a common language base of all therapies is both a logical requirement and a public need. However, integration of the various conceptual approaches cannot be done by reducing them into each other's terms. It is proposed in this article that the sole undeniable core of an integration of therapeutic modalities has to be founded on the essence of therapy as a whole—the ethics of caring. In this sense the dimension of the context of fairness becomes the overall guiding rationale of any valid unification of therapeutic schools.

Ivan Nagy briefly reviews those critical aspects of this therapeutic approach that deal with issues at the individual/family interface. The clinician will find this useful in understanding a theorist/practitioner who has been explicitly articulating issues involving the individual and the family for several decades. Of particular interest is Nagy's view that integration is both possible and necessary, but can only occur within a specific dimension (the ethical). In juxtaposition, he is critical of attempts to merge the individual and family paradigms on the level of procedures. [Editor's note]

"Market success" has produced an unprecedented number of therapeutic schools and professionals. Logic and clinical unity have created new modalities from individual psychotherapy; such as group therapy, family therapy, and marriage therapy. In turn, each modality has a variety of schools and orientations (e.g., analytic, behavioral, existential, experiential, Jungian).

In physical medicine, at least theoretically, the family physician refers the patient with a specific problem to a specialist, who determines whether pharmacological or surgical treatment is appropriate. The physiological logic of the human body provides a unifying guideline. The gynecologist or urologist does not ignore a serious heart condition, for example.

Psychotherapy and its derivatives lack a solid scientific underpinning; therefore, it is possible to represent the various modalities of therapy as whole solutions to a client's problems. For example, the individual therapist may ignore the substrate of what the family therapist would address and vice-versa.

Furthermore, without a scientific explanation, the mechanism of cure is also questionable. Can group therapy work because it is a more effective psychotherapy of each individual? Can its effect be assumed to penetrate via each member's changed family relationships, even though relatives have never visited the group therapist? Can it be that the client got better because participation in the group helped a close relative who, in turn, has affected the client beneficially?

The development of an integrated therapy approach has been discussed by several authors in the family therapy field. At times, the suggested integration appears to be based on a wish for a fusion of all schools, as if by throwing all authors' concepts into a big basket.

The therapeutic concepts of one realm are virtually nontranslatable into those of another, however. The unity of therapy lies beyond the level of therapeutic concepts.

Individual therapy's concepts address the psychological processes and phenomena *within* one person, such as ego strength, displacement, projection, transference, paranoia, narcissism, internal objects, externalization, wish to be loved, aggressive or sexual drive, despair, and anger. The transactional-relational concepts of classic family therapy address processes *between* persons, including triangulation, double bind, power of helplessness, marital skew, pseudomutuality, enmeshment, and homeostasis. Although the terms of individual therapy cannot be translated into those of systemic therapy, they can be subsumed into the terms of relational ethics. Each individual's self-gain is integrated into the ethical formula of multilateral fairness, and reciprocal fairness becomes an umbrella under which individual and transactional phenomena find a balance.

The integrative principle must be based on therapy's ultimate mandate for humanity. Responsibility for one's work does not require a perfect performance during the therapy session, but a lasting effect on the clients' lives. In other words, relationships represent areas for therapy far beyond their ephemeral, here-and-now effects on the partners' behavior. As a result of a parent-child relationship, for example, the child may acquire destructive entitlement (Boszormenyi-Nagy, 1981). Perhaps the child will be destructive for the rest of his or her life. The injury to the justice of the human order (Buber, 1957) that victimized the child will be sustained through the child's perpetration of new injustices. Such vindictiveness may manifest itself as insensitivity to other people's feelings or as nongiving, exploitative behavior when the child becomes a parent. Turned against the self, the vindictiveness can lead to self-destructive behavior patterns, psychosomatic illness, suicidal inclinations, or psychotic withdrawal from the interpersonal world.

Despair over bad faith in relationships is an ever present threat to an individaul's internal security and capacity for behavioral mastery of everyday living. Despair and bad faith rise out of the parenting world's mistrust toward the helpless child. To a degree, most of us have earned the entitlement to be destructive. Destructive entitlement is thus primarily a tragic derailment of an originally justifiable claim and only secondarily a psychic distortion. Some children were treated by the world more unfairly than others. Even if their resentment of the world is therefore justifiable, the switch to carelessly hurting an innocent third party can never be justified. The inner dilemma about one's relational core integrity is a great source of despair and escape into "pathological" patterns of behavior. Subsequently, the reliance on the self-motivating process of fulfillment through the earning of constructive entitlement gets lost. One's capacity for creatively fair solutions, trust, investment in relationships, and psychosomatic relaxation, as well as the willingness to give posterity a fair chance may become lost. Consequently, reliance on destructive rather than constructive entitlement is not merely an "intrapsychic pathology"; it is a self-fulfilling prophecy that creates a matching untrustworthy relational context around the person.

The transgenerational consequences of parent-child relationships make it inappropriate simply to apply the symptom-curative or even the pathology-eliminating therapeutic framework of medicine to psychotherapy of any kind. Medical cure of a symptom or even of the substrate of pathology in the parents rarely is in direct causal relationship with the development of pathology in the offspring. The overtly symptomless "successful" parent is often invisibly dependent on his or her child's relational trust and integrity. It is possible for the parent to drain the child of inner security while appearing to be a realistic critic of the child's behavior. Therefore, the failure of psychotherapists to strive for a precise definition of transgenerational relational consequences amounts to cynical disregard of these consequences.

DEFINITION OF THE PROBLEM

In medicine, the subjectively felt or seen symptom is the patient's definition of the problem; the physician's scientific knowledge of the underlying causes provides another definition. The patient has no reason to doubt the scientific validity of medicine. The problems of the psychotherapist's patients are more complex and scientifically less definable, however. They are also subject to both consequential and teleological causation. The past contributes to consequential aspirations and to teleological determination of actions. Besides, life need not be filled with pathological behavior to create conflicts of interest that can contribute to people's problems. In contrast to most other psychotherapy and family therapy approaches, contextual therapy aims at a positive definition of workable relational reality, rather than at a mere elimination or perhaps reshuffling of pathology. Any behavioral changes are ephemeral unless they are anchored in a reconstruction of mutual responding and responsibility.

A problem, a concept inseparable from day-to-day living, easily becomes a tautologous equivalent of the need for help or intervention. It seems that the term *problem solving* has become widely accepted as a synonym for therapy, yet it has a much broader and vaguer meaning than does therapy. Similarly, the use of the term *conflict* as a synonym for pathology is unproductive.

INTERPERSONAL CONFLICTS OF INTEREST

The context of relational reality encompasses the inevitable conflicts of interest between persons. Such conflicts are not signs of pathology. They cannot be reduced to either intrapsychic conflict between two forces of one mind or to power conflict between two confronting persons or systems. Interpersonal conflicts pertain to all four dimensions of a relational reality: (1) facts, (2) psychology, (3) transactions, and (4) relational ethics.

Conflicts of interest do not connote only competitive struggles for the same object or territory (e.g., love triangles, loyalty conflicts). They are inherent in giving and receiving. Conflict is implicit in the asymmetry of options for giving and receiving between parent and child, for example. If the asymmetry is ignored and the child is expected to repay all, the conflict becomes enormous. If the parent has been developmentally deprived, the parent and the child may find themselves in an existential conflict.

In contrast with contextual therapy, neither classical psychodynamic nor classical family therapy approaches explicitly take into account the therapeutic significance of interpersonal conflicts of interest. In his early career, Freud was interested in the ways in which young children may actually be harmed by their parents. As he dropped his "seduction theory," he examined conflict as it emerges between the psychic forces and structures of one mind. Thus relational conflicts were relegated in part to a historical, formative past that had been internalized.

Classic systemic family therapists extended their interest to all family members and emphasized the therapeutic options that exist in changing transactional and communicational patterns. A whole new framework of transactional pathology has evolved (e.g., triangles, collusions, power alliances, games, role distributions, generational boundaries, double binding, scapegoating), but it has failed to stimulate thinking in terms of dialogues or conflicts of interests among unique whole persons. Yet, relationships are resources for therapy far beyond their here-and-now behavioral characteristics. The conflict of interests between the possessive needs of the parent and the individuation needs of the offspring are lifelong. Furthermore, intergenerational relationships are determined by procreation rather than by the psychology of affects or the cybernetics of transactions between participants. Legacies from the past and mandates for posterity affect the distant offspring unilaterally, since there can be no feedback to the long-deceased ancestor.

Even therapy approaches that are aimed at the fostering of differentiation and individuation of each person's self within the context of the family still tend to lack a definition of the dialogue or conflicting interests among well-differentiated selves. Having differentiated himself from an all too powerful fused, deindividuated, enmeshed system of transactions or from the dependent clinging between himself and others, the person nonetheless continues to affect the lives of the others. The individual reality of (centripetal) consequences for the self is complemented by the rational reality of (centrifugal) consequences for others. Neither psychological nor transactional-systemic reductionism can capture the whole of relational reality.

Factual circumstances of relationships can by themselves create conflicts of interest. For example, the fact of parental divorce inadvertently places the interests of the children in conflict with those of the parents. The children have a vested interest in family continuity, yet at least one of the parents wants the divorce. It is in the children's interest not to blame either parent, yet one parent usually blames the other. It is better for the children to stay out of the adult conflict, yet one or both parents tend to put them in the middle. The children have an interest in continuous relationships with all grandparents, yet divorcing parents may hate their in-laws. The children need an opportunity to ventilate their frustrations, yet the parents need listening and understanding from their children. The children may resent any intruder into the injured family intimacy, yet the parents may need new partners.

Parental remarriage leads to new sources of conflict of interests. The children's loyalty binds them to their natural parents, but a parent's remarriage establishes a rival to the other natural parent. Remarriage can result in a complex set of six or eight possible grandparents whose interests seem to conflict.

In contextual therapy, the very acknowledgment of the multilaterality (i.e., the inevitability of interpersonal conflicts) is by itself considered a healing resource. Relational ethics begin with the recognition of the different sides of conflictual situations and, subsequently, with an attitude of responsibility for the various consequences for the participants.

METHODOLOGICAL IMPLICATIONS
OF MULTIDIRECTED PARTIALITY

· The recognition of conflicts of interests among family members plays a great part in the methodology of contextual therapy. Because of the extension of concern to include everyone potentially affected by the intervention, the multidirected professional commitment and contract leads to the therapeutic method of multidirected partiality (Boszormenyi-Nagy, 1966, 1972). One by one, every family member is expected to define his or her side of conflicting interests as a first step toward a constructive contribution.

As family members take turns defining their own interests, the therapist helps them make clear points, commit themselves to relational positions, and benefit from hearing the others' uninterrupted exposition of their respective interests. The therapist shows partiality to every family member by deliberately being empathically understanding toward the fairness or justifiability of the position of each person. In that process, the therapist may have to be partial against the opposing side. This approach encourages each family member to invest renewed trust into both talking and listening. The long-abandoned dialogue may start again.

Every affected person's interests must be included in multidirected partiality, even if the person does not attend therapy sessions. The view that all persons affected by therapy are entitled to fair regard is more than a moral position. In essence, the underlying principle of multilaterality is an important clinical guideline as well. Its implications apply whether work is done with individuals, couples, or families. An all-inclusive therapeutic concern is by itself therapeutic, because it addresses life as a context of interdependence.

The bulk of the therapeutic literature shows how difficult it is to conceive of the dialectic of separation and individuation in a relational context. Therapists who isolate individuation from the context of relationships not only deceive themselves conceptually, however, but also deprive their clients of chances of success. Therapists who become unilateral advocates for their individuating adolescents, for example, may not clearly realize that they become adversaries to their clients' parents in the process. The therapist may endorse apparently advantageous attitudes that cause injury to the parents. In truth, adolescent clients cannot lastingly benefit from callous indifference toward their parents' suffering. Adolescents can achieve a more mature stage of individuation through responsible concern for the consequences of their growth to their parents. They are also less likely to feel guilty over actual disloyalty. The therapist would stand on much firmer ground if he or she could responsibly review with the patient the possible pitfalls from the latter's parents' vantage point. In this sense, the ethics of multilaterally responsible caring is the umbrella under which to integrate adolescent individual care, parental psychology, parental marriage counseling, and three-generational leverages.

ATTEMPTS AT AN INTEGRATION

The wide range of theories and concepts on the complexities of human experience and behavior can overwhelm the student of therapy. The more mature and experienced therapist is less likely to expect to find one theory that is preferable to all others. Naturally, the experienced therapist increasingly relies on personal resources and on resources within personal relationships. A well-informed, experienced therapist does not ignore the thoughtful efforts of other therapists who have tried to capture an essential factor in therapy, however. Obviously, it is useful to know about: defenses, transference tendencies, resistance, learning theory, conditioning, basic trust, generativity, inborn patterns of behavior, imprinting, double-bind, games, scripts, gestalts of emotional patterns, feedback, power alignments, role boundaries, relabeling, paradoxes, etc. The question is how best to put all these efforts together. Should the therapist simply run after each clue as they come to mind? Should he or she pursue a transference element now, a double-bind next, and a power coalition clinician afterwards? (See Figure 19-1).

Family therapy has demonstrated that it is important to consider relational as well as individual reality in evaluating health and dysfunction. The integration of therapeutic approaches must take into account the ordering of relational reality. Comprehensive therapy requires first a clustering of the various factors that determine relational reality, then a hierarchical ordering of priorities of goals and procedures. In contextual therapy (Boszormenyi-Nagy, 1979), a parsimonious clustering still involves four units (dimensions): (1) facts, (2) psychology of needs, (3) transactional systems, and (4) balance of fairness.

Few psychotherapeutic schools emphasize the determinative significance of factual circumstances. Yet the discovery of cancer in a parent, for instance, can reshuffle options for constructive transactions and may open up options for bypassing the parent's neurotic defensiveness.

Omission of the psychological dimension from strategic planning can deprive the therapist of the leverages of the family members' motivational forces. Addressing the failing liver function of a severely self-destructive alcoholic man may not create the highest therapeutic lever-

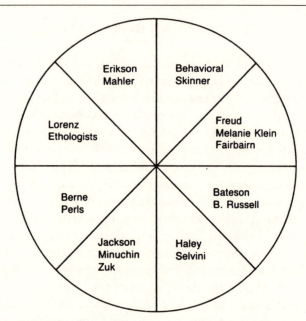

Figure 19-1. Therapeutic Conceptual Sources and Rationales

age, for example, but he may be deeply motivated by the fear that his 8-year-old son will see him in a shameful drunken state.

Omission of the transactional, systemic dimension can deprive the therapist of important clues concerning the mutually reinforcing nature of complementary roles. Berne (1964) was among the first to describe such transactional Gestalts as "games." The therapist of the alcoholic man should not ignore the man's recurrent patterns of interaction, for example, with his mother or with his wife. Building therapy entirely on the manipulative "restructuring" of transactions unnecessarily limits the therapist's role, however, and may render the family members passively compliant. Furthermore, it leaves interpersonal conflicts of interests undefined.

The balance of fairness constitutes an ethical factor of relationships. It represents concern about the consequences for any relating member. The therapist may never see the alcoholic client's son, but realizes that the person most profoundly and lastingly affected is the son. At the

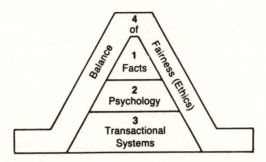

Figure 19-2. The Four Dimensions (Clusters) of Relational Reality

same time, as mentioned earlier, an appeal to the interests of the son may be the strongest motivational factor in changing the behavior of the desperate alcoholic. The hierarchical ordering of the clusters of relational (therapeutic) reality then resembles (Figure 19-2).

The translation of therapeutic theoretical terms and conceptual frameworks is neither necessary nor possible. As the number of therapeutic concepts and procedures increases, it is becoming less and less feasible to reduce them into any common denominator. On the other hand, therapeutic accountability to all affected persons remains a sound clinical and ethical guideline. Subsuming methods under the umbrella of the ethics of fairness rather than mutual integration becomes then the unifying principle of a comprehensive therapeutic practice.

REFERENCES

Berne, E. *Games people play: The psychology of human relationships.* New York: Grove Press, 1964.

Boszormenyi-Nagy, I. From family therapy to psychology of relationships: Fictions of the individual and fictions of the family. *Comprehensive Psychiatry, 7*(5), 408–423, 1966.

Boszormenyi-Nagy, I. Loyalty implications of the transference model in psychotherapy. *Archives of General Psychiatry, 27,* 374–380, 1972.

Boszormenyi-Nagy, I. Contextual therapy: Therapeutic leverages in mobilizing trust. In *The American family,* Philadelphia: Smith, Kline and French Laboratories, 1979. Reprinted in Green, R. J., & Framo, J. L. (Eds.), *Family therapy: Major contributions.* New York: International Universities Press, 1981, pp. 393–416.

Boszormenyi-Nagy, I. Interview with Margaret Markham. Contextual therapy: The realm of the individual. *Psychiatric News, 16,* 20, 1981.

Buber, M. Guilt and guilt feelings. *Psychiatry, 20,* 114–129, 1957.

Index

Accountability, xviii, 134, 139n, 162, 170,
192, 236, 275, 313
  multidirectional, 216
  relational, xvii, 171, 239
  transgenerational, 124, 147
Accreditation, record keeping and, 184–185
Activeness, 166, 203, 278
Adolescents, individuation of, 326. *See also*
  Children; Delinquency; Individuation
Adoption, 166, 220, 222–223, 224, 228,
269
Alcoholism, 220–221, 327–329
Ancestral shame, legacy of, 178–179
Assessment, in contextual therapy, 197–200,
227–228
Asymmetry, 79, 274–275
Attachment, 236
Attitudinal change, 280–281
Autonomy, 15–16, 21, 28, 88, 225–227. *See
also* Individuation

Basic trust, 87, 162, 270
Bateson, G., et al., 84, 273, 300
Behavior, 152, 159–160
Behavioral therapy, 142, 273
Being and Nothingness (Sartre), 84
Being the object, 62, 93
Benedek, T., 40
Berne, E., 328
*Between Give and Take: A Clinical Guide to
Contextual Therapy* (Boszormenyi–Nagy
and Krasner), xv
Blaming the family, 196
Boszormenyi–Nagy, I., xv, xvii, xviii, 3, 21,
36, 41, 44, 54, 55, 79, 80, 82, 85, 88,
89n, 118–120, 129, 139, 140, 147,
148, 155, 156, 158, 162, 163, 167,
177, 178, 181, 213, 235, 252, 255,

258, 272, 274, 275, 280, 295, 296,
298, 302, 303–304, 306, 307, 308,
312, 315, 321, 325, 327
Boundaries, 61–62, 83
  intrasubject, 91
Bowen, M., 14, 84, 162
Bowlby, J., 236
Buber, Martin, xvi, 107, 140, 257, 304,
306, 321
  "dialogue" of, xvi, 140, 160, 241, 303
Burton, A., 168–172

Causation, 23, 149, 194
Change, 35–52, 134, 137, 138, 140–142,
148–153, 156–162, 168
  basic dynamic of, 43–49
  criteria of, 52
  "desirable," 134
  direction of, 35, 39, 40
  dyadic or triadic, 41–42, 51
  in family therapy, 37–43
  as goal, 142, 168, 246
  individual/relational concepts of, 49–52,
134, 142–148
  inducements to, 156–162
Child(-ren), xviii, 21, 31, 66, 298
  exploitation of, 55, 125–127, 275, 289–
290, 305, 308
  loyalty of, 111–117, 127, 146, 303
  parentified, 21, 29–30, 55, 99, 111, 113,
226, 275–276, 303
Child abuse, 299, 305, 306
Child guidance, 59, 273
Collusion, 55, 84, 251, 259
Collusive postponement of mourning , 35,
49, 71, 134
Commitment, 101, 116, 121, 125, 130,
155, 191